SCHILLEBEECKX, Edward. The mission of the Church, tr. by N. D.
  Smith. Seabury, 1973. 244p (Theological soundings, 4) 73-6436.
  9.75.   ISBN 0-8164-1144-1
The present collection of articles and addresses, which were previously
published in various periodicals or given to diverse audiences between
1962 and 1968, provides the devoted readers of Edward Schillebeeckx
with further evidence of his theological expertise in expounding on
several important documents of Vatican II. The amazing Dutch Roman
Catholic theologian deals here with the reformation of the Church,
the "sacrament of the world," Christian anthropology, the respective
roles of laymen, religious, priests, and bishops in the mission of the
Church, and finally, with the Catholic understanding of office in the
Church. Schillebeeckx steers a middle road between loyalty to the
letter of official documents, on the one hand, and on the other, the
spirit of Christian missionary openness to the world. Recommended
for theological collections.

THE MISSION OF THE CHURCH

The Mission of the Church

EDWARD SCHILLEBEECKX

Translated by N. D. Smith

A Crossroad Book

THE SEABURY PRESS · NEW YORK

1973
The Seabury Press
815 Second Avenue, New York, N.Y. 10017

© Sheed and Ward 1973

Originally published as *Zending van de Kerk*, Uitgeverij H. Nelissen, Bilthoven
(Holland) 1968

Nihil obstat : Lionel Swain STL, LSS *Censor*
Imprimatur : David Norris *Vicar General*
Westminster, 28 March, 1973

Library of Congress Catalog Card Number : 73-6436

ISBN : 0-8164-1144-1

Made and printed in Great Britain by
William Clowes & Sons, Limited
London, Beccles and Colchester

CONTENTS

INTRODUCTION

In this fourth volume of *Theological Soundings* I have grouped together those of my articles concerned with the church's mission which remain relevant to the contemporary situation. The church's mission is in the first instance directed inwardly, for constant self-reformation is something that the church always needs, but this has to take place in her service to the world and is thus also directed outwardly. The theme of this volume differs from that of its predecessor, *World and Church*, in that it is particularly concerned with the variety of functions in the church: laity, priests and religious, and their mutual co-operation in service to the world.

EDWARD SCHILLEBEECKX, OP
Nijmegen,
December 1972

I
THE REFORMATION OF THE CHURCH[1]

Ecclesia semper purificanda
(Constitution on the Church 1, 8)

According to the scriptural warning, God's 'judgement begins with the household of God' (1 Pet 4:17–18). In a chapter on the 'mystery of the church' contained in his remarkable and sympathetic analysis of the Vatican Council and the new theology,[2] Professor Berkouwer made the following critical comment: 'The real question now is whether and to what extent it will be possible to understand this warning completely and to make it function fully and in all its implications in the light of the factual identity of the church and the body of Christ. Is there not a danger that a duality will come about between the urgent gravity of the warning which is issued to the church and the certainty of the guarantee given to the *visible* Roman church?' (254–5).

If the catholic church traces her lasting character or indefectibility to the eschatological character of redemption and thus interiorises this in the visible church as the sacramental presence of eschatological salvation, how can she then make the gravity of the apostolic warning, which is heard 'precisely where the community is seen as the eschatological people of God' (*op cit*, p 255) fully true? It is certainly impossible to deny that this is a serious and radical question. The catholic church cannot take this warning to heart if she thinks of the divine guarantee as an automatic assurance of salvation.

In the new dogmatic constitution, however, the catholic church says that she is essentially 'always in need of purification'—she is the *ecclesia semper purificanda*. In this, any guarantee which would make salvation automatically available or which would deprive the church, both as the community of salvation and as the institution of salvation, of her need to seek salvation 'in fear and trembling' is clearly rejected. In this chapter, I will try to throw light on this aspect in particular, although inevitably only in flashes. In the first place, then, it is necessary to consider how and to what extent the Council's constitution on the church affirms an identity between the catholic church and the body of Christ and how she connects the indefectibility of the church with this identity.

I. The catholic church according to the second Vatican Council

A. The pre-conciliar draft constitution

The preparatory commission had no intention of writing a treatise *de ecclesia*. It had decided to develop a number of ecclesiological themes which needed to be thought out again in contemporary terms or even reaffirmed explicitly, since it believed that there was still a danger of a division between the 'church of love' and the 'church of law'. Virtually the central idea in the pre-conciliar draft constitution, then, was this: 'The community of the church and the mystical body of Christ are not two things, but only one (reality) with a human and a divine aspect' (*Schemata Constitutionum et Decretorum*, Series secunda, Vatican City 1962, 1, 6, p 12). Except in a few insertions, this formula can be found literally in all the later drafts and even in the definitive version of the constitution. But because of the context within which this text is contained in the various versions, including the final version, this confession of faith by the church is given certain important shades of meaning.

This first draft said that this one church, which was identified with the body of Christ, was no more or less than the 'Roman catholic church' (*op cit*, 1, 7, p 12). When this idea was, however, brought up for discussion in the plenary assemblies during the first session of the Council, it was at once sharply attacked by the world episcopate because of its oversimplified character. Apart from other fundamental objections, one of the many reasons why this pre-conciliar draft constitution was referred to the conciliar commission —which had been chosen by the fathers of the Council themselves—for its members to formulate a new version was this indiscriminate identification.

B. The second draft constitution

Partly at the request of the fathers of the council, this new commission was also not to write a treatise 'on the church', but to precede the fundamental questions by dealing more incisively with the 'mystery of the church'.

Just as in 1961 at New Delhi confession of belief in the Trinity was made the basis and condition of membership of the World Council of Churches, so too did the new draft constitution see the mystery of the church against the background of the saving activity of the Father through the Son in the Holy Spirit (*Schema constitutionis dogmaticae de ecclesia*, Pars prima, Vatican City 1963, 1, 2–4, pp 7–8). On the basis of the mission of the Son and the special mission of the Holy Spirit, the church is connected with the gratuitous saving initiative of the Father.

Whereas the first schema, in its attempt to find a closer definition of the church, had mainly looked for a link with the encyclical *Mystici Corporis*, which placed emphasis on the social and juridical and the corporative aspects of the church (although not without some reference to Romans and 1 Corinthians), this second schema looked for inspiration above all in the Pauline concept of *corpus* as found in the letters written by the apostle when he was in prison, namely that believers are the 'body of Christ' because they are, by virtue of God's saving activity, personally united with the humbled and raised body of Jesus, the Christ. This union *in corpore Christi* is realised in faith by baptism and by the celebration of the eucharist. It is only in this light that the social and juridical aspect of the concept of *corpus* is situated, that is, the church seen as a differentiated and organised entirety of gifts and ministries. In this way the second draft surmounted the narrow perspective of *Mystici Corporis*, namely by including the aspect emphasised in this encyclical in a broader and more biblically orientated perspective, in which stress was laid on the saving activity of the raised Christ who, active in the Spirit in visible forms of the church, incorporates believers personally in his body. Thus the church is, at least 'in germ and beginning', the kingdom of God (*op cit*, 1, 5, pp 9–10).

The ideas contained in the first schema were then included within this new perspective: 'The visible community (of the church) and the mystical body of Christ are not two things, but one reality, composed of a human and a divine element', not without some correspondence with the Word made flesh (*op cit*, 1, 7, p 11); similarly 'This church, founded in this world and directed towards a community, is the catholic church, guided by the pope and the bishops in union with him', to which was immediately added: 'although there are, outside her structure, various elements of sanctification which, as realities which are characteristic of the church of Christ, direct people towards the catholic unity'. The church and the mystical body of Christ, then, are one reality, but they point to two aspects of that one reality. The church is, as it were, the sacrament, the realising sign of God's redeeming presence as grace.

Despite this, the second draft constitution was also strongly criticised by many of the fathers of the council. Cardinal Lercaro especially objected to an identification without any light or shadow between the mystical body and the catholic church. He blamed a lack of eschatological tension in the church for this, resulting in a tendency to regard the church's completion in heaven as already fulfilled in the church that is still on the way and thus to anticipate an inadmissible identification. With the same thought in mind, many bishops asked for the kingdom of God to be made central so that the need for redemption of the church on the way could, in a sober and realistic manner, be more clearly brought out.

4

It was only if this were done, Cardinal König and the English Abbot Butler in particular stressed repeatedly, that the dogmatic constitution itself could be called ecumenical in its structure and that the *ecclesial* reality of the non-catholic churches could be confessed.

C. *The amended second draft and the dogmatic constitution*

In correcting the second draft constitution, all the interventions made by the bishops who had criticised it were taken into account, if not fully, at least to some extent, since those responsible for the amended version did not wish simply to force the views of the majority on the minority who held different views. The final draft was therefore to a certain extent less advanced in character than the views of the majority as expressed in the council.

Since this third schema was not a new draft constitution, but only an emendation of the second draft, the same positive elements which I have outlined in my discussion of the second draft still apply to this third schema and all that I need to do now is to throw light on the new emphases that it contains. Within the trinitarian perspective, the amended schema above all stressed the 'kyrial' value of Christ who inaugurated the veiled beginning of the kingdom of God in the old testament on earth in his life, works and person and founded his church for this purpose (*Relatio super caput primum textus emendati schematis constitutionis de ecclesia*, Vatican City 1964, p 3). For this reason, the amended second draft interpolated, between the fully elaborated confession of the Trinity and the proclamatory description of the mystery of the church, the kerygma of the kingdom of God. This divine kingdom is manifested in Christ's words, actions and miracles and finally in the whole of his person. The raised Christ sends his Spirit and gives his church the task of proclaiming the kingdom of God and, in this way, of proclaiming itself as the 'germ and beginning' of this kingdom, still on the way and directed towards eschatological completion (*Schema constitutionis de ecclesia*, Vatican City 1964,

1, 5, pp 9–10). The kingdom of God and the church are not in this way identified, but at the same time they are not separated from each other either—the church proclaims the eschatological kingdom, but does so in the first place in and through her very being, since she is the beginning of that kingdom.

After summarising the various biblical images referring to the church, the amended schema concentrated on one of these, namely the 'body of Christ'. This image was worked out even more perspicaciously than in the previous schema within the biblical context of the dead and glorified body of the Lord and of the eucharistic bread which guarantees communion with Christ's body. Yet, in spite of this, the idea of the structured social body was not lost sight of (*op cit*, 1, 7, pp 12–14).

Within the whole of this amended schema with its new emphases, the substance at least of the statement which was made in the first schema in connection with the visible and pneumatic character of the church was once again repeated: 'The community, built up of hierarchically structured elements, and the mystical body of Christ, the outwardly visible group (*coetus*) and the pneumatic community (*communitas*), the church on earth and the church endowed with heavenly gifts—these cannot be regarded as two things. They form one complex reality composed of a human and a divine element' (*op cit*, 1, 8, pp 14–15). The explanatory memorandum defined this more clearly: 'There are not two churches, but only one church, which is simultaneously both heavenly and terrestrial' (*Relatio super caput primum, op cit*, p 3). This is, according to the dogmatic constitution, the church that we confess, in the creed, to be 'one, holy, catholic and apostolic'. The amended schema then went on to say, of this same church: 'This church, founded in the world and directed towards a community, is found in the catholic church, guided by the successor of Peter and the bishops in communion with him, although there are, outside her structure (*compago*), many elements of sanctification and truth which, as the proper gifts of the church of Christ, direct people towards the catholic unity' (*Schema constitutionis de ecclesia, op cit*, 1, 7, p 15). The 'identification' between the biblical mystery of the church, as first outlined, and the *ecclesia catholica* was expressed literally as follows: *Haec* ecclesia...subsistit in *ecclesia catholica*. This *subsistere in* has not, however, the specifically scholastic significance of the word. On the contrary, it is clear from the *acta* of the council that the word was deliberately chosen in an attempt to weaken the first and far stronger formulation: *Haec ecclesia* ... est *ecclesia catholica* ('Loco est dicitur subsistit in, ut expressio melius concordet cum affirmatione de elementis ecclesialibus quae alibi adsunt'; *Relationes de singulis numeris, Relatio in* 8, p 25). This weaker formulation was used so as not to eliminate the reality of ecclesial elements in other christian churches. In justifying the acceptance or rejection of the amendments that were put forward, it was said that the intention of the commission was to indicate, by the choice of *subsistere in*, that 'the church, the inner and concealed essence of which was described..., is concretely found here on earth in the catholic church' (*Relationes, op cit, Relatio in* 8, p 23), to which was immediately added: 'This empirical church reveals the mystery (of the church), but she does not do this without shadows. She will continue to do this until she is brought into the full light, just as Christ passed through humiliation to glory' (*op cit*). It is therefore easy to see that the word *subsistere in* was used because of its power of suggestion. In this connection, the prefix *sub* is not without significance—*sistit sub* meaning that the biblical mystery of the church is present in the catholic church under all kinds of historical concealments.

The intention of the dogmatic constitution is therefore clear—the mystery of the church of Christ, as previously outlined in its essential characteristics, is not an idealistic or unreal vision, nor is it a purely future reality which is not *de facto* present anywhere today. No, the mystery of the church is really present in a very concrete community, the catholic church, although this catholic church conceals it in shadows (*op cit*). Although the catholic church deprives this mystery of its lustre, this does not, however, make its manifestation or visibility entirely impossible (*op cit*). The amendments accepted by the commission were further justified as follows: this church is *unique*, 'although ecclesial elements are also found outside her' (*op cit*, p 23). In the decree on ecumenism, it was stated not only that many ecclesial values are present 'outside the visible boundaries of the catholic church', but also that this could be 'to our edification' and moreover that the existence of different christian churches is a hindrance to the church's 'expression of the fullness of catholicity in all its aspects in the reality of life' (Decree on ecumenism, 1, 4; cf the title of ch 3). In the concrete, the 'mystery that is the church' becomes visible in the catholic church, 'both in strength and in weakness', 'in sin and in purification' (*Relationes de singulis numeris, Relatio in* 8, *op cit*, p 23). The overcoming of this weakness can only take place 'through the power of Christ and through love' (*op cit*). For this reason, the constitution on the church says that the church is *sancta simul et semper purificanda*, at the same time both holy and always called to purification, *metanoia* and renewal (*Schema constitutionis de ecclesia, op cit*, 1964, 1, 8, p 16, and the constitution on the church, 1, 8).

This schema was approved in the second instance by 2144 out of a total of 2189 votes. The opportunity that was provided to improve this text even further by submitting *modi* or, as it were, last minute corrections and more subtle shades of meaning did not produce any essential changes in connection with the particular theme under discussion here, with the result that the text which I have just analysed was the final version and therefore accurately reflects the dogmatic constitution itself. All the same, it is interesting to note that several of the fathers of the council wanted to give further shades of meaning to the already ecumenically open formulation, 'this church . . . is found in the catholic church', in order to stress even more strongly the ecclesial nature of

8

the non-catholic churches (*Modi a patribus conciliaribus proposi, a commissione doctrinali examinati, op cit*, 1964, 1, p 6).

The dogmatic constitution on the church clearly bears witness to a climate of theological opinion which was noticeably different from the one-sided catholic theology which was current, at least in certain circles, before the council and constructed its teaching on the church exclusively on the emphases contained in the encyclical *Mystici Corporis*. In fact, the rejection of the pre-conciliar draft constitution was a reaction against the one-sided emphases made in this encyclical. A clear distinction was made in the constitution between the church on earth and the kingdom of God, while the intrinsic bond between them was maintained. What is more, the biblical mystery of the church and thus the mystical body was not identified with the catholic church without some more subtle shades of meaning. In the first place, the identification, originally so strongly expressed in the word *est*, was later deliberately weakened to *subsistit in*, in the sense that this mystery of the church is found in the catholic church and even then not without all kinds of historical concealments (to which the explanatory memorandum referred).[3] It follows from this that this *subsistere in* does not exclude the presence, in various degrees, of the same mystery in other christian churches as well, which consequently includes a certain identification with the mystical body of Christ. In the second place, the constitution says that the empirical catholic church contains this biblical mystery of the church 'concealed in shadows' and 'covered with weakness'. For this reason, the catholic church is 'at the same time both holy and always called to purification'.[4] Finally, even though it is not explicitly stated in so many words, it is quite clear from the whole of this dogmatic exposition that the constitution accepts a certain distinction between the church as the 'institution of salvation' and as the 'fruit of the redemption',[5] in other words, a distinction between the institutional element in the church and the eschatological community of faith and grace, a distinction which nevertheless remains inadequate. In the second chapter of the constitution, this statement about the 'people of God' is found: 'God has called together and made into a church the assembly (*congregatio*) of those who, in faith, look up towards Jesus, the bringer about of salvation and the principle of unity and peace, so that this church may be for all people and for each individual the visible sacrament of this unity which brings salvation' (Constitution on the church, 2, 9).

Finally, this is said about the actual community of salvation, the church: 'She strides forward (*procedens*) straight through all tests and vicissitudes, comforted (in the biblical sense, also, that is, strengthened) by the power of God's grace, pledged to her by the Lord's promise, so that, in the weakness of the flesh, she may not defect in perfect trust (*ut . . . a perfecta fidelitate non deficiat*), but remain the worthy bride of her Lord and, thanks to the activity of the Holy Spirit, never cease to renew herself until she reaches, through the cross, the light which knows no setting' (*ibid,* 2, 9).

My theme is thus summarised by the constitution in the witness that it bears to the fact that the mystery of the church, as the eschatological community of faith and grace of those who believe in Christ and, guided by the world episcopate in communion with the pope, look forward to the eschatological completion of the kingdom of God, may hope for the powerful promise of the Lord that the church will remain the faithful and worthy bride of Christ and always renew herself in the weakness of the flesh through the Holy Spirit.

This promise is equally applicable to the church's *diakonia*,[6] both in its task of proclaiming and teaching (*op cit,* 3, 25) and of cultic and sacramental sanctification by leading in prayer and administering the sacraments (*op cit,* 3, 26) and in its task of pastoral and guiding authority (*op cit,* 3, 27). In the constitution, the biblical warning that renewal in the weakness of the flesh through the Spirit is always necessary is given in the first place to the whole people of God, even before there is any question of a functional or ministerial distinction between the faithful and those holding office. This means that both the hierarchy and the believing people of God are subject to the biblical warning that there must be unceasing renewal and a constant inward return to the christian sources.

Thus we may conclude that the church, both as a community and as an institution of salvation, is, according to the dogmatic constitution of the second Vatican Council, subject to the powerful promise of her Lord, who will not allow her to be unfaithful. Nonetheless, she must constantly renew herself in the power of the Holy Spirit—and thus we come back again to Berkouwer's question: 'Is there not a danger that a duality will come about between the urgent gravity of the warning which is issued to the church and the certainty of the guarantee given to the visible Roman church?'

II. The indefectibility of the church and the biblical warning

The dogmatic constitution on the church thus on the one hand regards the biblical mystery of the church as being present in the 'Roman church', that is—expressed formally —as present in the church that is guided by the successor of Peter and the college of bishops in communion with this successor,[7] with the result that the full promise of the Lord's assistance applies to this church. On the other hand, the constitution also gives this church an urgent warning of the need for constant purification. Both of these facts point clearly to the complete absence of any tendency on the part of the constitution to make salvation and the divine guarantee—or rather promise—in the catholic church automatic. This does not mean, however, that this simultaneous affirmation of the church's indefectibility and her need for constant purification does not give rise to certain delicate and radical problems. It is in any case clear that, according to the constitution on the church, the biblical mystery of the church is certainly found in the church of Rome, but hidden under historical concealments and even misgrowths which cannot, however, result in fundamental unfaithfulness on the part of the church as a whole because of Christ's promise. In other words, it is impossible for the church to become the synagogue again, to be unfaithful to her fundamental task and mission, though she owes this not to her own perseverance, but to the unmerited grace of God which makes her persevere.

The two facts—indefectibility and purification—give rise to a powerful tension. The one element does not do away with the other but, because of the situation 'in the flesh', evokes it. Precisely because of her promised indefectibility, the church is in the concrete the church which is always purifying and reforming herself. To put it in a different way, the church's constant reformation of herself in faith is the historical modality of her indefectibility. What is at once clear from this is that this indefectibility is not something that displays itself in triumphalism, but something that consists of a weakness in which God's grace triumphs. Consequently, there is no indefectibility *despite* weakness or possessed automatically, but only an indefectibility in faith, hope and love. It is precisely on the basis of the Lord's powerful promise that the church's continued existence takes on the historical form of *metanoia*, renewal and self-correction carried out again and again. Even though outside stimuli are certainly able to help in this process, this constant renewal undertaken in God's grace must be understood literally as self-correction that is always subject to the lasting norm of scripture, which has after all, throughout the whole biblical tradition of the church, always had the function of leading the people of God and their hierarchical leaders again and again back to the original sources.[8]

The indefectibility of the church, then, is not a static, an essentialist quality which can overlook the church's existential faith and obedience to the Lord's promise. It is, on the contrary, a quality which functions *within* the church's faith and trust. If the catholic church regards this indefectibility as a dogma, this naturally means that it functions within the church's faith. The concept of guarantee—which is incidentally far less frequently used now by catholic theologians—is no more than a juridical extrapolation of the supremacy of grace, which is so powerful that it functions within the church's response in faith. This indefectibility, which functions within faith and the church's correction of herself in faith, cannot, however, be objectivised juridically, because the essence of the church as founded by Christ implies the existential experience of the community of salvation precisely as the fruit of the redemption. If, on the other hand, the church and her qualities are defined separately from the actual faith of the community of the church in Christ's promise, then what is described is a non-church. It is after all essential for the church to be Christ's salvation insofar as this manifests itself visibly and tangibly among us in the historical act of acceptance by faith and love, in which grace appears precisely as triumphant grace. It is in and through faith, hope and love which constantly impel us to *metanoia* and renewal that the promise of indefectibility —which is therefore not a purely juridical or forensic promise—is interiorised in the church. 'The *a priori* character of the guarantee which is related to the visible church in her concrete form' (G. C. Berkouwer, *op cit*, p 266) does not therefore weaken the gravity of self-examination and reflection—it is only in the church's examination of and thinking about herself that this guarantee can function properly. It is only permissible to view this guarantee in connection with love and faith and walking in the truth. That is why the dogmatic constitution places the church's indefectibility under the constant *epiclesis* to the Holy Spirit: 'So that . . . she may . . . thanks to the activity of the Holy Spirit, never cease to renew herself.' This indefectibility is not a claim, but the fruits of trust 'in fear and trembling' in God's promise.

The catholic view of the church's indefectibility has often been misrepresented, as though it were fundamentally and primarily connected with the structures of the church as distinct from the church as the community of grace and faith. Now the constitution on the church has strongly emphasised that there are not 'two churches'—the church of the structures and that of the community of grace. One may say that the church is the institution of salvation precisely insofar as she is also the loving community of grace and faith. She is also the body of the Lord precisely insofar as her members are the recipients of the grace of the Spirit of Christ. One is bound to affirm, together with Y. Congar that, on the basis of the definitive and eschatological character of the incarnation, the idea of the 'people of God' has to be supplemented by the idea of the 'body of the Lord', in order to express the fact that, unlike ancient Israel, the new people of God cannot be superseded.[9] Between Christ's resurrection and his *parousia*, the church is situated in the tension of the 'already' and the 'not yet', but the 'not yet' should not allow us to forget that salvation has been definitively realised in Christ. This has placed the people of God in the situation of the 'body of Christ' and this is an entirely new condition, in which speaking about sinfulness and defectibility means something quite different from what it does in the case of the people of God who were not yet the 'body of the Lord'.[10] The 'body of the Lord' of its very nature also means 'inhabited by the Holy Spirit'. John's statement has to be taken very seriously: 'For as yet the Spirit had not been given, because Jesus was not yet glorified'.[11] The gift of the Spirit as a person is the eschatological gift, presupposing the death and resurrection of Jesus. This gift is the principle which makes the church move *effectively* towards eschatological fulfilment and which distinguishes her from ancient Israel, which was still able to be fundamentally unfaithful to the promise. The church is the extension of the earlier 'people of God', but in the totally new mode of the 'body of the Lord' and thus as the temple of the Holy Spirit.[12] This implies that, unlike ancient Israel, the church not only lives from God's gifts, but also is borne by God in his own person and therefore effectively and irrevocably towards eschatological fulfilment. Through the incarnation, completed in Christ's resurrection from the dead and resulting in the sending of the Holy Spirit, God begins in a different and extremely personal manner, to be God for people, thanks to his absolute communication of himself, culminating in the personal gift of the Holy Spirit.

This is manifested in the church precisely as the body of Christ. The basis of the indefectibility of the church is not purely the fact that the people of God has been constituted into the body of Christ since Easter and Pentecost, but the fact that this body is the dwelling of the Holy Spirit. The Spirit is in fact effectively and irrevocably the eschatological gift and it is he that therefore leads the church from within indefectibly towards eschatological fulfilment.

This same reality is also the basis of the catholic view of the saving efficacy (*ex opere operato*) of the sacraments of the church, of the power of the church's ministry of the word and of the so-called 'infallibility' or indefectible faithfulness of the church's teaching office to the apostolic *paradosis*, the gospel of Christ. This efficacy of the church as the people of God and as the official ministry stems from the 'soul' inhabiting the 'body of the Lord', in other words, the Holy Spirit. After all, however necessary it may be to stress the unity of the plan of salvation—the unity of mankind, Israel and the church—it is important to remember that Easter and Pentecost introduced an entirely new element into the history of salvation. Before the incarnation, God was certainly personally concerned with mankind in grace and care and in an absolutely transcendental manner which allowed secular history to take its course, but at the same time made it a history of salvation. The personal appearance of the Son as a man among other men within human history, however, visibly established an absolutely new datum in world history —the terrestrial, personal body of Jesus, the Christ, which took up its abode with us: 'For in him the whole fullness of deity dwells bodily' (Col 2 : 9), the *corpus Christi*. After Christ's resurrection, this same body has continued to be with us under the sacramental form of the eucharist—the *corpus eucharisticum*. Moreover, this body also has a lasting, historical, sacral and visible form in the 'body of the Lord that is the church'—the *corpus ecclesiasticum*.

This fundamentally changes the situation of the people of God after Easter and Pentecost, which are God's *eschatological* acts. It is from this that the indefectibility of the church comes—on the basis of this beginning of the eschatological gift, the church goes forward towards the ultimate fulfilment of this gift and cannot be diverted from this aim. She cannot be diverted from this end in her progress towards the unveiled and full epiphany because the end is already given in faith. The Holy Spirit, the *telos* of the Trinity, and God's gift to the church herself, takes her to this 'end'.

It is therefore quite clear that the indefectibility of the church is not a claim, but pure grace. It is, however, a grace that is interiorised *in* the church herself, the body of the Lord, by the personal in-dwelling of the Holy Spirit. The church is not only the sacramental presence of salvation, the sign of Christ's rule—she is also the presence of this salvation to which consent is given (in grace). Just as the body of Christ is not only the visible form of God's grace, but also that within which Christ as the 'servant of God' expressed constitutively his consent and obedience to the Father, so too is the church as the 'body of Christ' not only the concentrated presence of grace, but also praising and thanking consent in Christ to this grace. The body of Christ that is the church is therefore not only the constant gift and the continuous flowing through of God's saving power, but also the flowing through of this power to which consent is given, in the existential experience of the gift of grace itself.[13] It is precisely in our giving consent in faith and our obedience to the

16

will of the Father, in the footsteps of Christ, that God's rule becomes a historical reality and that the kingdom of God grows in the visible world.

But it is also this existential consent—which is essential for the church herself—that makes the indefectibility of the church a *history*, a history not only of human actions, but also of grace itself. The church reveals herself as holy in God's sight wherever and insofar as consent is given existentially to grace in faith and love. Because of our life in the flesh, the church cannot, however, give adequate consent to grace in her members—in each one of us there always remains some part which is immature and sinful. Sin is a very personal event. Mankind does not sin collectively but, through an accumulation of personal sins, the church, in the actual form in which she appears, that is, in our supposition, as the church of Rome, can be responsible for all kinds of errors, lost opportunities in history, cases of lack of understanding and so on. The church derives her reality from grace to which consent is given, the grace which is effectively in man's living response to it, and because this always lags behind the gift of grace itself, the church is 'at the same time both holy and always called to purification'. Being church is essentially a covenant relationship—this is why the dogmatic constitution supplements the image of the 'body of the Lord', which might too strongly suggest an identification, with the image of the covenant between the bridegroom and the bride (Constitution on the church, 1, 7), two subjects in one covenant and love, but still two subjects. I sometimes wonder whether christians of the reformation do not regard the church too much as the *object* of God's activity in grace, instead of regarding her as a *subject* in the inalienable sense of the word, although, in this case, purely as the subject of grace, for which the *gratia* is really *domestica* (*forma inhaerens*), precisely because of her supremacy and sovereignty, in other words, as a subject which is in grace and yet at the same time 'in the flesh'.

The history of the church is therefore, in reality, a history

of constant fall and constant renewal. This renewal is, however, always self-correction on the basis of the church's
evangelical principles—her going back to the evangelical
sources on the basis of the indwelling Spirit who makes
everything new and yet only reminds of Christ. (On the
basis of the ecclesial and therefore non-alien values in the
non-catholic churches which were recognised by the Council,
we may add to this that, precisely because of their reformed
character, the other christian churches have an essential
function historically with regard to the church's indefectibility in the mode of constantly renewed purification. These
other churches therefore belong to the historical mode of
indefectibility which the Council attributes to the church of
Christ.) For this reason, all the qualities of the church—her
holiness, her one-ness, her indefectibility—are dynamic
realities which have a history and go through good and less
good periods, but which nonetheless always find the principle of continuous self-correction and purification in themselves (as interiorised grace by virtue of the indwelling of
the Holy Spirit), in the light of the scripture. This means,
however, that, viewed at one particular point of history,
what is reformable and what is not reformable in the church
are so closely and so mysteriously interwoven that the church
cannot always, in reflection, make a precise distinction between them. The church cannot boast of a triumphant
possession of the truth, but she does have a faith, in fear and
trembling, in her dynamic indefectibility, the essentials of
which are gradually deposited in the history of the church
and included in a constantly renewed questioning. But, in
this, the church continues to be the community of faith
which, guided by her office, confesses together that God's
grace, which is forgiveness and power to renew from within,
is effectively triumphant. The church's confession is an
inner element of this victory, projected on the screen of
history. The church's authentic proclamation of definitive
and irrevocable salvation is therefore no longer able to cease
in the history of mankind. In obscurity and disunity, the

church is the epiphany on earth of this irrevocable salvation
—*sancta et simul purificanda*. In this way, the church also
confesses herself when she expresses her faith in the
church. Her faith in herself is faith in the supremacy of
grace, despite the disunity of man. Although she is bound to
go through good and less good periods in her history, the
church cannot be diverted from her orientation towards the
eschatological gift because she always carries this gift as
grace within herself, at least in germ. This is the consequence
of the eschatological and therefore definitive basis of the indefectibility of a church which is still on the way towards
the ultimate kingdom. Since grace to which consent is given
forms an essential part of the church, since this grace constitutes the church, the church is both indefectible and
'called to purification'. The church on earth is self-correction
in grace, either in sloth or in urgent zeal. She is subject to
the new testament warning.

2
IS THE CHURCH ADRIFT?[14]

I. An outline of the situation

In the past, the church has often been compared with an island in the middle of the frantic and rapid traffic of the world. In reality, however, she is far more caught up in that rushing traffic. Almost unrecognisably, but certainly unmistakably, she takes part in it, in life and thought. Even the fathers of the church, who were so much closer to nature than we are today in our modern technical world, as witnesses to the church in the first centuries of her life, did not regard the church as a motionless figure looking anxiously from the safety of the shore at the raging sea and everything that was driven along in it. They saw the church herself as a boat at sea, tossed by the waves and often creaking in all its joints, but always with its helm pointing towards the one goal—the safe port. Her master, Christ, had promised that she would arrive intact—not that she would not encounter storms, but that she would overcome them.

The church is not a static, unchangeable factor, a granite block, a solid rock in the sea around which the changing, ever-moving tide of the world flows while she remains calmly fixed and not swept along in the movement of time. 'Stat crux, dum volvitur orbis'? No, it is not true that the cross remains motionless while the world whirls and eddies around it. Ought we not rather say that the cross is caught up in the current of history and is, precisely for this reason, our comfort, our strength and our foundation? It was not when he was on the shore that Christ was the comfort of the apostles struggling in the storm, but when he was with them in the boat and seemed to disregard the storm.

Those who do not experience the church as an insecure boat at sea that is safe because of Christ's presence, but as a solid rock—these are the christians who find faith in the church difficult these days. The church is showing herself to be so flexible and is introducing so many changes and renewals. These christians cannot sincerely bring themselves to take part in these changes. Very often they are genuinely afraid that this renewal is simply a lenient adaptation to the world, a concession carried out in an attempt to make the church sympathetic. But such small concessions made in the beginning soon become bigger and more fundamental. Is it not necessary, in the end, to protest against them? Is the christian birthright not being sold for a mess of pottage?

The beginning was very inconspicuous. Permission was given to drink water before going to communion, at first plain water. In itself, this was insignificant, but for many christians it was revolutionary. In the past, they had endured raging thirst in order to be able to go to communion. They had even had severe qualms of conscience after cleaning their teeth and had wondered anxiously whether they could still receive the sacrament. People with a more easy-going disposition had long since ceased to worry about this, others felt a sense of liberation, but others felt cheated and asked themselves, 'We have had to suffer torments for so long because of this and now, quite suddenly, we are allowed to do it.' And very soon this first 'concession' was followed by others. Permission was given to eat up to three hours before receiving communion and to drink up to only one hour before, and not only water. Later on, permission was even granted to eat one hour before communion. In the meantime, the rules of Lent and fasting were virtually abolished in their traditional form.

The unchangeable block that was, as a whole, called 'christianity' seemed to be slipping. Almost every month seemed to bring some new change and some christians began to think that everything in the church could change now. Others, who regarded all aspects of life in the church as equally important, whether it was a point of faith like the Trinity or to do with the snake in paradise, the mass or benediction, the rosary or the stations of the cross, the official creed or a hymn to Mary, regulations like Lent or remaining sober or the commandment of chastity, became extremely uneasy. What had previously been venerated in the church was now, so it seemed, being publicly burnt. It was as though Clovis' action long ago was being repeated now in reverse. But the burning of the pagan images by the proud king of the Franks was an action taken to prevent an unchristian attitude from entering christian life. Now, however, it seemed as if the church was intent on burning her own familiar images—forms that had been known since time immemorial. For years she had opposed cremation, but now this was officially accepted by the church. The celebration of the mass had for long been associated with a mysterious language, Latin, and with music that was unknown to the rest of the world, Gregorian chant, that it was scarcely possible to think of mass without these things. Now, however, it seemed as though they could disappear, slowly but surely, from the service of the word and even from the whole celebration of the eucharist. Even the characteristically catholic vocabulary, familiar for so long from the catechism, for example, gave way to a brand new language. In some countries, even the children's catechism itself was abolished. The bible, which had frequently been regarded in the past as typically protestant, is now displayed all day long on many catholic altars; and what is more, the same bible is now read, as a whole, by catholics.

It looks, then, as though what had become the skin of catholicism is being stripped from the living flesh. No longer are heretical books burnt amid general rejoicing at the entrance to the church—the catholic has now to throw his own familiar traditions on the pyre while the church calls on him to recognise the presence of christian truths and above all of a more profound evangelical inspiration in his 'separated brothers', to whom the door was always firmly shut in the past whenever they dared to knock with the bible in their hands.

Moreover, whereas catholic priests in the past always said
that a catholic family had to be a big family, the church
now says that a sense of responsibility is required in the
founding of a family. Even more than this—with precisely
this idea of human responsibility in mind, ways and methods
which were previously subject to excommunication now
appear to be open to catholics.

In addition to all these changes approved or undertaken
by the highest authority, countless opinions which seem to
assail the very essence of the church's confession of faith are
current within the church. One of these tendencies, many
catholics believe, is the 'movement' aiming to abolish the
law of priestly celibacy. Priests are now going around like
laymen. The cassock and the cowl have disappeared and
although priests continue to wear the Roman collar in some
countries, in many others they no longer have a single outward sign to distinguish them from laymen.

But it is above all what priests say and preach that seems
to be a different faith from what was heard in the past from
the pulpit. The word 'God' is rarely heard now. A great
deal is said, and in greater detail, about Christ, but it is said
about 'the man Jesus' who is like us except for sin, although
he was not free from temptations, according to modern
catholic preachers. In the past, it was impressed on catholics
that the central christian virtue was submissive obedience to
bishops and priests. Now, however, they are told that christians have come of age and the church is no more the business
of her priests than it is of the laity. Whereas the hierarchy
was previously regarded as unassailable—even though no
notice was frequently taken of a particular person holding
office in the church because of his character or temperament
—decisions made by those in authority in the church are now
publicly attacked and the people of God, who have now
become active, often point in a direction which is different
from that indicated by the hierarchy. Sometimes the official
church even sanctions these different paths afterwards. Was

this not so in the case of the liturgical renewal which the Council approved in broad outline?

The church that once proclaimed that evil and error had no rights has now proclaimed, in the second Vatican Council, the freedom of religion, the right of every man (while observing the general well-being) to conduct his life, as far as religion is concerned, according to his own conviction and within a church or religion chosen in accordance with his own conscience. Previously, it was always stated that there was no salvation outside the church of Rome. Now, however, the Roman church herself teaches that all men of good will, even atheists, can attain salvation. In the past, the church preached a flight from the world, but now the Council has urged us to transform our world into a better place for man to live in and has even stated that a glimpse of the eschatological kingdom can be seen in this process of transformation. The christian is even called upon to take part in social and decolonialising 'revolutions' aimed at getting rid of religious, racial and linguistic discrimination, although, at an earlier stage in her history, the church went to war against the Turkish threat to christianity. In America, France and Spain today, young priests take part in protest marches against social injustice but, in the past, it was taught that charity had to transcend this injustice and, as it were, cover it up. In some places, it is still being disputed whether or not a catholic university should be under the direct control of the episcopate, while in other countries, where the catholic university is directed by laymen, there is already fierce discussion as to whether a 'catholic university' has any meaning at all in our present-day society. In still other countries, there are no catholic universities at all, but the theology taught at these 'secular' universities sets the standard for the whole world. Many of the achievements, customs and traditions inherited from the past are in this way being revised today.

It would be possible to go on for hours in this vein, but what I have said already ought to be enough to provide a picture of a church that is in the world and to give a good idea of the extent to which historicity, the process of becoming, enters the church's very being.

Many catholics are very alarmed and disturbed by all this and this is to some extent understandable—they had to make serious sacrifices in the past to fulfil faithfully what the church ruled and now the church is simply doing away with many of these rules. It is not surprising that some catholics feel cheated and regard what is taking place now as a kind of mockery of all their hard sacrifices. Some leave the church because of this. Others remain faithful to the church, but cannot understand her any longer. They try to understand and do succeed in understanding certain aspects of the church's new attitude, but they are still seriously disturbed. Others again are looking forward to an *aggiornamento*, but it is all taking place far too quickly for their liking, in too perfunctory a manner and with too much improvisation. But above all it is the *infallibility* of the church and her teaching authority which seems to so many catholics to have suffered most in the present situation. They inevitably make comparisons with the past, when so many catholics were convinced that the pope only had to say one word and everyone knew infallibly what was right and what was wrong.

II. The christian courage to change

Anyone observing the rapid pace of life in the world today is bound to say that the church can sin more by omission than by too great haste and more by adapting herself too slowly than by adapting herself too quickly, because she runs the great risk of being left behind as an incomprehensible relic dating from an earlier age. That was the charismatic vision of John xxiii when he applied the 'secular' word *aggiornamento* to the church as a demand. This Italian word means 'bringing up to date'. The church has to become a church 'of today'. In her concrete manifestation, she must free herself of anachronisms. This implies far more than a mere external adaptation. It is a question of enabling the church to function in the present-day image of man and the world, in the real life of man today. We have to listen to the good news of Christ, as he left it to the faithfulness of his church, once again in such a way that it sounds in our ears as real and good news. We must not think of this as having, for tactical and educational reasons, to restore an old picture of faith that the church has had in her keeping for a long time, to put it in a new frame and display it again in order to gain more recruits. Our task of bringing the church up to date goes much deeper than this. The good news must be heard, now, in our times, as the original christian message and as none other. It must also be practised as the original christian message. Otherwise it will no longer be possible to assimilate it in our lives.

Any christian who realises that this new and repeated preaching of the whole evangelical message is the church's constant task is bound to become less disturbed by renewals in the church. Even more particularly, any christian who recalls that what is done away with now is frequently no more than something with a very recent and short tradition behind it and was possibly even a renewal itself at the time of its introduction, compared with a quite differently orientated christian life. Let me give one example of this. According to certain late medieval texts, the *small* family was then the mark of a genuinely christian marriage, since the conviction prevailed at that time that even marital sexuality was to some extent sinful because of the enjoyment associated with the sex act. Christians who gave way to sexual desire as infrequently as possible and consequently did not have a large family were therefore able to give their marriage the stamp of a truly christian community, and marriage in which the partners had freely chosen to have no children was regarded as the highest form of christian marriage. It is clear, then, that faith is never entirely dissociated from a historically conditioned view of man and the world. Various practical conclusions may therefore be a 'commandment of the hour'—a task which, given that particular human presupposition, follows from christianity—and these consequences should not be identified with christianity as such. If, because of our changed way of associating with the things of this world, our view of man changes, then the earlier consequences of christianity will also change—they must be changed if they are really to remain consistent with christianity.

A new view of man and the world, however, is not something that forces itself suddenly on the whole world at the same time. Human society consists of people who, as far as their view of man and the world is concerned, belong to different historical periods, although they are all living at the same historical time. There are probably no people living in the Western world of today whose view of life is still that of the stone age. But we are all aware from our everyday experience that there are among us people who are still living according to a view of man and the world which goes back to a rather less remote historical period—the middle ages, the *Ancien Régime*, the nineteenth century, the period between the two world wars, the immediate post-war years and finally the period of the last five or so years. These people, whose mental attitude is that of the early nineteen-sixties, are those who are in fact growing towards an entirely new view of man and the world. This great diversity in human assumptions confronts our experience and expression of faith with far greater difficulties than those experienced in the past. The same expression of faith may be felt by one person to be the authentic form of his experience of faith, but by another christian with different basic assumptions as an intolerable modernism. One believer would choke if he had to express his faith in the forms that have such deep meaning for another christian.

It is therefore clear that all believers, in other words the church, should, in mutual trust, allow each other a certain diversity in the expression and experience of faith. On the other hand, it is equally obvious that the church as a whole is bound to look ahead and must therefore risk the *aggiorna-*

mento. In principle, she *must* be fully behind the will to change, because it is precisely this that constitutes the essence of the church—she is the visible presence of grace in and for this world. This was her task in the 'ancient' world, and in the early middle ages, when the fusion of the later ancient christian civilisation with other younger cultures, especially the so-called barbarian Germanic, Frankish and Celtic elements, caused the world to acquire those characteristics which we now call typically medieval. It is also her task now, in the world of the twentieth century, to be the visible presence of grace in our society. She would be failing in this essential task if she were to continue to present grace visibly in medieval forms, for example, since modern man is quite simply not medieval. Although every period has its special dangers, it also and primarily has its special grace and any christian who remains deaf to this is being unfaithful to Christ here and now. On the basis of God's plan, the christian believes primarily in the goodness of creation and therefore in the good aspect of a fundamental change in human society, even though this will not make him blind to its dangers. But the christian who is primarily aware of the danger is in fact doubting faith in creation which is confirmed by the redemption and is turning things completely upside down. For contemporary man, then, the church must be the effective and visible presence of grace and she must therefore, while remaining true to herself, that is, in faithfulness to Christ, speak the language of contemporary man. Of course, sin is included within this new language, but not because it is new and no longer medieval (as those christians whose view of man and the world is still medieval are inclined to think). Language and style—not simply conceived in the purely grammatical sense, but as a living structure and the expression of man's attitude—cannot therefore still be 'medieval' (or tied to any other past period whatever), but must be contemporary, existentially relevant. This may become nothing but a series of cries, a *theologia exclama-*

28

tionum, and has in fact become just this in some places, but this is no reason for putting an end to the urgent task.

It is, of course, true that grace continues to be actively present, for example, in out of date liturgical celebrations, but in the long run people will cease to come to these services because they are no longer able to experience the presence of grace in them. The assertion that grace is also active in older structures may be quite orthodox, but it is above all purely abstract, empty and existentially heterodox. Anyone who really cares for the whole people of God will therefore be able to make personal sacrifices and, out of love for the church, for living people, will not be disturbed because of all the changes that are taking place, but will welcome them, even though he may put his own wishes with regard to faith at least partly aside. It is, of course, true that changes and renewals, even though they may be extremely necessary and should, in themselves, be welcomed, do demand, from people who all their lives have had to think, act and react differently, a rather difficult adaptation. They have to break away from deeply rooted habits which have supported, comforted and strengthened them throughout the whole of their christian lives and which are not easy to leave behind, precisely because they are so closely entwined into their lives. And what is new still has to prove its worth. For example, the plan to replace driving on the left-hand side of the road in Sweden by driving on the right, which offered a great advantage to world traffic, meant that many drivers, whose habits were deeply rooted, have had difficulty in adapting themselves. But this sacrifice is required of them for the sake of everyone's well-being.

But in addition to these rather more psychological and sociological difficulties of adaptation to new forms, there are many other and deeper questions which are coming to light in the church. It is easy enough to understand the discussion about whether the liturgy should be celebrated in Latin or in the language of the people as a question that does not belong to the *essence* of the church (however much

it may be existentially a question of faith!). Similarly, it is
not difficult to understand that eating or not eating before
communion or eating one or three hours before communion
does not form an essential part of christianity. The diversity
that is found in various spheres of 'secular' life—driving on
the left or driving on the right, the different priorities on
roads, the various forms of state, such as republics,
monarchies and so on—has certainly taught modern man that
the organisation of the church, although it is necessary, can
also vary. There must be a definite organisation, but the
form that is given to this may change according to the
situation.

This variety in secular life can also teach him not to be
astonished when, for example, missionaries preach to certain Eastern people that Christ sits at the left hand of the
Father, although the bible says that he sits at the right hand.
They do so, of course, because a seat at the left hand is, for
some people, the place of honour and it is this place of
honour that the bible wished to stress. The Western catholic
is no longer alarmed by the fact that Japanese catholics
never kneel before the blessed sacrament, but make what is
in their country the highest mark of honour, a deep bow,
although, in the past, a long controversy was conducted about
whether the Japanese could be 'dispensed' from kneeling.
Because of our present-day understanding of diversity in the
world, we judge such cultural differences very differently
now. The pastoral constitution of the second Vatican Council affirms that the church is not exclusively bound to any
culture and the decrees on ecumenism and on the Eastern
catholic churches state that even dogma, liturgy and legis-
lation are not bound to Western concepts, forms of worship
and Roman jurisprudence.

The modern christian is no longer shocked by the fact
that native dancing takes place within the framework of
African or Indonesian liturgical ceremonies. Because the
world has been made one by the press, the radio and television, people have come to accept things that were origin-

ally strange here and this is bound to have an influence on the experimental liturgy. But, in this sphere especially, what may well be a really religious experience for one christian may at the same time be almost blasphemous for another. He may believe that he is bound to resist such liturgical attempts as 'a member of the church', but, in so doing, he is forgetting that his resistance is really a *cultural* appreciation and should not be identified with membership of the church as such. We should also remember that the frequently very moving Gregorian chant was partly derived from secular music, sometimes even quite 'light' music. The melody of the beautiful Advent hymn *Creator alme siderum*, for example, was in the first place a folk song with a secular text sung at medieval markets. There must be a difficult period of transition, with tentative efforts and some failures, before really good and contemporary church music can evolve. A transitory period of this kind requires patience and courage on the part of the christian to get through the inevitable discomforts.

But all these difficulties, however radical they may be, are only, as it were, external changes in faith. The transition becomes more delicate when it concerns the church's teaching about faith. But here too, a better insight into what this teaching really is can dispel a great deal of alarm.

Since the definition of the first Vatican Council of the dogma of papal infallibility, in the sense that, in certain clearly defined cases (in fact, exceptional cases), the pope is able to establish a truth of faith infallibly, many catholics have been practically convinced that everything that the pope says, in his addresses to audiences, his sermons and encyclicals, are quite simply infallible statements. It is in this way that a myth has come about concerning the church's teaching authority. It is, however, in practice frequently forgotten that the church's teaching office takes as its point of departure not only revelation, but also human assumptions (which may or may not be true) and that furthermore it is only rarely that it appeals to the fullness of the apostolic authority. The teaching office has always made a distinction between fallible and infallible statements, at least in abstract, formal definitions. Even the fallible teaching authority of the church is always a real authority and thus calls for obedient consent (which allows for various degrees), but it is certainly not infallible, which means that it can make a mistake. But quite apart from mistakes, there is, between error and truth, a whole range of certainties, greater, less great and smaller. Our human opinions are, after all, very rarely entirely true or entirely untrue. They are usually, so to speak, profiles of the truth in which a great deal remains unexpressed and in which what we have expressed in a main clause might have been better said in a subordinate clause, thus giving our perspective of the truth a more subtle shade of meaning. Our words may also embrace a truth which is formulated in such a one-sided way that the most important element is not expressed. It is also possible that the omission of this important datum may reduce our statement to the level of a nuance of secondary importance, whereas it was in fact affirmed as the major truth.

The mistake that many catholics, both leaders of the church and faithful, have made is that they have tended to believe, on the basis of the rightful conviction that we are really in touch with the absolute, we already possess this absolute truth in an absolute manner. This opinion is based on an unjustifiable theory of knowledge, an attitude of mind which has failed to grasp in particular that the christian revelation is a mystery that will never be exhausted. Even dogmatic definitions can only inwardly point to this mystery —they can be meaningful, but only from a historically conditioned point of view as concepts taken from a particular culture. It would seem that it is not too difficult a task to define faith concretely in a society that is uniform, but great difficulties arise if the society is pluriform. There were, of course, purely terminological difficulties even in the earliest period of the church's history. For centuries the debate continued about the precise formulation of the mystery of Christ and the Trinity—what 'person' meant for one group of theologians meant 'nature' for another and the one group maintained that there was only one nature in Christ, while the other insisted that there were two natures in him. Each group declared that the other was heretical. In our present society, however, there are more than simply terminological differences. There is great diversity in the meaning of concepts and above all in philosophical assumptions, making it very difficult to formulate a unanimous definition of faith. This is why the second Vatican Council tended to resort to broader and rather vague definitions. In the prevailing circumstances, these did more justice to the indescribable character of the mystery of salvation, because they avoided the risk of taking one precise element out of the total content and, as it were, defining this in itself. In a broader definition, the whole of the content of faith is given a fairer hearing, whereas there is always a danger, in a more precise definition, of distorting the total content and of forgetting the complementary aspect that is not included in the definition. This danger is all the greater nowadays, because the concepts used in such a precise definition will no longer be so uniformly understood by everyone as they were, for example, in the middle ages. A clearly defined formulation of faith does not therefore give us greater clarity. On the contrary—a precise understanding of such an exact definition requires volumes of commentary.

This modern diffidence to formulate faith precisely is an indication of the fact that reverence for the mystery, which is offered to us for our experience, but which constantly eludes us, has sharpened our awareness of the inadequate and vulnerable nature of definitions of faith. Every precise definition is, as such, vulnerable, because it points inwardly to one aspect of the totality of faith which has its value as a reality within this totality. As a precisely defined aspect, however, it is, so to speak, separated from this totality and threatens to become an ideology and to lead an independent existence. The best example that I can give of this is the definition of papal infallibility made at the first Vatican Council. It became quite clear at the second Vatican Council that this papal privilege had to be seen as an expression of the lasting character of the whole of the people of God, the church, in which the Holy Spirit dwells, and at the same time as something that is embedded in the collegiality of the world episcopate. Anyone who simply reasons in accordance with the definition of the first Vatican Council will therefore come to the following conclusion. As the church's defined and revealed teaching shows, infallibility is a privilege that is connected with the papal office. The believing community therefore possesses infallibility only insofar as it is open and obedient to what the pope teaches. Faith therefore means the obedient acceptance of truths which are put before us as revealed by the church's teaching authority for us to believe. But such a view is bound to come into conflict with the dogmatic constitution on revelation of the second Vatican Council, which states that this infallibility is also based on the collective sense of faith of the whole of the people of God, which has received the anointing of the Holy Spirit. The people of God receive these gifts of the Spirit so that they may also listen faithfully to the word of God. The faith of the whole church is itself infallible, but it is guided by the church's teaching office. It is precisely because it guides an infallible faith in the church that this teaching authority must itself possess a certain *charisma* of infallibility. Otherwise, by virtue of its authority, it would be able to separate the people of God from its faithfulness to God. Regarded in this light, then, the infallibility of the church's office is to some extent secondary in comparison with the infallible faith of the whole church. And this is quite the opposite to what could be concluded from the isolated datum of the first Vatican Council. The teaching office of the church can only, critically, authoritatively and selectively, bring forward what is already present and living in the tradition of faith of the whole church. Thus the teaching authority of the church in fact functions quite differently from how one might conclude that it would function according to the definition of faith as formulated in isolated precision at the first Vatican Council.

It should therefore be clear, from what I have said in the preceding paragraph, that the definition of the first Vatican Council is still irrevocably true, but that this truth is only realised in its full authenticity within the totality of faith as defined by the second Vatican Council. Any christian who accepts the pronouncement of the first, but denies the statement of the second, Vatican Council is clearly formally heretical. The first Vatican Council did not, of course, intend in any way to ignore the richer content of the second Vatican Council. It is quite clear from the *acta* of the Council that the dogma of papal infallibility was seen against the background of the church's consciousness of faith, which was later clearly formulated at the second Vatican Council. All that the first Vatican Council did not do, however, was to define this background dogmatically. But this failure to define the background makes it possible for us to understand that an isolated definition is, in the mind of believers, able to function almost 'heretically', and those who have experienced this dogma in this way naturally have the impression that the second Vatican Council has proclaimed a faith that is different from the faith that they had always confessed. The faith has not, however, changed—what has happened is that one precise datum of faith has been given its place in the totality of faith within which it is an authentic catholic truth.

It is therefore possible to say that the growth of insight into the content of the evangelical message is not simply a growth of knowledge, but always a 'conversion', the discarding of a certain element of blindness to other truths of faith.[15] A deep conviction of the saving significance of the church made earlier generations of christians, for example, blind to another truth, that of religious freedom and of the activity of God's grace in the whole of the world. For this reason, they regarded all those who were not baptised and even all who did not belong to the catholic church as doomed. Anyone who denied this was censured by the church, yet now the second Vatican Council has solemnly proclaimed that this is not so. Is the church in conflict with herself, then—is she accepting a different faith? No, she is not, but her defence of one particular datum of faith (the church is the universal sacrament of salvation—the second Vatican Council still teaches this, and even with special emphasis) made her, because of human motives, blind to other aspects of faith. In the past, she really defended one datum of faith but, in so doing, her gaze was too narrowly concentrated on herself and this made her blind to other, complementary truths. The declaration on religious freedom is therefore a manly discarding of an earlier blindness which had been partly conditioned by the clan spirit of the closed society of the time. But even this explanation cannot conceal the fact that the church did not, at that time, listen to another authentic word of God and in fact only listened to what was flattering to her self-esteem in that word of God.

Does this observation diminish the church in our eyes? No, it makes her more real and enables us to see her more as a church on the way, trying, 'in fear and trembling' (1 Cor 2:3; Eph 6:5), to keep intact the mystery of faith, that inexpressible mystery which always eludes us and which only yields its wealth to us gradually and after great difficulty on our part throughout the history of the church. What is broken, then, is an unreal image of the church, but this is a grace. In the past, many catholics (and because of this, many non-catholics as well) had unreal views about the infallibility of the church's teaching authority. Unconsciously, they gave rise to the impression that the pope, for example, had a permanent telephone line with heaven and was therefore always able to give an immediate, cut-and-dried answer to everything.

The church is enduring—this is the promise given to us by the master. What we call infallibility in the church's teaching is an inner consequence of this, in other words, in its original authenticity, the christian message will never cease to be heard on earth. The infallibility of one particular dogmatic definition is a weaker and further deduced manifestation of this primary significance of infallibility which has to be seen against the background of the whole course of history. This implies the fundamental faithfulness of the whole people of God and their leaders. And, according to the dogmatic constitution on revelation of the second Vatican Council, this faithfulness, or fidelity to faith, comes about by means of a constant interaction between the people of God as a whole, the witness of scripture and the authoritative and critical guidance of the church's teaching office. The way in which this lasting, faithful listening of the church is taking place is coloured by the tepidity or the liveliness of the church as a whole at any given time. If we say, then, that the church remains faithful to the Lord in the historical dynamism of her existence on earth, this does not mean that this faithfulness is equally great, equally profound and equally generous at every moment of her existence. In the history of the church too, there is always a rise and fall. There are always periods when certain data of faith are given such a one-sided emphasis (usually partly prompted by the need to defend them against false ideas) that other truths of faith, although they are not positively denied, are thrust into the background of the church's consciousness of faith. It may therefore happen that a temporary development takes place in which elements of secondary importance become central, with the result that the equilibrium of the christian message is upset and central mysteries of faith are, as it were, suppressed. The reformation, for example, frequently led the church to give such a one-sided emphasis to certain secondary aspects of faith. Centuries passed before she was converted again and was able to give the correct emphases—partly under the influence of the evangelical inspiration which she now recognises in the continuing protest of the reformation. Ultimately, however, everything is made right again—this is our faith in the enduring church.

This being made right again is, however, not something automatic. It requires a faithfulness to the Holy Spirit which is always renewing itself (cf pp 10–11 above). Insofar as it is concentrated on the faithful handing down of the christian message, the infallibility, in other words, the enduring character of the church thus clearly reveals a rise and fall, an entire history of human impotence, in which infallible grace ultimately triumphs in the reflective faithfulness of the church.

The fact that every conceptual formulation is insufficient and is always open to further development within the same faithfulness to the uniqueness of the gospel—as such, a question for the theory of knowledge—is therefore at the same time both a moral and a religious question in the life of the church. High-handedness may make the church cling so much to one particular conceptual formulation of faith, even when this has long since lost its validity because of the growth of man's consciousness, that authentic fidelity to faith is endangered—once again, the church may believe that she possesses the absolute, which is so near to us in grace, in an absolute manner. This attitude—and the church cannot be absolved entirely from the charge of having this attitude—makes the relative absolute and therefore endangers the mystery itself. In many respects, then, the second Vatican Council was an examination of conscience undertaken by the church herself, a search for greater faithfulness to the christian message and a straightening out of perspectives that had, in the meantime, become distorted.

In the past, the church, for example, encouraged crusades and reacted strongly against the reformation because she was so convinced that God was entirely on her side. Now, however, she has learnt that she must pray incessantly that she herself may be allowed to stand on God's side.[16] She has become more humble, even though she has not lost faith in God's election.

But, on the basis of her enduring character, promised to her by her Lord, the church knows that, in her formulation of the christian message, she can never fall away from the truth. Despite the constant rise and fall that takes place in her history, we continue to have trust in the church and her hierarchical teaching authority because of this conviction. We do not have any mythical faith that the church only needs to open her mouth in order to proclaim heavenly and infallible truths to us, but we do have an unshakeable trust, in grace, that, despite these ups and downs, the Holy Spirit will set the church's compass on the right course and that the definitions of dogma will be like beacons placed at intervals to mark the long voyage to the safe port—though of course the voyage is not yet over. Looking back over the course that the church has taken, we can see that these beacons mark a zigzag route. Indeed, looking back, we can even say that this diversion or that one could have been avoided. But the Holy Spirit has piloted the church safely. Despite her weaknesses, the promise that the Lord made to the church continues to be with her.

Of course, a delicate situation may arise when an individual, not in a spirit of carping criticism, but rather in a spirit of genuine self-criticism, sees at a given moment that the church is about to make a diversion while he himself clearly sees a more direct route and in conscience feels bound to follow it. This is, however, a problem that I cannot deal with separately here. All that I can say is that a fundamental obedience in faith to the word of God, subject to the guidance of the authority of the church, does not stand in the way of the freedom of the children of God. Such fundamental conflicts will not, however, be a daily occurrence.

It should therefore be clear from what I have said that the christian faith always functions within the prevailing view of man and the world and consequently has to be re-interpreted again and again in the light of its original authenticity, if it is to remain true to itself. Thus the church has, at the moral level, always sought to safeguard the dignity of man, for example, in marriage. In the past, however, the prevailing view of man, both inside the church and outside, was tinged with

dualism. It will be obvious that the norm of human dignity—
now, as in the past, the human norm of, for example, marriage, as safeguarded by the church—will have various consequences, differing according to whether mankind, and
therefore the church as well (since the church does not have
her own, quite distinct view of man), regards man as dualistic
or not. If, however, this dualism is overcome—and the idea
of man as a unity, which had its origin at the end of the
eighteenth century and the beginning of the nineteenth, is
now becoming a generally accepted view—then the unchanged norm of human dignity in, for example, married
life is bound to lead to ethical conclusions which are very
different from those in the past. A change in man's view of
nature and consequently in his view of man naturally results
in a change in ethical imperatives, even though a realisation
of, for example, married life which is worthy of man will remain the unchanging norm. In the sphere of ethics, the
changing character of what is (partly wrongly) known as the
'teaching of the church' is the direct result of the historical
character of man's being as man, which is, after all, a concrete understanding of himself. In this sphere too, many believers have had too inflexible a view of the church's teaching
and of its unchanging character, with the result that they
are astonished whenever the church changes the emphasis in
her moral teaching. Again and again, this same misconception emerges—the mistaken view that we, and especially we
who belong to the church, possess the absolute in an absolute manner. This qualification, 'in an absolute manner',
indicates a failure to appreciate the most profound experience of christianity and also a failure to appreciate the true
place of our being as men. Any christian who thinks like this
is in danger of becoming an intolerant integralist, a propa-
gandist of the 'established order', a person who is always de-
manding that those who do not think as he does should be
condemned, and in the end perhaps even a man who accuses
the church of falling away from Christ because she is listening flexibly to God's word. He becomes resolute in his re-

jection of all renewal in the church and is constantly lamenting the decline of morals. Finally, he becomes an isolated figure, enclosed in his own bitterness. After all, the renewal of the church, which draws its strength from the church's enduring faithfulness to Christ, will continue, despite all protests. The duty to adhere faithfully to God's word is the special task of the pioneers of true renewal.

I have, in this section, briefly surveyed some of the factors which may cause alarm in the present renewal of the church. I have, however, deliberately not discussed one fundamental problem, which I should, however, mention. This is the problem of the hermeneutics of the christian confession of faith in what has been called the period 'after the death of God'. Although it did not perhaps always have the truly christian perspective of the early church, the 'death of God' movement was basically a return to the conscious ignorance, the *docta ignorantia*, and the 'negative theology' (which, of its very nature, also includes a theological 'negative anthropology') of the early church and of the best of scholastic theology, re-interpreted in accordance with the modern view of man and the world.

The essence of the christian message, which includes the new commandment to love God above all and one's neighbour as oneself, teaches us that we must love our fellow-man so radically that this radical love can only be realised and understood as the other side of the coin of the absolute and generous gift of God's unconditional love for us, in other words, that such a radical love of man is only possible as love of God, whether this is conscious or not. This has been revealed to us in Jesus, the Christ, and the church's teaching about the Trinity, Christ, the church, the sacraments and the last things is the further elaboration in detail of this revelation. The teaching of the church will therefore only acquire its full and dogmatic significance within this basic christian vision and after it has in fact become christian *life* within this vision. Every dogma thus serves the love of christian life. Outside it, it quickly deteriorates into a meaningless ideology, giving scandal to non-believers who, in their care for their fellow-men, in fact often practise the christian dogma more than believers, who are frequently more concerned with ideological orthodoxy, 'right thinking', than with christian orthopraxis, 'right doing'. But surely this 'right doing' is the best guarantee for authentic 'right thinking'?

3

THE CHURCH, THE 'SACRAMENT
OF THE WORLD'[17]

In the various documents of the second Vatican Council, the statement that the church is the universal sacrament of salvation is encountered again and again:

'Christ. . . has, through the Spirit, instituted his body, that is the church, as the universal sacrament of salvation' (Dogmatic constitution on the church, 7, 48).

'The church is the universal sacrament of salvation which manifests and at the same time realises the mystery of God's love for man' (Pastoral constitution on the church in the modern world, 1, 4, 45).

'In Christ, the church is as the sacrament, that is, the sign and instrument of the inner union with God and of the unity of the whole of mankind' (Dogmatic constitution on the church, 1).

'God has called together and made into a church the assembly of those who, in faith, look up towards Jesus, the bringer about of salvation and the principle of unity and peace, so that this church may be for all people and for each individual the visible sacrament of this unity which brings salvation' (*ibid*, 2, 9). 'For it was from the side of Christ as he slept the sleep of death upon the cross that there came forth the wondrous sacrament that is the whole church' (Constitution on the liturgy, 1, 5).

It will, of course, be clear to everyone that these statements about the mystery of the church which are to be found in various conciliar documents are extremely important and above all that they will, by their pregnant content, stimulate not only theological reflection, but also and especially the christian life of future generations.

43

I will confine myself, in this brief introduction, to an analysis of two aspects of the content of these conciliar statements; on the one hand, the relationship between the church and the divine decree as expressed in the history of salvation and, on the other, the relationship between the church and the whole of mankind, since the church is, after all, the sacrament of divine salvation with regard to the whole world, the *sacramentum mundi*.

I. The church as the epiphany and historical completion of God's plan of salvation

Without denying the legitimacy of a more technical concept of sacrament that has become current since the theology of the middle ages,[18] the council nonetheless went back to the richer and more dynamic and universal concept of the bible and the church fathers. The Greek word *mystērion*—in the Latin of the church *sacramentum* and *mysterium*—denoted the divine decree, or God's plan of salvation, insofar as this is and has been manifested in a veiled manner in time and is accessible only to faith. In this sense, the concept of sacrament embraces the whole of the christian plan of salvation, visibly prepared in the old testament, but given a completing manifestation in the life, death and resurrection of Jesus, the Christ, of whom the church is the visible presence in this world (*ibid*, 14, cf 7), although 'under shadows' and 'under the assumption of constant purification' (Constitution on the church, 8). According to this concept, then, sacrament is the history of salvation itself as the active manifestation of God's plan of salvation.

What the council meant precisely by the word 'sacrament' is most profoundly expressed in the decree on missionary activity, although the word itself is unfortunately not used in this context: 'Missionary activity is nothing other and nothing less than the revelation of epiphany of and the completion of God's plan of salvation in the world and in the history of the world, in which God, through the mission, visibly completes the history of salvation' (9). But because 'the church on the way is, by virtue of her being, orientated towards mission' (*ibid,* 2), one is quite justified in replacing words like 'mission' and 'missionary activity' in this conciliar text by the word 'church'. Consequently, the text that I have just quoted might just as well have read: 'The church is nothing other and nothing less than the revelation or epiphany of and the completion of God's plan of salvation in the world and in the history of the world in which God, through the church, visibly completes the history of salvation.' In yet other words, using the concept 'sacrament': 'In Christ, the church is the universal sacrament of salvation which manifests and realises the mystery of God's love for man' (Pastoral constitution on the church in the modern world, 1, 4, 45), 'God's love for man' being 'for all people and for each individual' (Constitution on the church, 2, 9). The church, then, is the universal and effective sign of the salvation of all people. She is the epiphany, in other words, the active and historically tangible form of God's plan of salvation, a form which makes the source of salvation, Christ, present for us. The church is the 'instrument of redemption', because she is the 'visible sacrament' (Constitution on the church, 2, 9) of this redemption on earth—'she is the germ and the beginning of the kingdom of God on earth' (*ibid*, 1, 5). But the church is this only 'under shadows'— 'she is always in need of purification' (cf pp 1–19 above). Indeed, the *Relatio,* the justification of this text provided by the commission during the council, makes this even clearer: 'This empirical church... reveals the mystery (of the church), but she does not do this without shadows' and the mystery in the catholic church becomes visible 'both in strength and in weakness' (*Relationes in singulus numeris, Relatio in* 8, pp 23 and 24). Partly in her *metanoia* and conversion, the church is therefore the historically visible form of salvation, in other words, salvation itself becoming visible in human history and, as such, the way to salvation for all people.

II. The church, sacrament of salvation for the whole world

According to the first aspect that I have considered, the church is the active presence of God's salvation in the world, in a veiled, but nonetheless perceptible form. It is precisely in this quality that the church is the sacrament of salvation offered by God to the whole world. In other words, salvation, which is in fact actively present in the whole of mankind, is given, in the church, the completed form in which it appears in the world. What God has already effectively begun to bring about in the whole of mankind in an activity of grace that is not clearly expressed and recognised as such, is expressed and accomplished more clearly and recognisably as the work of grace in the world in the church, although this expression and accomplishment are to some extent always deprived of their lustre because of our human failure.

The council did not state explicitly that the church is the visible sacrament of that salvation which is already active wherever people are to be found, but so many conciliar texts point in this direction that it is even possible to say that a dialectical tension exists which is not resolved in the texts themselves and which consequently calls for further theological clarification. Indeed, the constitution on the church says, on the one hand, with reference to the church as the 'messianic people', that 'although this does not yet in fact include all men and often seems to be a small flock', it is nonetheless 'the most powerful germ of unity, hope and salvation for the whole of mankind' (2, 9). This small flock, then, is the sacrament of salvation for all men. On the other hand, however, the same constitution also explicitly states that 'the church on the way is necessary for salvation' (*ibid*, 14). Other conciliar texts intensify the dialectical tension between these two statements. This tension is illustrated, for example, by the statement: 'Even those who, through no fault of their own, remain ignorant of the gospel of Christ and the church, but who are nonetheless honestly seeking God and, under the influence of grace, are really trying to do his will, which they recognise in the voice of their consciences, are able to achieve eternal blessedness' (*ibid*, 16). The pastoral constitution on the church is even more emphatic. After having depicted the christian as the 'new man in Christ', it states explicitly that this new mankind is present 'not only in christian believers, but also in all men of good will, in whose hearts grace is active in an invisible manner' (1, 22). The council's declaration on the non-christian religions, moreover, says that christianity is the 'fullness of the religious life' for all these other religions (2), thus indicating clearly that the relationship between the church and the non-christian communities is not a relationship between a religion and a non-religion, but a relationship between a fullness and something that simply does not possess this fullness. Finally, the decree on missionary activity states clearly: 'God's all-embracing plan for the salvation of the whole of mankind is not only realised in, so to speak, a hidden way in the hearts of men or by initiatives, including religious initiatives, through which they seek God in many different ways, "in the hope that they might feel after him and find him; yet he is not far from each one of us" (Ac 17:27)' (1, 3).

These texts—and there are probably others which could be quoted—show that the council has made two fundamental statements which are to some extent dialectically opposed. On the one hand, we have the statement that the church is necessary for salvation and, on the other hand, that those who are 'outside the church' not only are able to achieve salvation, but also frequently do in fact share in it. What, then, we are bound to ask, is the real meaning of the conciliar statement that the church is the 'universal sacrament of salvation'? Does it mean that God's salvation cannot in any sense reach the world except in and through this world's gradual and historical confrontation with the church? Or does it mean that universal salvation, which has already been offered to the whole world on the basis of God's universal will to save all men, and which is already active in the world, only reaches its completed appearance in the church? It is, I believe, abundantly clear from the texts that I have quoted that the council tended to think in the second direction. What God's grace, his absolute, gratuitous and forgiving proximity, has already begun to do in the lives of all men becomes an *epiphany* in the church, in other words, completely visible. There is no doubt that, because she is the completed manifestation of God's saving grace, the church is a very distinct and separate gift of grace and opportunity for grace. There is equally no doubt that the other, non-christian religions are not, as such, special and distinctive in this sense, because they need this completing grace. In order to fill this gap, the church, as the 'universal sacrament of salvation', is, by virtue of her very being, truly missionary —she is orientated towards mission.

From this, then, a certain 'definition' of the church according to the second Vatican Council becomes crystallised, namely that the church is the completed and active manifestation, confessed explicitly in thanksgiving and praise to God, of that salvation which is already actively present in the whole world of men. In other words, the church is the 'primordial sacrament' of the salvation which is prepared for all men according to God's eternal decree, the salvation which is, moreover, not a monopoly of the church, but which, on the basis of redemption by the Lord who died and rose again 'for the sake of the salvation of the whole world', is already in fact actively present in that whole world. The church is therefore both the sacrament of herself, in other words, the visible appearance of the salvation that is present in her,[19] and, at the same time, the *sacramentum mundi*; in other words, what is present 'outside the church' everywhere, wherever men of good will in fact give their consent personally to God's offer of grace and make this gift their own, even though they do not do this reflectively or thematically, is audibly expressed and visibly perceptible in the church. The church is the 'sacrament of the world' precisely as the sacrament of the salvation which is offered to all men—she is hope not only for all who belong to her; she is also, quite simply, *spes mundi*, hope for the whole world. The mystery of salvation which God is always bringing about in the whole history of mankind and which he will never cease to bring about—the enduring fact of the living prophecy of the church bears witness to this—appears fully in the church and is present in her as in a prophecy. It is possible to say that the church is the making public of existential salvation in the world. She reveals the world to itself. She shows the world what it is and what it is able to become by virtue of God's gift of grace. Because of this, she hopes not only for herself, but also for the whole world, which she serves.

Since the conciliar texts can only be interpreted in this light, the council has in fact, with its key statement, 'the church is the universal sacrament of salvation', laid the foundation on which a new and practical synthesis can be built up, a synthesis which may help to banish 'the discrepancy which exists in the case of many believers between the faith that they confess and their daily lives', a breach which 'must be regarded as one of the most serious errors of the present time' (Pastoral constitution on the church, 1, 4, 43). This will be a synthesis in which the church and the actual world no longer confront each other as strangers. On the contrary—in this synthesis, the church, as the sacrament of the world, will clearly express, for the benefit of the world of men, the deepest meaning which men have already experienced, in tentative search and without being able to express it, in the world, even though this meaning does not have its origin in the world. The world will then see, in grateful recognition, its meaning and hidden inspiration fully expressed as a sign in the church.

III. Pastoral consequence

This brief exposition of one conciliar theme leads to the following pastoral consequence. I have argued from the conciliar texts that the church is the visible epiphany or the effective sacrament of God's salvation which is active not only in the church, but also in the whole world, and that the church, in this capacity, has to show herself in the whole of her historically situated life as an active appeal to the conscience of all men, so that they, in grateful recognition of the gift of grace which God offers to them, 'may know God and him whom he has sent, his Son, Jesus Christ'. If this is true, then it is not only a grace bestowing a clear privilege, but also a task implying a grave responsibility for the church 'to make God the Father and his Son, who became man, present and, as it were, visible, by constantly renewing and purifying herself under the guidance of the Holy Spirit' (*ibid*, 1, 1, 21). This special grace which is only given to the church, the grace to be the *sacrament* of the world, is, after all, partly concealed by the life of the church and is therefore shown 'both in strength and in weakness', 'in the situation of sinfulness and conversion'. In a very special way, the church is *simul iusta et peccatrix*—sanctified and yet failing. Her enduring quality and her holiness do not have their origin in herself, but in the redeeming grace of Christ, the bringer of salvation.

It is quite clear from repeated statements made by Pope John XXIII that the real aim of the second Vatican Council was the renewal, purification and conversion of the church. The success or ultimate failure of the council will be measured by the successful renewal and purification of the church.

4

CHRISTIAN FAITH AND MAN'S
EXPECTATION FOR THE FUTURE
ON EARTH[20]

It was only during the last week of the first session of the
second Vatican Council (December 1962) that the idea was
put forward of the schema that was known for a time, from
January 1963 onwards, as Schema 17, until it was re-
christened Schema 13. In the pre-conciliar period, several
basic data about man had already been included in the draft
of a constitution on the church—data relating to his condition as a creature, his raising to the supernatural order, his
sinfulness and his relationship with this world. This pre-
conciliar draft was brought up for discussion during the last
week of the first session but, because of the criticism that
it encountered, it was decided to make a new draft, to some
extent on the basis of this earlier schema, for a dogmatic
constitution on the church. Leo Cardinal Suenens took
advantage of this opportunity to suggest that all texts which
were especially concerned with the presence of the church
in the world should be included in a separate conciliar
document, *De ecclesia ad extra*. This was the origin of the
schema to which the title 'The Presence and the activity of
the church in the modern world' was first given. This title
was later changed to 'The Task of the church to promote the
well-being of modern society'. The document was finally
entitled, in 1965, the 'Pastoral constitution on the church in
the modern world'.

A closer analysis of the pre-history and a comparison of the
six or seven different versions of this schema would reveal
the great change in attitude that took place during the four
years of the council, but a task of this kind would also go
beyond the aim of this chapter. Nonetheless, if the pastoral

constitution is to be properly understood, it is, in my opinion, necessary to indicate a number of clear turning points in the difficult course that the schema took before the definitive edition was made.

The first versions of the draft included an outline of a christian anthropology followed by a few moral problems. A subsequent version still retained this framework, but at the same time had all the marks of a traditional treatise on God's creation and grace, with the basic problem of the relationship between 'nature and the supernatural' approached in the medieval and Augustinian sense. This schema was also found unacceptable and was never discussed in the aula of the council. Consequently, a new draft was written in the course of 1964 and discussed in the third session (1964) in St Peter's. The bishops welcomed this schema as an advance on the previous schema, but still criticised it radically. Both the concept 'world' and the concept 'church' were used with different meanings, with the result that the whole document made an untidy impression. What is more, it presented a very dualistic picture of the church and the world and did not seem to be sufficiently aware of the fact that christian believers did not regard the world as something outside themselves, but as their own lives. The attempt to provide a 'christian anthropology' in outline also failed because the view of man expressed by the document remained static and firmly individualistic, with the result that man's social and historical dimension and his relationship with nature did not emerge sufficiently clearly from the background. Above all, however, the document threw no light whatever on the relationship between man's expectations for the future on earth and the christian expectation for the future. Despite the modern wording of the document, it remained basically medieval and Augustinian in its inspiration—the 'world' seemed in it to be no more than an opportunity for christians to practise charity.

With these criticisms in mind, Bishop Guano, the chairman of the commission concerned, decided to enlarge the group working on the schema considerably and include a number of lay people. Between the third and the fourth sessions of the council, this extended commission worked hard, in Ariccia near Rome, at a new draft, which was discussed in St Peter's during the last session and, after a number of more or less fundamental changes had been made in the text, ultimately approved by the council as the 'Pastoral constitution on the church in the modern world'.

I propose to discuss here the relationship between man's expectations for the future on earth and the christian expectation, a theme that is dealt with in the four chapters of the first part of this constitution. In this part of the document, chapters I and II provide a basic outline of a christian view of man, in other words, a 'christian anthropology', chapter III gives an introduction into what may be called a 'theology of terrestrial values' and the concluding chapter (IV) offers, on the basis of what is said in the preceding chapters and also in the light of what had already been said about the church in the constitution *Lumen Gentium*, a few insights into the problem of the 'church and the world'. A large number of commentaries have already been written about the pastoral constitution, but many of these have forgotten to make clear what the constitution really has to say to us. It is therefore most important to consider the theological view which emerges from these four chapters before going on to a critical reflection. Let us first listen, then, to what the fathers of the council have to say to us.

I. The view of man in the pastoral constitution

A. *The two fundamental principles of part I*

After giving an outline of the evolutions and revolutions in the world of man today, the council asks this question: what does this all mean for the believer who belongs to the church? The fact that the world and all that it contains is there for man may be regarded as a prior datum that is accepted by almost all men (12). The great human enterprise to control this world and to place it at the service of man's plans for life, however, raises the question, what are these plans, and then the questions, what is man himself, what is the meaning of his life and what has God's revelation really to say to us about the grandeur and the misery of our being man?

One of the fundamental insights of the pastoral constitution, in the light of which many of the other statements contained in the constitution become clear, is that God gives man an insight into his own conditions, that God reveals man to himself precisely by revealing himself as love to man. This is stated explicitly no less than four times in different contexts in part 1 (22, 38, 40 and 41; see also 1, 11). This insight is basic to the theological foundations of the constitution. Every theological statement, that is, everything that is said about God, is at the same time[21] a statement about man. The consequence of this, which, although it is not explicitly formulated, is clearly felt in the constitution, is that man's new experiences also have something to say to us about God's intentions with us. This is evident from the problem posed in the third chapter (33), which establishes as a new fact of human experience that man is now able to realise himself much of what he expected, in the past, from God. The increasing application of science in the sphere of man's work is making his control of nature greater and greater—one of the most obvious facts of modern life is that the world can be completely managed. After establishing this, the constitution then goes on to say that it aims to *illuminate* 'the way that mankind has been following for some time'. There is no protest against this new view of man and the world mentioned in the constitution; on the contrary, there is only a desire to lay bare what is taking place in this concrete human experience in the light of the revelation of the word.[22] The conciliar text does not state explicitly that this new human experience is an event of salvation which is then illuminated by the revelation of the word. But this view is implicit in the whole of the constitution—this is clearly brought to the surface, for example, when, after describing the social evolutions of today, the constitution says explicitly: 'The Spirit of God . . . is actively present in this development' (*huic evolutioni adest*—26). It is obvious that the social dynamism that permeates the whole world is seen in its relationship with, indeed as a dimension of, the history of salvation today.

This brings us to the second statement that is fundamental to the whole pastoral constitution: 'the *same* God who is the creator is also the redeemer; the *same* God is also the Lord both of the history of man and of the history of salvation' (41). Creation and covenant—these form one divine structure and this is also seen in its historical consequences. The pastoral constitution therefore recognises, for example, that all that is good in the dynamism of modern society—man's striving towards unity in the world, the process of socialisation and so on—is closely connected with the religious mission of the church (42), because, to quote from the dogmatic constitution on the church, 'the church is the sacrament, that is, the sign and instrument of the inner union with God and of the unity of the whole of mankind' (1).

The whole of the first part of the pastoral constitution is included in these two fundamental statements—an outline of a christian anthropology and an outline of a theology of terrestrial values. This, then, is the perspective within which the problem of the 'church and the world' must be situated.

B. A basic outline of a 'christian anthropology' (chapters 1 and 2)

In answer to the question, what has the revelation of the word to say about man in his grandeur and his failure, the council refers to the biblical statement that man was created in the image of God and that this image was disfigured by man's sinfulness and restored by Christ's redemption. Creation (goodness), sin (badness) and redemption (superabundant restoration of the good)—these are the three threads from which the fabric of the first part of the constitution is woven.

Man as the 'image of God' is given a clearer outline in three perspectives: (a) man is a being who is able to know and love God; (b) he is at the same time God's representative on earth with regard to the non-human world, which he has to humanise by controlling nature, a process which is a glorification of God's name; (c) interpersonal relationships also form part of this basic structure of creation, in that man is essentially a fellow-man, living in a human community, so that the twofold realisation of being man—as man and woman—is, as it were, the primordial type of this (12). Sin deprives the image of God at all of these three levels, but man's restoration by Christ's redemption is also effective in all three dimensions. The constitution develops this view in the first two chapters, the first dealing with man in his being as a person, the second in his essential fellow-humanity.

The constitution did not set out to provide a fully elaborated anthropology. What it did aim to do was to provide an outline which was carefully directed, and this for two reasons. Certain aspects which had become more clearly conscious in modern man's understanding of himself are confirmed by the council in the light of the church's view of the man Jesus, the Son of God made man. Thus, the argument of these two chapters is made intelligible in the light of the last paragraph of each: 'Christ, the new man' (1, 22) and 'Christ and human solidarity' (2, 32). These two concluding paragraphs are at the same time the directing point of departure of the preceding text. Some of the fathers of the council would have preferred them to be placed at the beginning of each chapter rather than at the end, but the decision was made in favour of a rising curve. The 'anthropology' of these two chapters is also selectively directed in that they give additional emphasis to aspects which come into play less or not at all in contemporary man's understanding of himself precisely in order to avoid a distortion of that view of man.

1. *The value of the human person* (*chapter 1*)

The themes selected here are first man in his essential unity, as a corporeal being who, because of a transcendent principle of life, nonetheless rises above the material world. The first chapter then goes on, with the present situation of mankind in mind, to point to some fundamental characteristics of man—his intellect, his conscience, his freedom and the mystery of his death—and, because of the atheistic and agnostic view of man held by a very large part of the human community in the modern world, to discuss atheism at some length. Finally, the significance of man's being is considered in the light of the 'perfect man', Jesus, the 'image of the invisible God'. It is, then, possible to call this an outline of a christian anthropology that is 'situated' in the life of present-day man.

As man was created good by God, his body also shares in this fundamental goodness, with the result that any under-estimation of the human body is pernicious. On the other hand, however, man is not an integral part of the material universe or any anonymous element in history. He has an inner centre of action which transcends the purely corporeal sphere and is able, because of this, to take the world and his own life into his hands. He is not, as it were, lived—he himself makes his own life. His appearance as man manifests a spiritual and therefore an immortal principle of life in man (14).

The fact that the humane and natural sciences are flourishing in the modern world is evidence of man's intellect. Man is able to control the world by means of his intelligence, but his success in this sphere should not allow him to forget that he needs wisdom. True human civilisation requires not only science and expert knowledge, but also a wisdom which penetrates to the most profound meaning of things. Without this wisdom, human society itself is threatened (15).

Man's conscience, a kind of 'inner voice' which is in us,

but not ours, gives a direction to all man's activities, so that he does not make just what he likes of his own life. Man's conscience makes him aware of fundamental values and of the need to build up and extend his life in the light of these values. Since this conscience is the privilege of all men, they should try together to solve the moral problems of life (16).

Fundamental values are not, however, imposed by force. Man has to give himself to these values or basic moral norms in freedom and out of personal conviction. It is this freedom which is the living sign of the 'image of God' (17).

Man's pattern of life which is subjected to moral norms and the advance of the humane and natural sciences cannot, however, throw light on the fundamental mystery of life—the incomprehensible enigma of death. Precisely because he is also spirit and consequently transcends corporeality, man has a deep, reverent fear of death. His spiritual principle of life points to a survival after this death. It is only revelation which opens a perspective here—because man is called to personal community with the living God, death cannot be the last word for him. Death is overcome (18).

Apart from this existential problem that is so frequently the theme of modern literature, there is also the much discussed problem of atheism, not in the sense of the 'Death of God movement', which is probably only a reaction against false ideas of God, but in the sense of a real denial of all religion. This atheism takes many different forms (see the conciliar text, 19 and 20)—from an explicit denial to agnosticism. The reasons for this denial are also different. Some atheists are convinced that everything can be solved by scientific methods, even the problem of God, or else hold a relative view of truth. Others regard the existence of God as in competition with or as an attack on our being as man, in which case their basic intention is to save man's being as a person, which, in their opinion, is impossible if the existence of a divine, absolute being is accepted. Many so-called atheists are opposed not to God, but to a caricature of the image of God. Others, on the other hand, appear to be simply content with a purely human sphere of life—the problem of God means nothing to them. For many people, denial of God is a protest against the immeasurable evil and suffering in the world. Not in itself, but because of its purely terrestrial interest, modern society undoubtedly makes it more difficult for man to find God.

We can only speak of guilt in the case of somebody who goes against the conviction of his own conscience and deliberately refuses to pose the problem of God. In this, however, believers often have a share of the guilt, since atheism is not an original or a spontaneous attitude, but a reflective attitude of mind, a reaction against, among other things, existing and especially christian religions. By failing in their education of themselves in faith and thereby giving a false picture of faith or, what is even more harmful, giving the impression that there is a cleavage between their professed faith and their actual lives as christians, believers often obscure the true face of God and of religiosity (19).

But there are also atheistic ideologies, which are opposed to any form of dependence on a higher being, There are basically two forms of ideological atheism. On the one hand, human freedom, because of which man is really *faber suiipsius*, a being who determines and makes himself, is seen in its exclusive sense. In other words, man is free without being dependent, as a creature, on God, and his technical and scientific achievements are not regarded as a purification of the older concept of God, but as an apparent stimulus to and confirmation of the denial of all forms of faith in God. Another form of systematic atheism has its ideological basis in the ideal of man's liberation from all forms of alienation brought about by social and economic pressures. This form of atheism also regards religion and all expressions of religiosity as an implication of social enslavement and as something which would be automatically banished from society by a new social and economic pattern, with the result that it is militantly anti-religious, all the more so whenever it is taken over as an ideology by the state (20).

It goes without saying that christianity and atheism are in contradiction with each other. This is why christianity, partly out of respect for the dignity of man at the deepest level, is itself a condemnation of atheism. It is, however, most important to try to discover the reasons for this absence of religion. We christians must therefore remain fully conscious of the fact that our hope for an eschatological future does not diminish the importance of our task here on earth and thus of our future on earth, but that it on the contrary provides new motives for our commitment on earth. The pastoral constitution stresses this again and again in its later chapters. On the other hand, outside religion, many fundamental existential problems remain unsolved (problems such as death, suffering and guilt) and this leads to a distorted image of man and also leaves man himself dissatisfied, since these problems are certainly apprehended, however vaguely, by every man as real problems of life. The only real remedy against atheism is an integral and authentic christian life on the part of the church and those who belong to her. The church must, so to speak, make God the Father and Jesus, his Son who becomes man, visibly present for all men, show God to all men and therefore constantly renew and purify herself in the power of the Holy Spirit. What is necessary is not a naive faith, but a living, mature and lucid faith which is strong enough for martyrdom. In this strong faith, christians must be in the vanguard of those who care for their fellow-men and who work for greater justice and love in society. They must above all be in the forefront of the struggle to help the poor. They must show, by their love of each other and of all men as brothers, what human solidarity means.

The conflict between christianity and atheism should not, however, be allowed to stand in the way of dialogue between christians and atheists and, since they live together in the same world, they must work together to make this world a place that is more worthy of man. Discrimination between believers and non-believers on the part of the state is pernicious. The church asks for freedom so that her members may be allowed to build the house of God in this world and she invites all atheists sincerely to consider the evangelical message, which does not alienate man from himself, but comes forward to meet his deepest longings and does not deprive his being of its lustre, but is a light and life-giving liberation for its completion (21).

Finally, the dignity of the human person is seen in its deepest foundation—in Christ Jesus, the 'new man'. Revealing himself in the man Jesus, God reveals man to himself— in Christ the image of God, obscured by sinfulness, is restored in new lustre. Christ, a man like ourselves, thinking, working, willing and loving like ourselves but, unlike us, without sin, loved men to the end. Christian life makes us conform, in conflict and hope, to his humanity. But this 'new humanity' applies to all men of 'good will', since God knows only one destiny in life, the same for all men. In this, the council affirms most explicitly that the man renewed in Christ is not a monopoly for christians (22).

2. *The human community: fellow-humanity and social structures (chapter 2)*

This christian anthropology would be no more than a bare torso if it took no account of man's social dimension. There are social structures and there are interpersonal relationships; both are closely related, but there is a difference in their value (23).

Created and called to be the 'image of God', the image of the triune God, man is also orientated towards the human community. Being man means living in one great family of men, which comes from God and goes back to the one God. The love of God and fellow-humanity are therefore two fundamental demands of life. The present-day process of socialisation above all offers a wonderful opportunity for man to realise his love of his fellow-men, because man 'only comes to himself in giving himself to the other' (24).

The person and the community cannot be separated, although the person is the subject, the principle and the aim of all social structures. In this, the emphases placed by the council are clearly different from those placed by the so-called catholic social teaching of the period between the two world wars. Because of the essentially social dimension of the human person, the church can only welcome the present-day process of socialisation, even though it does contain some dangers. There are, after all, many social structures which prevent full justice from being done to the human person. In this, some part is played by the conflict between different political and socio-economic systems, but deeper causes can be found in man's selfishness and pride. In this way, sin is also made objective in the social structures, with the result that these in turn give rise to sin (25).

Man's general well-being must make it possible for all individual persons and all communities to be really able to reach perfection. This is why the community has to champion the fundamental 'rights of man'. The social system and man's general well-being are not simply statistical data—they are an evolving reality which must be built up on the basis of truth and justice inspired by love. An equilibrium which is increasingly worthy of man must be achieved in freedom and, if this is to be attained, it is necessary both to renew man's attitude and to reform the structures of society (26).

Respect for one's fellow-man—the 'other self'—without any form at all of discrimination, is essential in this connection: a respect for man in his body, in his psychical and spiritual structures and in his social rights. A failure to respect these human rights is always a stain on human civilisation (27).

Even when there are differences in socio-political and religious convictions, there is still a need for respect and indeed love for the opposite party and for dialogue. This has nothing to do with indifferentism with regard to the truth or ethical indifference (28).

All men must be offered opportunities in life that are

equal, fair and worthy of them. Even though men may differ in their talents, all discrimination in the fundamental rights of man because of the colour of people's skin, their race, language or religion is quite pernicious (29).

Although this chapter of the pastoral constitution lays great stress on the need for the community to allow the individual person to develop fully, it also insists that this should not be understood in an individualistic sense—the individual person is also at the service of the community (30), he is responsible for it and he should therefore share in political responsibility as far as he is able (31).

Finally, the christian basis of the community and of fellow-humanity is concisely stated—God calls us in Christ to a community of brothers. The gift of grace is a covenant between God and his people, his great family. Because of this, the church of Christ is a fraternal community (32).

C. A theology of terrestrial values (chapter 3)

Chapter III of the pastoral constitution discusses the *navitas humana,* a classical Latin word ('human activity', with the emphasis on 'exertion and attempt') which can best be translated in this context by man's activities within this world. In number 34 of the constitution, this *navitas humana* is described as 'the great individual and collective effort by means of which men attempt to improve their conditions of life throughout the course of time'.

The problem that is dealt with here is this. Man himself is becoming more and more the subject of history. He makes history and his aim is to build up a future for himself on earth in which it is good for him to live. What, then, is the connection between this expectation for the future on earth and the christian hope of eschatological completion? What is the relationship between humanisation and the kingdom of God? This chapter is clearly a reaction against a misunderstood 'flight from the world'. One of the basic errors of our present age is the cleavage that exists between life within this world and religion, in which religion is reduced to a cultic and moral activity alongside life here in this world (43). In this chapter, the constitution therefore sets out to throw light on the christian meaning of a secularised and humanised world (33).

At the beginning, it is stated that the whole process of humanising this world as such corresponds to the *propositum Dei* (34), which means, in the terminology of the council, not only God's plan of creation, but also his saving intentions, thus creation and covenant as one structure. Competition between God and man's process of humanisation is senseless. This progressive process of humanisation and the achievements of man's gigantic exertions are a sign of God's greatness, the fruit of his intentions with mankind. The evangelical message does not take man out of the world, but on the contrary stimulates him to a more intensive commitment within this world (34).

But, just as man is the immediate source of this humanisation, he should also be its immediate goal. The humanisation of the world should serve the humanisation of man himself. Technical progress in itself is certainly not the ultimate end of the process of humanisation, which is greater justice and brotherly love and a way of life which is more worthy of man. Man's authentic good, which, expressed in religious terms, is God's will, must become the norm of all man's activity within this world (35).

The link which the council establishes between life here in this world and religion cannot, however, give rise to any misunderstanding, since it does not in any way do away with the autonomy and the values which are distinctively those of the world. God's creation constitutes things precisely in their distinctive quality and value and a failure to respect this is an infringement of these things and consequently of God's will. The creator and the bringer of salvation cannot be played off against each other. Anyone who affirms the autonomy of terrestrial values will naturally not in any way wish to deny their condition as creatures. Such a denial would be a failure to appreciate their deepest distinctive value and would in this way deprive them of their lustre (36).

But man's sinfulness also impairs his humanisation of the world. Because of selfishness, his relationships with his fellow-men are also impaired by sin—they become the vehicle of sinfulness. Thus man's increasing control of the world can become a danger to mankind. In this context, Paul warned us not to allow ourselves to conform to 'this world' (Rom 12:2), that is, to the sinfulness of the world of men. The christian possesses the world authentically when he loves it with a love that is redemed and resurrected by the cross (37).

The whole of man's activities within this world must therefore be integrated within the mystery of Easter. The christian knows, on the basis of this mystery, that fellow-humanity and the building up of a 'city of man' in which brotherly love predominates will not be in vain. Man's longing for an eschatological kingdom inspires, purifies and strengthens his longing for a situation here on earth in which life is more worthy of man and nature is controlled. This inner relationship between man's future here on earth and his eschatological expectation, however, allows for two types of christianity. The one type will above all bear witness to this eschatological expectation of the future. The other type will, as it were, prepare the matter for the eschatological kingdom by committing itself to the task of making a better future on earth.

The whole of the history of man is therefore permeated with dynamism towards a humanity which is entirely an offering that is acceptable to God. This is the eschatological kingdom. In this movement, the eucharist is earnest-money for the journey, since 'humanised nature' becomes, in it, the glorified body and blood of Christ. It is the meal of brotherly love and a foretaste of the heavenly meal (38).

Little can be said about the eschatological kingdom itself —the time and manner of it are unknown to us. But the form of this world, insofar as it is distorted by sin, is already passing. (The original text, 'will pass', was deliberately changed into 'is already passing', so as to express once again that the *eschaton* itself is already active in the world's progress towards the future.) In this way, God is preparing a new dwelling, a new earth, in which justice lives and in which all man's longings for *shalom* (in the rich biblical and patristic sense of the word) will acquire an inward but transcendent completion. In this new dwelling, death is overcome and what is sinful disappears from the body. Charity and everything that has been brought about by charity in the world is perpetuated into eternity. What is transient is invested with an enduring character and the human world is transfigured.

This christian vision of the future stimulates our commitment to this world, our attempt to build up a dwelling-place on earth in which the human family can grow together. Man's attempt to make mankind one by making this world a better place is already to some extent a foreshadowing of the eschatological kingdom.

This process of humanising the world should not, however, be identified with the growth of the kingdom of God, although it is most closely related to the growth of the kingdom insofar as it really contributes to a better regulation of the human community and thus means care for our fellow-men.[23]

The good fruits of humanity and of human activity—especially human dignity, brotherly love and freedom (there is an echo here of the slogan, 'égalité, fraternité, liberté')—which are propagated on earth in the spirit of Christ will be found again in the eschatological kingdom, but purified from all stains and inwardly transparent and transfigured. At the end of time, there will be a kingdom of justice, love and peace. But this kingdom is already present in a veiled form in this world. It will be ultimately completed in Christ's *parousia* (39).

D. The church and the world (chapter 4)

On the basis of the preceding three chapters and partly in the light of the constitution on the church, *Lumen Gentium*, chapter IV of the pastoral constitution aims to throw further light on the relationship between the world and the church, both as the community of all believers and as their hierarchical leaders. In this context, the 'world' is regarded both as the community of all people who are not explicitly members of the church and as the sphere of life and activity within this world of all those who are explicitly members of the church.

This chapter takes as its point of departure the fact that the community of believers that is the church is not a separate entity, but a community which lives and acts within the whole world of men and together with it, since it is composed of people who are members of that community of men on earth, but who are at the same time called to fashion that world community into a family of God. Thus believers, who belong to the church and form a special and spirit-filled community with a visible social structure, stand shoulder to shoulder with all people in this world and share the same fate as these people. The community of believers that is the church must be an inspiring ferment within this greater community of all men, with reference to whom the pastoral constitution had already observed in chapter 1 that, if they are men of 'good will', they have already been transformed into a 'new humanity' in Christ. The church must, moreover, be the inspiring ferment of this renewal in Christ and of the transformation of mankind into the family of God. This is not put forward in the pastoral constitution as a definition of the church as such, but rather as a definition of the church's function with regard to the whole world of men.

There is therefore an interpretation between the church and the world and it is only in faith that light can be thrown on this process, which in fact constitutes the mystery of human history. In realising her own, purely religious mission, the church also performs a humanising task. In communicating divine life, she also illuminates, as in a reflection, the whole of the world of men. In this way, the value of the human person is confirmed, healed and raised, the bonds which join the human community together are strengthened and man's activity within this world is permeated with a deeper meaning. This humanising function is not a monopoly of the catholic church and for this reason the council also includes the other christian churches within this perspective. The pastoral constitution also affirms that the church herself is helped in her task by the world (40).

The fourth chapter of the constitution sets out the basic principles of this mutual help in the realisation of what the church and the world have in common, although in different respects. These are the help that the community of the church gives to individuals (41), the help that the church gives to the whole community of men (42) and the help that the community of men gives to the church (44). The council also draws the attention of believers (bishops, priests and lay people) to their duties with regard to the world (43) and finally points to Christ, the alpha and the omega of the whole of human history (45).

The fact of the church reminds men of the problem of life, which is raised above all by the existential theme of death, something that no one can escape. God's revelation is also an illumination of man's understanding of himself—christianity makes man 'more' human. For this reason, the church champions all human rights, but at the same time warns man that freedom cannot be identified with exemption from God's laws, since this is far more a depersonalisation (41).

As far as her service to the whole human community is concerned, the church has a religious mission, not a political or socio-economic mission. But this religious mission certainly has an influence on these activities within the world and, if the circumstances require it, the church herself can also set up organisations to help people, especially the poor.

As the 'sacrament of the world', the church shows that true social unity has its source in the unity of heart and mind, since the unity of the church is based on the unity of faith and of love. In this, the church is a realising sign of true unity for the world. Her influence on society is therefore based not on positions of power within the world, but on acts of faith and love. She is, then, not tied to any specific form of civilisation and any political, social or economic system and is therefore able to collaborate intensively with all men. She does demand complete freedom of movement for herself, but no state political structure is an obstacle to her if it recognises the basic rights of the individual person and the family and the demands of the general well-being of the community (42).

Turning to believers themselves, the council urges them to take up their tasks in this world. A flight from the world which implies an avoidance of worldly responsibility is as pernicious as a commitment to the world which is alien to religion and confines this to the sphere of worship and morals. Although the lay christian's task is not restricted to his activity within the world, this is nonetheless the task that is characteristic of him. It requires expert knowledge and skill, an enterprising spirit and co-operation with others. In this work, the priest brings him the 'comfort of the gospel', but he ought not to believe that he can provide an answer to everything. Many different choices are possible in the affairs of the world within the christian vision and no one should accuse his fellow-believers of failing as christians in this, or put forward his own choice as the solution that is specifically that of the church.

The bishops in particular have the task of showing the true face of the church to the world. They must support everything that can promote unity. Everything that divides is pernicious.

The church, the sign of salvation for the world, often

shows herself without lustre and this is always an obstacle to the gospel. Constant renewal and purification are necessary to make the sign of Christ shine on the face of the church (43).

The church also learns a great deal from the whole world of men and must therefore listen attentively to the language that the world speaks so as to be able to proclaim her message of salvation in a suitable way. Everything that the world does for the family, for society and for the political, social and economic structure of life is in fact also a promotion of the church as the community of faith, which is, after all, situated within this world (44).

The first part of the pastoral constitution concludes with a view of Christ as the alpha and the omega, the beginning and the end of both the church and the world, of the history of man and of salvation. The church, the 'universal sacrament of salvation', manifests God's love of men in Christ visibly on earth. That is why she longs to see the redeemer of the world again—*Maranatha!* (45).

II. An examination of the conciliar view of man and the world

The pastoral constitution tried to strike a new note, but its tone still often has an 'unsympathetic' effect on lay people. The frequent magisterial statements about the church's 'integral view' of man and the human community do echo a kind of 'noetic triumphalism'. Clearly what is meant by this integral view of the church is that what sociologists, psychologists and other scientists have to say about man and the community of men is only a partial view and that the church has above all the religious dimension, man's salvation, in mind; this is not simply another aspect existing alongside the other aspects of man and the human community, but something that embraces all these other aspects. To clarify this by saying that the church has a 'total insight' into things is, however, both very misleading and very irritating, and rightly so. This so-called total insight often seems to close our eyes to partial views and can therefore change rapidly from an 'integral view' to 'integralism'. What is more, the emphasis on 'true civilisation' and 'authentic civilisation' implies some kind of doubt that the civilisation of non-believers is 'sincere'. Again and again the question rises as to whether a council can really determine all that easily what authenticity or non-authenticity in human society means. On the other hand, the council is almost naive in its enthusiasm for our technical civilisation, but pays little attention to the enormous significance of art and literature (novels, films, etc) in man's understanding of himself today.

Let us, however, leave these—and other—possible comments and observations on one side and examine more closely the content of the council's view itself.

If we disregard the discrepancy that often exists between the fundamental views of the council and the way in which the church in fact appears both universally and locally—something which the council explicitly regrets—then we may say that, in comparison with the traditional teaching of the church about the 'world' and the process of secularisation and humanisation, the pastoral constitution certainly strikes a fresh note. In it, some of the basic ideas which have been elaborated by theologians since the second world war have become officially the common property of the church. These ideas themselves come from the post-war theologians' attempt to interpret, in the light of the christian revelation, the new existential experience of mankind. The watchword is no longer flight from the world, but flight with the world towards the future, a taking of the world itself with us in our christian expectation of the future, which is already transforming the earth here and now. It is precisely because the christian hopes for a 'new heaven and a new earth' that he can never reconcile himself to an 'established order' in the world, since this would be, by definition, a forsaking of his eschatological hope. Because this hope had faded in the past, reactionary powers which aimed to preserve the established order inflexibly in its static and given character were often able to find protagonists among christians. In the pastoral constitution, the church has, in principle, broken with this attitude. At least in a limited sense, the constitution expresses something of the will to take part in the 'revolutions' that are taking place more or less all over the world as a result of man's care for his fellow-men. The view that there is a mysterious bond between man's expectation of the future here on earth and his eschatological expectation is fundamental to the constitution. The consequence of this is that christian hope for the *eschaton* also stimulates christian commitment to the building up of a better world on earth. This conciliar statement may seem rather harmless, but it is really new and it has enormous consequences.

Harvey Cox has shown in his book *God's Revolution and Man's Responsibility* (Valley Forge 1965) how God in fact revealed himself in the old testament in political and social revolutions, how the God of the old testament was precisely a God who revealed himself in the exodus from Egypt, in the conquests of Israel, in Israel's exile and in the collapse of the monarchy. He has demonstrated convincingly that political and military revolutions were the sphere of God's revelation of himself and that God frequently allowed non-Israelites to play a part in this process. Ought we not in the very first place to see, he goes on to ask, not what the church is doing in this world, but the great dynamism that we are now experiencing in the world itself as God's activity in the modern world—the anti-colonial revolutions, the scientific revolution of the present age, the movement against racial discrimination, the peace movement and, in a word, the whole revolution of secularisation (*op cit*, p 32)? What, he then goes on to ask, is the church's position with regard to these movements? Should she remain neutral? Is God not present in the modern age above all in the Marxist revolution, in the Freudian revolution? Man's liberation from the supremacy of the 'principalities and powers' to which the bible refers means in modern terms, Cox argues, man's liberation from the fate of infrastructures, from the many different uncontrolled powers which condition man economically and socially and keep him a slave. We have overstressed the church, we have overstressed worship in the church as something separate and have forgotten that the people of God assembles on Sundays and disperses afterwards to work for a better world. Cox does not, in this context, minimalise the importance of sin. On the contrary, he devotes a whole chapter to it (37–50). Man's capital sin, however, in his opinion, is pride and selfishness, which causes man to fail to commit himself sincerely and totally to the improvement of the human condition.

Although their emphasis is one-sided, the 'death of God' theologians do confront us with a real problem. The council has provided us with an *initial* answer to this problem in three very striking statements. Firstly, the discrepancy between religion and life in the world is un-christian. Secondly, there is a veiled but nonetheless real relation between man's future here on earth and his eschatological future. And finally, 'the Spirit of God . . . is actively present in these evolutions (on earth)'. These are, as I have said, striking statements, but they leave very many problems still unsolved.

A. No christian anthropology; rather God is close to man in grace

Quite correctly, emphasis has been laid on the fact that the council's re-evaluation of the concept of the 'people of God' has introduced a very sensitive change into our view of the church of Christ, and that this new assessment has enormous consequences for the future. But however important it may be, this new emphasis is still, as it were, confined to the church and one may even go as far as to say that the danger of the earlier division between clergy and laity which, in the past, worked to the advantage of the clergy, being turned now to the advantage of a laity that is coming of age is present in it. In such a perspective, the old dualism may still continue, but with a shift of emphasis.

Far more important than the concept of the church as the

people of God is the theme that is to some extent implicit, but nonetheless really present in the pastoral constitution, the theme that the church of Christ is the 'sacrament of the world'—the church is the people of God, but she is that people as the *sign* in the world and for the benefit of the world (42).

At the present moment, membership of the catholic church amounts to only 18% of the world population. Taking the increase in world population and the slight increase of catholicism in certain parts of the world into account, but leaving aside particularly surprising changes which can at the most only be hypothetical, catholics will, in about thirty years' time, constitute no more than about 8–9% of the whole of the human race. Viewed in this light, this is a negligible quantity of the whole of the great community of men. This percentage is, of course, made higher by the inclusion of all christians of all denominations, but even the whole of christianity is a very small flock in a great meadow of humanity. Seen in this light, the problem of the 'church and the world' lies ahead of us in life-sized proportions and christianity is compelled to reflect about itself anew. The word 'conversion' cannot disappear from the christian vocabulary, but christianity is nonetheless faced with the need to think about itself in rather different terms. After all, if the church is purely an institution set up for the 'task of conversion', we are bound to conclude, after two thousand years of carrying out this task, that the result is, quantitatively at least, a very meagre catch of fish—the very opposite of John's vision of the wonderful catch made by Jesus' apostles. Even though it has not been in vain, the catch does not amount to much more than a few bream and carp. But let us, then, leave this pessimistic consideration (pessimistic because of the point of departure from which we have approached the subject) and look at the matter from another point of view.

Man is not brought into contact with the God of salvation for the first time when he is explicitly and historically confronted with the church of Christ. The grace of God's redemption is not only and for the first time effective when it is officially proclaimed by the word of the gospel and of the sacraments in the church. On the basis of God's universal will to save and of the central fact of Christ's death and resurrection for all men, grace is concealed but active in the whole of human life, in everything that we call human. It is evident from the fact that the Son of God was truly man, that Jesus' personal humanity was the revelation of grace. In him, the deepest meaning of our being man was made manifest to us. Personal humanity is therefore always a possibility of revelation, the sphere in which revelation and grace are accomplished. What is human is thus the material through which the revelation of God's grace is expressed. The mystery of salvation is concretely and actively present wherever man experiences his own existence, even before there is any question of his coming into contact with or becoming a member of the church.

Philosophy and literature attempt to interpret this nameless mystery or at least they try to evoke it. But it is only in the perspective of the prophetic interpretation of the revelation of the word that theology will be able to expose the deepest meaning of the mystery of human life. In any case, our consent or our rejection of the mystery of salvation is, if not always consciously and explicitly, then certainly implicitly present in the attitude that we adopt towards the reality that surrounds us and especially towards our fellowmen. For us christians, then, this means that our membership of the church is not a suprastructure built on top of our everyday life or on top of our attitude towards our fellowchristians and towards non-christians, people who do not belong to our political, social or religious 'party'. On the contrary, our christianity has to make itself true precisely within these relationships.

The same fact, that is, that a consent to or a rejection of the mystery of salvation is already present in man's actual relationships, leads to the insight that even people who do not belong to the church make decisions for or against salvation in their relationships with their fellow-men. In this sense, contact with the church is not the first decisive element. This means that we cannot divide the people of the world into those who belong to the church, that is, christians, and those who do not, that is, non-christians. There are true christians who do not belong to the christian churches and there are purely nominal christians who do belong to the church of Christ. This way of looking at the matter does not do away with the unique value of the church, but it does give a more relative value to certain overstrained ideas about the church. We must learn to think in more modest terms about the church herself, without minimising her value and significance. The church is not the 'world', but she is not 'non-world' either. What the church has to offer us explicitly is already implicitly active in human life as a whole, that is, the mystery of salvation. The profound content of what is being brought about in the world is exposed, proclaimed and celebrated in thanksgiving in the church and reference to the world is therefore an essential element of explicit christianity, the church. The church is the world where the world comes to itself in complete consciousness, recognising and proclaiming the most profound mystery of its life, the mystery of salvation brought about by Christ Jesus.

In this way, the church is a sign. She is a visible sign to the whole world, the sign in which the mystery of life in this world is made visible. God's plan with the whole world must be apparent in the *koinonia* or community of love of the church and this plan is to bring all men together in a community of brothers on the basis of their community with God in his representative, Christ Jesus.

What must be done to make this real, to make the church *de facto* the sign of this *shalom*, this community of love among all men? In my view, the first and most important post-conciliar task facing all christians is to overcome the social, cultural and human distance that has come about over the years between the church and the world. What is more, this gulf has to be bridged above all in all those places where the church is concretely visible—in the parish, in the diocese, in every country, in every family, in every type of community and in the world church. The setting up of this sign is the task of all believers, both laity and clergy, but the bishops are officially responsible, together with their priests, for the face that the church shows to the world. The priest's task is not to establish a 'church' oasis in the world, a kind of refuge from the world's traffic. Because of the three aspects of his office in the church—proclamation of the gospel, administration of the sacraments and guidance of the community of believers—which simply point to three directions in his work as a priest, his task is basically to raise the community of the church to the point where it becomes the *sacramentum mundi,* the sign of salvation in and for the whole world and the revelation of the world to itself.

In the bible, the word 'world' is always used in a basically anthropological sense, but with a variety of meanings within this, ranging between the two extremes of 'Do not be conformed to this world' (Rom 12:2) and 'God so loved the world' (Jn 3:16). The physical world is included in the biblical concept of world, but always as something that is essentially involved with man and connected with his fate. The biblical world is, in any case, always an existential world, a world of men, a humanised world and this is the sense in which the pastoral constitution regards the world. The following statement is made at the very beginning of the document, in the introduction: 'The council has the world of men in mind, that is, the whole family of men together with all the things of the world in which this family lives.' The constitution then goes on to clarify this statement: 'A world which is the stage on which the history of mankind is enacted, a world characterised by assiduous activity, by defeats and victories, a world which christians believe to have been created out of love by the creator and to be preserved by his love, to have become subject to the power of sin, but to have been liberated from sin by the death on the cross and the resurrection of Christ, who thereby broke the power of evil in order that the world might be transformed in accordance with God's saving intention and attain its ultimate completion' (2).

Revelation, then, is concerned with God's love for the world. The bible does not provide us with an anthropology or a cosmology. All that it tells us is that man in the world is divinely loved by God. Precisely what man in the world is has to become apparent from human experience and therefore from human history. Revelation does not tell us what man appears to be in the course of history. It only tells us that whatever that man appears to be in the course of history is sustained by the love of God, who does not regret the gift of his love. Revelation tells us no more than this about man in the world. That is borne out in the appearance of the man Jesus on earth. This absolute love of God to the very end appeared in him—'God so loved the world'. It is apparent from the sinful history of mankind that God's love for a sinful mankind is of its nature a redeeming and forgiving love. And it becomes clear in the human life of Jesus that the only adequate human response to this love of God is *radical* love for our fellow-men, a love that is so radical and absolute that it is inwardly an absolute witness to God, in other words, that it only becomes intelligible in its radical character in the light of the gift of God's love for us. This is really the whole of revelation. The church's teaching about God, about Christ and the church herself, about the sacraments and about eschatology—this is no more than man's thematic and reflective expression of this revelation of God's love. This thematisation should not, however, allow us to forget the fundamental datum of revelation itself. This thematisation moreover only has meaning if it creates the possibility of man's deeper experience of radical love of his fellow-men, which is the other side of the coin of God's absolute love for us.

Christianity therefore knows no more about human anthropology than this—whatever man is, this is included in the mystery of God, in other words, the mystery that is man is in the deepest sense the mystery of God. As history moves forward, man learns how to discover the dimensions of his being man, so that light has to be thrown again and again on every new understanding that man gains of himself from the vantage-point of the one datum of revelation and, in this newly discovered dimension of his own being, man has to realise love for his fellow-men which is sustained in its radical character by God's absolute love for man, for which man owes God no debt. The 'anthropology' is therefore extended or exposed in its formal structures by man's experiences in this world, the experiences of christian and of non-christian man, and revelation continues to invite us again and again to perform our task of love in this 'anthropology'.

An impasse often occurs here in the case of christians. A definite image of man and the world, the product of a particular historical period in the history of man—and thus also in the history of the church—is identified with faith in the christian revelation and, because of this, christians are often fiercely opposed to any new image of man and the world and adopt a reactionary attitude. In so doing, they forget that revelation does not provide us with a 'christian' anthropology—all that it does is to tell us that we are called upon, in our concrete life as men (which always embraces, either implicitly or explicitly, a view of man and the world), to realise radical love for our fellow-men precisely as the absolute gift of God's love for us. This faith in revelation of course implies that man is a *personal* being, otherwise the church's proclamation of the love of God and of men would be inwardly meaningless. In this sense, the church will always leap to the defence of human, personal values. But what these are in the concrete is always gradually discovered by man in situations within this world. The church will always affirm the demand of revelation within actual human situations—that is why she always speaks about this demand in the light of the prevailing image of man and the world. This is, of course, evidence of the church's sober sense of reality in her affirmation of the demand for revelation. But man himself does not remain motionless in history. It may therefore happen that the demand of revelation is still being affirmed rightly in the church, but wrongly in the light of an image of man and the world that has been superseded. In this case, the christian faith is often unconsciously identified with an anthropology and an outdated view of man is defended in the conviction that it is 'orthodoxy' which is being defended. The consequence of this is that true orthodoxy— the demand made by faith to love our fellow-men, a love which only becomes intelligible in its radical character through God's gift of his absolute love for us precisely in *this* particular situation, our particular situation in the world —is, in the meantime, misunderstood in practice. In other words, christians are attempting, in this case, to realise the demand of faith in a world that is no longer their own contemporary world. They are acting as though they were still living in the ancient world or in the middle ages and as though the world had never been radically changed since then by science, Marxism or Freudianism, to mention only a few of the recent phenomena which inevitably require christians to realise the demand of revelation in a different way. It is an impasse of this kind that gives rise to the church's alienation from the world.

The task of revelation continues to acquire constantly new forms in the light of man's increasing understanding of himself. Christians are as much involved in this increasing self-understanding as non-christians. It must, however, be freely admitted that, apart from some noteworthy exceptions, christians have, in the past, simply tended to go along, often unwillingly, with the crowd and have not generally been among those who have provided the impulse.

What, then, is the new view of man and the world to which man has come at this present moment of his existence? It is important to know this, because it is in the world of today that the demand of revelation, our radical love of our fellow human beings which is the gift of God's absolute and forgiving love, has to be realised. The following is a brief outline of this new image of man.

In the past, nature was directly experienced as God's creation. Now, however, it is regarded as the rough building material from which man creates his human world. Nature is no longer the subject—it has become the object of man's control. This change in man's view of the world has brought about a change in his view of man. Man now experiences himself as a being who makes history. Humanising nature, he humanises himself. Man's control of nature contains within itself the temptation for man to regard his fellow-man as a world to be mastered, as a thing that can be subjected to man's power by technical means just as the things of nature can be controlled by technology. Man is tempted to apply his control of nature to man himself in the whole of his bodily and psychical structure, since man too can be manipulated. But this control of nature must be at the service of the human person and give free scope to man's fellow-men. It does in itself offer this possibility, but it can also be abused by man's sinfulness. Alongside man's control of nature by technology and the greater human possibilities that have been brought about by this control, then, there is in the modern world a very characteristic urgent call for human fellowship and a powerful attempt to reform the world socially, economically and politically and to make it more worthy of man, arising from man's care for his fellow-men. The new image of man and the world is thus directed towards the future. This new image, unlike the earlier image of man and the world, is basically a project for the future. Man's aim is to build a new world. Paradise, the 'golden age', is no longer in the past. It lies ahead, in the future, and nature is the raw material with which man is to build this new world for the benefit of all men.

It is clear, then, that post-conciliar christianity will in the first place have to come to terms with this modern reality and in particular in the concrete form in which man's building up of a future world is presented to us—the marxist expectation of the future. All that the christian knows in the light of revelation is that this expectation of the future on earth is included and secure in the absolute, gratuitous and forgiving proximity of God's grace. This is why this dimension of the future has a central position in contemporary theology. Speculation about the relationship between 'nature' and the 'supernatural', which preoccupied theologians in the past, has been transformed, in modern theology, into the problem of the relationship between man's expectation for the future here on earth and the eschatological kingdom. Theology has become eschatology in confrontation with the building of the 'city of man'. The light that the theologian has here has remained the same—man is 'of God', he is included in the mystery of God that was manifested in the life and death of Jesus who was brought to life by God. In other words, man's radical love for his fellow-men, the gift of God's absolute love for us, is not in vain. That is the only datum of faith that is revealed to us in Christ. The question then is, how is this datum of faith to function in the new image of man and the world which looks forward to a better 'new world' that has still to be made? How can the basic christian conviction, 'Nothing will be able to separate us from the love of God in Christ Jesus our Lord' (Rom 8: 39), be made actively true in this changed world of today, a world in which modern man, unlike man in the past, has taken his life and history into his own hands? That is the theme of the pastoral constitution. The fundamental problem has not been entirely solved in the constitution, but it has been stated in new terms—what does our christian hope for the *eschaton* mean to modern man whose aim is to build a better future for mankind on earth? Is christianity to leave the world to its own fate and to be concerned, in the liturgy and in prayer, with a better future for man after this earth or is it to work for a better future here on earth, in which the eschatological future is prepared, and to celebrate, in the liturgy and in prayer, that one future which unites the history of man on this earth with the *eschaton*?

B. The christian relativisation and radicalisation of the
   building of the 'city of man'

The answer to the problem posed in the preceding section
is already provided in outline in Jesus' own radical love of
man, which is intelligible in the light of God's personal love
for man. Jesus' death was, after all, not a 'liturgical cultic
mystery', set aside from the world, but a personal offering of
his own life, made in a historical context, a coming together
of conflicting situations in this world with the leaders of his
people. This secular event, an incident in Jesus' complete life
in the world, was later expressed, in the letter to the Hebrews
especially, in themes taken from the old testament liturgy of
sacrificial worship, but this should not cause us to forget that
this event was not in the first place a liturgical sacrifice that
took place alongside real life in the world, but a sacrificial
act in a concrete, living situation. Christ's death, in other
words, was not a liturgical flight from the world, but in the
deepest sense, his immersion to the very depths of his being
as a person in human life in the world, a radical love for
men, only intelligible in its completely radical character in
the light of the love of God himself for men. We celebrate
and give thanks for this event in Jesus' life that was accomplished so radically in the world in the liturgy of the church,
but we do so in order to draw from this celebration the
strength to be able to experience our life in this world in
giving ourselves radically and caring radically for our fellow-
men in a radical love that is only intelligible in the light
of God's absolute love for us. This is the basic intuition of
the pastoral constitution, clearly revealed by the fact that,
in the middle of a discussion of the 'church in the modern
world', the eucharist is seen as the earnest-money given to
christians in their commitment to the building up of life
within this world (38).

Another perspective is revealed by the fact that Jesus'
followers did not themselves choose the name of 'christian'.
It was non-christians who discussed something of that which

had inspired Christ himself in certain people and therefore called them 'christians'. Authentic christians are people in whose lives the Spirit of Christ himself is visible—'See how they love one another.' In the early church, this visible love functioned within the early image of man and the world. How must it function today? In other words, what is the relationship between christian love and the building up of a better world for men to live in? Quite correctly, the pastoral constitution warns us of two dangers; firstly, the danger of our not taking, as christians, the building of a better future on earth seriously and, secondly, the danger of our identifying, in an un-christian way, a self-made future with the kingdom of God. Because of the promise of the kingdom of God, the christian is, in his commitment to this world, placed in the very centre of the mystery—every result achieved in this world is always questioned because of christian hope for the *eschaton*, yet this commitment to the world is never in vain. There is a tension between relativisation and radicalisation in the christian commitment to the building of a better future on earth. I should like to conclude by throwing some light on this tension.

Every project to build a better future for man on earth has to come to terms with the problem of death, otherwise a utopia is planned without regard to real facts. The fact of death makes relative all attempts to build a better world for man to live in. On earth, humanisation has no definitive shape or form which can ultimately be called christian in content. The christian hope for the *eschaton* and faith in an eschatological 'new world', in which death no longer has any place, makes all humanisation here on earth and all man's building of a 'secular city' relative. It is clear that the council understood this from the section in the pastoral constitution referring to the need to include all activity within the world in the mystery of Easter (38). The ultimate world that is fully worthy of man can only be given to us as a gift of God beyond the frontiers of death, that is, in the act in which we ultimately confess our impotence to make this world truly human, in our explicit and effective recognition that the 'new world' cannot be the result of human planning, but must be a pure gift of God. It is only when man surrenders completely to God that any real future lies ahead of him.

But, however fundamentally christian this view may be, it is still not the whole of christianity. If this—authentically christian—aspect alone is emphasised, the objection raised by all those who are ready to lay down their lives in order to banish injustice and discrimination from the world of men still remains valid, namely, as Merleau-Ponty observed, if it ever comes to the point where there must be a revolution in order to banish injustice from the world, we can never rely on christians, because they relativise every commitment to the world. This is a very real objection and, what is more, one which is not closely examined in the pastoral constitution.

Any attempt to answer this objection would in the first place have to throw a much clearer light on the fact that the christian relativisation of man's commitment to this world is not inspired by a flight from this world, nor is it prompted by a conviction that grace enjoys an absolute priority. The christian makes this commitment to the world relative precisely because he hopes for an eschatological completion, in which man will possess himself and the world completely in a radical giving of himself. This hope for a 'new world' makes every result achieved on this earth in the process of humanisation relative because the result achieved is not yet and cannot be this hoped for 'new world'. In the past, christians drew the wrong conclusion from this correct assumption, namely that they had to be indifferent or even hostile to the building of a better world on earth. In fact, however, the only correct conclusion is that christians can never reconcile themselves to an already 'established order' in the world, because it can never be christian in content. In this sense, there is no such thing as a 'christian' social order, civilisation or policy. What is precisely christian in this context is the constant striving to go beyond the result achieved, the refusal to say, 'the result is satisfactory and everything is now in order'. Christianity is therefore the confirmation of a future which always remains open and this openness is not a static datum or a purely theoretical statement, but an active commitment to a better future.

The change that was made in the original text of the pastoral constitution from 'the form of this world, insofar as it is characterised by sin, *will* pass' into the final version, 'is already passing', was quite justified. This passing of the form of the world does not, however, occur automatically, but through eschatological hope, which is already working for a better world here on earth. This may seem to some people to be an unjustified leap in the train of thought. But in this case they are forgetting the precise content of the 'veiled relationship' between man's future on this earth and the eschatological future as affirmed by the council. This relationship certainly cannot be determined more precisely. Precisely because the christian believes in an absolute future, the future which is God himself for man, he cannot describe the precise shape of this future meaningfully—any more than the non-christian can—and he can never confuse or identify the result of man's historical striving on earth with the promised 'new world'. After all, if God is the intangible, incomprehensible mystery and man is embraced by this mystery, then man's being is, by definition, also a mystery that cannot be comprehended by faith. But christian hope in God, who is man's future, is not a theory, but an active hope, which only becomes a reality in man's working for a better future on earth, in other words, in his care for his fellowmen in concrete situations in this world. This radical commitment to our fellow-men is an incomprehensible love and this love, because it is incomprehensible, makes the commitment completely radical. We do not know where this love is leading us, but we do know that it is not ultimately meaningless and will not be in vain. This makes christian love incomprehensible for the world. It makes our commitment to this world thematically incomprehensible even to us christians—we are a mystery even to ourselves and have, in all simplicity, to confess this to our 'non-christian' fellow-men when they ask us why we are committing ourselves to life in this world. This thematic incomprehensibility, however, does not mean that we commit ourselves any less to the world. On the contrary, it makes this commitment completely radical. Our commitment as christians to our fellow-men is completely radical because it is the other side of the coin of God's personal love for man. This commitment is radical because, even though it is not possible to realise here on earth a world that is truly worthy of man, it continues to work, in complete surrender to faith, towards a situation that is more and more human. It is a hope against hope, a hope against all despair that comes from our human experience, which continues to suggest that all our attempts to build a better world are in vain. The radical character of this christian commitment and of the surrender to faith cannot be justified in the light of purely human experience. It is, of its very nature, a hoping in God (explicitly or implicitly) as the future for man. It is possible that many christians have not yet drawn all these conclusions from the radical nature of this view and that they are consequently still hesitant in their attitude towards the social and political dynamism of the modern age and the struggle to build a world that is more worthy of man. They may therefore feel too satisfied in their own welfare state, while more than half of the world is still hungering and thirsting for a strict minimum of human dignity.

Nowadays, christianity is discovering the 'political' dimension of christian charity and the worldly dimensions of christianity. The inspiration here comes from the present situation in the world and from contact with the bible and especially with the old testament. In the past, christians tended to live in a separate little world of the spirit, where God and the 'soul' of man made asides to each other. The bible, however, teaches us that God is active in the whole world of men and that the church is called to share in this activity of God in the world itself. In this age, God seems to be accomplishing more through men like Martin Luther King, for example, than through the church. As Harvey Cox so rightly said, 'We christians have been a very talkative people, talkative to the point of verbosity' (*op cit*, p 54). We christians used to interpret the world differently from non-christians, but we did not transform it—and this is what really matters. The church must show what the future world will be. And here we are confronted with the mystery of christianity, which relativises and at the same time radicalises man's work for a better world here on earth. The church therefore has to stimulate us continuously to transcend ourselves. In her liturgy, she has to celebrate the unnamed future, while, in the world, she has to prepare for this future. Non-christians often leap into the breach to bring the biblical *shalom* into the world, while christians are conspicuous by their absence. On the other hand, those christians who are actively beginning to make this secular dimension of christianity really true are quickly characterised as 'social gospel' christians. Of course, their emphasis is often one-sided because of their reaction to the 'unworldly' church, just as, in the past, a one-sided stress was placed on the cultic aspects of the church. It is above all the task of theologians to draw attention to every one-sided emphasis, whether his words are welcome or not. He has, for example, to warn christians if the radicalisation of their commitment to this world is correctly taken into account, but the relativisation of this commitment is suppressed, so that the absolute character of man's history here on earth is disregarded and man himself is ultimately misrepresented. On the other hand, however, every period in human history calls for its special emphases. And then we may ask ourselves whether christians ought not to be on the side of the great social, economic and political revolutions which are taking place in the modern world, not simply going along, as critics, with these revolutions, but as people taking (a critical) part in them. In this case, the real demand made by the present situation in the world may be for christians to stress, perhaps one-sidedly, this worldly dimension of christianity. The dangers inherent in such a necessary, but one-sided emphasis must therefore be obviated by an equally one-sided emphasis on contemplative monastic life (in a new form), which is also equally necessary to the totality of christianity.

Both its relativisation and its radicalisation of all commitment to man in this world characterise christianity as a radical self-emptying. In this sense, christianity is a radically committed love which cannot justify itself, which has again and again to transcend its achievement in this world and which has again and again to give itself away in profound darkness in a self-emptying which often seems to be in vain in this world, but which is nonetheless so radical that it is precisely in this giving away of itself for the benefit of others that the very essence of the kingdom of God breaks through into our world. But this is already the kingdom of God itself —only the form of this present world passes, nothing of what has been achieved in the world by man's radical love for his fellow-men. All this implies faith in the absolute God, whose being is the negation of everything that seems to be in vain. Everything that seems, from the human point of view, to be in vain is made meaningful and not ultimately in vain by faith in the absolute God and, in this faith, man is not an anonymous element in history and does not, as is affirmed by an authentically atheistic commitment to a better world, pass for ever into oblivion. But, for man, this christian attitude is a mystery that cannot be rationalised. It is an active surrender to the mystery of God and therefore to the mystery of man. It is a mystery which, as God's 'amen' or 'yes' (2 Cor 1 : 20) to man, appeared in a veiled form in the man Jesus, the Christ, The christian does not flee from the world, but flees with the world towards the future. He takes the world with him towards the absolute future which is God himself for man.

5

THE TYPOLOGICAL DEFINITION
OF THE CHRISTIAN LAYMAN
ACCORDING TO VATICAN II[24]

The question as to whether a theological definition of the christian layman ought to include the layman's relationship with the secularity of the world has frequently been discussed in theological circles, especially since the second world war. What is the position of the fourth chapter ('The Laity') of the dogmatic constitution *Lumen Gentium*, on the church of the second Vatican Council in this? In order to throw light on the full extent and meaning of the conciliar position, I shall trace the development of the council's 'definition' of the christian layman from the pre-conciliar schema, through the various stages of the document up to the final version.

I. In search of the true conciliar definition
Even in the first draft or schema of the constitution on the church, which was compiled by the pre-conciliar commission and, after it had been examined by the pre-conciliar central commission (the *Acta* of which are still inaccessible), was submitted in 1962 to the fathers of the council, there was a separate chapter on the laity, *Schemata constitutionum et decretorum de quibus disceptabitur in concilii sessionibus*, 1962, Series II, 6, pp 36–41, with the *Commentarius*, pp 42–5. At the end of the first session, the whole of this schema was referred to the conciliar commission proper to be revised, but the pre-conciliar text continued to serve as the basis of the new text, at least as far as the chapter on the laity was concerned. One could even say that the pre-conciliar text (*op cit*, 4, especially 24, *De vita salutifera ecclesiae a laicis active participata*, pp 38–9) was, in some of its parts, clearer

than the first version of the new schema (*Schema constitutionis dogmaticae de ecclesia*, II, 1963, 25 (corresponding to
24 in the first schema), *De vita et apostolatu laicorum*, pp 8–
10).

A. The pre-conciliar text

In connection with the 'definition' of the layman, this text
says: 'The sacred synod *here* (= in this context) means by
the word "lay people" those believers who have, by baptism,
been incorporated into the people of God, but who live in
the world and are guided only by the general norms of
christian life. The synod has in mind especially those believers who are not called from the people of God either to
the hierarchy of holy orders or to the religious state sanctioned by the church, but who have to strive towards christian holiness in honour of God in a special way also through
activity in the world. They are involved in activities within
the world but, led by the spirit of the gospel, they courageously oppose the evils of this world and indeed, by virtue of
their christian vocation, they sanctify the world, as it were,
from within.'[25] As I have said, this text formed the basis for
all further elaborations and revisions.

It was stated in the commentary of the commission that
there was no intention to give a theological definition of the
christian laity. In the text itself, the word *hic* (here) pointed
to the existence of other meanings of the term 'lay people'.
The aim was to describe the use of the word 'lay people' in
the church and in particular *sensu vulgato*, that is, according
to its current use in church circles. In this sense, the layman
is positively defined by his membership of the church, the
people of God. This membership is further defined restric-
tively—the layman is a non-ordained christian, in other
words, he does not belong to the hierarchy of holy orders
and he is not a religious. This is in fact the ordinary christian's idea of a layman—a christian who is neither a member
of the clergy nor a member of a religious order. The lay
people are those who are left among the people of God if

members of the clergy and of religious orders are not included. What is clear in connection with the restrictive definition 'non-cleric' is that this pre-conciliar schema is really saying 'non-ordained person'. Nothing is said about belonging to the hierarchy of jurisdiction (apart from the hierarchy of ordination) and this suggests that a non-ordained christian, who nonetheless may possess some form or other of jurisdictional power, must still be known as a lay person as opposed to what K. Rahner, for example, has said (see pp 109–110). This view is in accordance with that of the pre-conciliar schema on the consecration of bishops, which does not, as such, bestow any participation in the pastoral government of the church. In the later revision of the chapter on the bishops, consecration itself was regarded as the basis of three hierarchical powers and therefore also of the pastoral governing power of the bishop, even though the exercise of this office was determined by the regulations of the church. According to this second view, jurisdictional power is, at least fundamentally, bestowed by consecration itself, with the result that there can no longer be any question of an adequate distinction between ordination and jurisdiction. This view would therefore have a repercussion on the definition of the layman as a non-office-bearer.

Finally, a relationship was established in this pre-conciliar text between lay people and their being in the world by the positive definition of the laity, and it was also stated that lay-people exercise holiness in the glorification of God's name in a special way, that is also through their activities in the world, carried out in the spirit of the gospel.

From the very beginning, then, three aspects are recognised in the christian concept of the layman. Firstly, he belongs to the church as the people of God. Secondly, he is a non-ordained and non-religious clerical member of that people. Thirdly, he is, in a christian manner, involved in activities in the world. The third aspect is not explicitly linked with —or seen as a consequence of—the non-clerical character of the lay person.

B. The second schema, drafted by the conciliar commission

Almost the same formulation can be found in the second schema, drawn up by the conciliar commission for discussion during the second session of the council: 'The sacred synod means by the word "lay people" those believers who have, by baptism, been embodied into the people of God and who serve God in the general state of christian believers and who actively share in the mission of the whole christian people in the world, also through religious activity, but who do not belong either to the hierarchical order or to the religious state sanctioned by the church. The synod has in mind especially those who are actively involved in activities in this world, but who, led by the spirit of the gospel, courageously oppose the desires of the world and indeed, by virtue of their christian vocation, sanctify the world, as it were, from within.'[26] The basic view-point is the same as that of the first schema, but there is a change of emphasis which strikes our attention at once as soon as we compare the two phrases 'also through activity in the world' (first schema) and 'also through religious activity' (second schema). It is more clearly affirmed in the second schema that lay people are not outside the primary, in other words, the religious mission of the whole church and that they have an active contribution to make to this religious mission as non-office-bearers, not only through their christian secular activity, but also through their direct contribution, as non-office-bearers, to the church's work of evangelising. Properly speaking, according to this second text, the layman's 'relationship with the secularity of this world' does not come within the *theological* concept of the layman. This relationship is, according to the explanatory note of the conciliar commission, concerned with the 'actual condition of the layman in society' (*op cit, Notae*, 4, p 11; also as in the first schema: *op cit* (footnote 1, p 255), *Commentarius* p 43). According to this text, then, the 'laicity' or the secular character of the lay person appears to be a non-ecclesiological element. The ecclesiological element

93

is to be found in carrying out, together with others, the mission of the church. This carrying out of the church's mission takes place 'also through religious activity'. In other words, it is said, though only implicitly, that the secular activity of a layman is, in one way or another, an aspect of the carrying out of the mission of the church. In any case the emphasis is placed on the primary religious mission. Whereas the first schema stressed the christian significance of the lay person's secular activity, the second seems to contain an implicit reaction against tendencies which seek to define the christian lay person more in the light of his relationship with the secularity of this world. It is for this reason that the second part of the second text contains the phrase: 'The synod has in mind especially those who . . .', whereas the second part of the first text had: 'The synod has in mind especially those *believers* who. . .'. This confirms that, in this text, the membership of the commission were thinking of the 'actual condition of the layman in society' and were dissociating themselves from the tendency to include the relationship with laicity or secularity in the theological definition of the layman. Otherwise, there is no essential difference between the second text and the first, apart from the use of the phrase 'serve God in the general status of christian believers' (in contrast to members of the clergy and of religious orders), which replaced the rather moralising 'guided by the general norms of christian life' of the first text, and the correct alteration of the expression, not belonging 'to the hierarchy of holy orders' used in the first schema into the formula, not belonging 'to the hierarchical order' in the second text, so that there was no explicit mention of ordination or jurisdiction in the second text and all the detailed theological questions which are connected with this, such as the question as to whether a non-ordained person who possesses jurisdictional power is still a lay person, were avoided.

C. *Discussion of the amended second schema by the fathers of the council: the third schema*

The second schema was approved as the basis for discussion. The co-ordinating commission had decided, however, that the third chapter, 'The people of God and in particular the laity' (second schema, chapter 3) should be divided into two chapters. The 'people of God' were to be dealt with (third schema, chapter 2) in a separate chapter to be inserted between the first and the second chapters of the second schema and the rest of the original chapter was to be revised to form a separate chapter on the laity (third schema, chapter 4).

When the chapter on the laity in the second schema was discussed in St Peter's, many bishops commented that the definition of the concept of the layman was too negative and too concise. The layman's being in the world had to be brought out more clearly, the mysterious formula 'sanctifying the world, as it were, from within' ought to be defined more precisely and the rather colourless expression 'the general (common, universal) state of christian believers' had to be formulated more meaningfully. As a result of these interventions on the part of the fathers of the council, the amended second schema (in other words, the third schema) which was submitted before the third session to the fathers for their approval and ultimate correction (by the handing in of *modi*) took on the following form. (Additions to the second schema and corrections are shown here in italics.)

The first half read: 'By the word "lay people", we *here* mean all christian believers *outside the members of the priesthood of holy orders* and of the religious state recognised by the church; those christian believers namely who *have been embodied into Christ* by baptism and set up as the people of God, who *participate in Christ's priestly, prophetic and royal office in their own way* and who consequently for their part carry out the mission of the whole christian people *in the church and* in the world.'

The second half read: '*A secular characteristic is peculiar to lay people....* Lay people *... are called to take care of and according to God to set in order temporal things by the whole of their lives in their own, albeit not exclusive way.* It is in the world that they live. It is there that they are called by God, in order to contribute *in the manner of leaven,* so to speak, from within to the sanctification of the world *by carrying out their own task,* inspired by the spirit of the gospel: *in this way, it happens that they excel especially by the witness of their lives, their faith, hope and love and make Christ known to others. They are therefore entrusted in a special way with the task of throwing light on and setting in order all temporal matters with which they are often closely connected, so that all this constantly takes place and goes forward according to Christ and proclaims the praise of the creator and redeemer'.*[27]

What strikes one immediately is that the commission did exactly what the fathers of the council asked it to do—in the new version, the 'general state of christian believers' was more meaningfully expressed, the lay people's 'sanctification of the world' was made more explicit and the layman was more closely connected with the reality of this world. At the same time, it is also striking how a more balanced formulation was achieved of a twofold tendency among the fathers of the council—some of them were anxious that the task of the laity *in the church* should be emphasised, whereas others wanted more prominence to be given to the christian task of the laity *in the world.*

These two requests were satisfied simply by saying that the lay people actively participated in the 'mission of the whole christian people in the church and in the world'. In this way, the contrasting emphases of the first schema ('also through activity in the world') and the second schema ('also through religious activity') ceased to apply. The text of the third schema was no longer concerned with any special emphases of this kind and stated simply that the layman, actively involved in the total mission of the whole church (although, of course, as a non-office-bearer), had a task both in the church and in the world. As opposed to the rather one-sided formula in the second schema (a one-sided emphasis which was, unjustly, called a 'clericalism'), the layman's christian relationship with the secularity of the world rather than simply his relationship with that secularity was included in the ecclesiological concept of the 'layman' in the third schema: participation in the mission of the people of God not only 'in the church', but also 'in the world'. Mgr J. Wright's *Relatio* or explanatory memorandum pointed out that this amended schema insisted both on the differences between the layman's religious tasks and his secular, civil tasks and on their harmonious association (*Relatio super caput* iv, *textus emendati schematis constitutionis de ecclesia*, 1964, p 6). It was also said more clearly than before that there was no intention of providing an 'ontological' definition of the layman, but rather a 'typological' description (*Schema constitutionis de ecclesia*, 1964, 4, *Relatio de singulis numeris, Relatio de* 31, p 127). This course was chosen firstly in order to avoid all kinds of disputed theological questions. A further reason was so that there might be no confusion arising from the use of the words 'laicity' and 'secularity', which had a clear meaning in many Western European countries, where they were kept distinct from words implying complete secularism, but which were unknown in other countries and might therefore give rise to confusion there. Finally this decision was taken because members of the clergy and religious communities also performed certain secular functions, although usually in a supplementary way.[28]

The original terms of the 'definition' of the layman, then, were kept. First of all, the generic and positive content of being a believer was brought out (*Schema constitutionis de ecclesia*, 1964, *Relatio de* 31, p 128). As far as this content was concerned, no change was made here, but the 'general (common, universal) state of christian believers' was expressed more suggestively and clearer emphasis was given to what the clergy and the laity had fundamentally in common—the layman shares as a non-office-bearer in the priestly, prophetic and royal mission of Christ and of the whole church, both in the world and in the church. These generic qualifications were then made more precise by the restrictive additions to the effect that the layman is not a member of the clergy or of a religious community. These restrictive definitions point to the characteristic aspect of being a layman (286–7). In this, the controversy between K. Rahner and H. Urs von Balthasar (see pp 109–110), whether members of so-called secular institutes should be called lay people or religious,[29] was left unresolved.

According to the commission, nothing new was said in the second part of the 'definition' of the layman. Apparently all that the members of the commission aimed to do was to enlarge on the statement made in the first part of the text that the layman participates in the mission of the church *also* in the world (that is, not only in the church). The schema said that 'a secular characteristic' was peculiar to the laity and that lay people were 'called to take care of and according to God to set in order temporal things by the whole of their lives in their own, albeit not exclusive way' (*Schema constitutionis de ecclesia*, 1964, 4, 31, p 118). This idea was already present in the previous schemas, but what is particularly noticeable here is the search for a correct placing of the secular qualification of the christian laity. Secularity was in this way included to some extent in the typological definition of the layman, since the constitution meant, by saying that the layman was not a member of a religious community, to regard 'to some extent' the 'secular characteristic' peculiar to the laity as a 'specific qualification' of lay life.[30] The negative formula ('non-religious') thus implies, according to its content, a positive relationship on the part of the christian layman with activity in the world. This christian lay institution in the world is therefore a 'special call' ('peculiariter . . . *vocantur*') for the layman. This is why, when all is considered, the laity is a *state* in the church, although this should be taken in the wider sense of the word 'state in life' (*op cit*, p 127). The world is, so to speak, the layman's proper place, but it is also his task to recognise the real value of that world, to set it in order according to God and to sanctify himself and others in it.[31]

D. The introduction of the final corrections (modi) and the final version: the fourth schema, the constitution itself

Although there is no essential difference between the final version of the 'definition' of the layman in the church and that of the amended second schema, one *modus* or correction was requested and accepted both by the commission and later by the council which introduced a subtle difference and made the text agree more closely with the original intention of the earlier schemas. In other words, one passage was formulated more happily. The amended text read: 'Lay people ... are called to take care of and according to God to set in order temporal things by the whole of their lives in their own, albeit not exclusive way.' This was changed in the definitive text of the constitution to: 'The *proper vocation* of lay people (*laicorum est, ex vocatione propria*) is to be found in their *search for the kingdom of God* (*regnum Dei quaerere*) *by* taking care of and according to God's will setting in order temporal matters' (*Schema constitutionis dogmaticae de ecclesia*, 1964, 4, 31, p 35). The phrase used in the previous, amended schema for the characteristic activity of the layman ('to take care of and according to God to set in order temporal things') did not as such point to the specifically christian character of this task. The new text included this characteristically lay activity explicitly within the perspective of theological life—the proper vocation of lay people (in the ecclesial sense) is not to set the things of this world in order on a purely ethical basis (this is a universally human task) but, in common with all the members of the people of God, to 'look for the kingdom of God' and to look for it as christian lay people, with the result that the search will take place characteristically in and through the humanisation of the world according to God's demands. What was the reason for this fortunate change at the last moment?

Five of the fathers submitted this *modus* because they feared that there was too exclusive an emphasis in the amended schema on the secular character of the christian laity (*Modi a commissione doctrinali examinati, a patribus conciliaribus propositi*, pt 4, 1964, *ad numerum* 31, p 7). I would rather put it this way: there was a danger that this secular character would not be sufficiently understood in its explicitly ecclesiological sense, but rather in its universal human sense. The new text did not therefore weaken what was characteristic of the laity, the ordering of life within this world, but integrated this into the only true christian perspective—the search for the kingdom of God. This was in any case the intention of the various schemas from the very beginning. Even in its commentary on the first, pre-conciliar schema, the commission said explicitly: 'lay people are not merely "secular" people, but members of the church in the temporal world' (Pre-conciliar schema, see footnote 1, 1962, p 44). In other words, looking for the kingdom of God, lay people are actively involved in the activities of this world. The conciliar commission also took up this position from the very beginning (*Schema constitutionis dogmaticae de ecclesia*, 1963, 4, *Notae* 17, p 15). The correct perspective was thus given to the religious character of the christian laity, and at the same time the constitution explicitly dissociated itself from all forms of clericalism ('Intentio est vitare omnem speciem clericalismi'; see *Schema constitutionis de ecclesia*, 1964, 4, *Relatio de* 34, p 130).

The definitive text, then, was as follows:

By the word 'layman', we here mean all christian believers outside the members of the priesthood of holy orders and of the religious state recognised by the church; those christian believers namely who have been embodied into Christ by baptism and set up as the people of God, who participate in Christ's priestly, prophetic and royal office in their own way and who consequently for their part carry out the mission of the whole christian people in the church and in the world.

Temporal characteristics are proper to lay people. The

members of the order of priesthood may sometimes, it is true, be occupied with secular affairs, even by practising a secular profession, but by their special vocation they are principally and professionally directed towards the ministry, whereas the religious bear eloquent and exalted witness by their state to the fact that the world cannot be transformed or committed to God without the spirit of the beatitudes. The proper vocation of lay people is to be found in their search for the kingdom of God by taking care of and according to God's will setting in order temporal matters. It is in the world that they live, namely in all secular professions and employments, in the ordinary circumstances of family and society—their very existence is, as it were, interwoven with these. It is there that they are called by God, in order to contribute from within, in the manner of leaven, to the sanctification of the world by carrying out their own task, inspired by the spirit of the gospel: in this way, it happens that they excel especially by the witness of their lives, their faith, hope and love and make Christ known to others.

They are therefore entrusted in a special way with the task of throwing light on and setting in order all temporal matters with which they are often closely connected, so that all this constantly takes place and goes forward according to Christ and proclaims the praise of the creator and redeemer (Dogmatic constitution on the church, 4, 31).

II. The basic view and special emphases of the conciliar definition

Three elements may be distinguished in the typological definition of the layman in the ecclesial sense according to the second Vatican Council:

(1) In the first place, the lay person is generally defined by his (active) membership of the church as the people of God—he participates in the total mission of the whole church. In this way, the christian wealth of this membership is positively emphasised and what both the priest and the layman have in common in all that they are and do as christians is insisted on. The destiny of the whole church is thus placed in the hands of lay people as well—in this it is clear

that the church has taken up a firm position against all tendencies which would give the church to the clergy as their sphere of work and the world to the laity. In their own way, lay people are as responsible for the church as the clergy. In this way, the purely negative, canonical definition of the layman according to present canon law (CIC, canon 948) is supplemented—or rather, the wealth of the similarly canonical concept of *christi-fidelis* is more closely connected with the concept of 'lay person'. In addition to the essential difference in function in the church between the clergy and the laity, the life and activity which are common to both as the one people of God emerge clearly in this definition— within the fundamental *koinonia*, the unity and community of the people of God, there is a certain 'antithesis' or difference between priest and layman which evokes a powerful solidarity, combination and mutual involvement.[32]

(2) Secondly, the layman is more precisely defined against this common background by drawing attention to the special character of the layman as opposed to that of the cleric—in other words, the layman is a non-office-bearer. In this way, the distinctively lay character of his participation in the whole mission of the church is typified as a non-official mission—as non-office-bearer, the layman is co-responsible for the church's mission. In this way, the non-clerical character of the layman's active care for the building up of the mystical body is formulated. The active involvement of the laity in the church's task for the benefit of the church and the world must therefore not be allowed to show any tendencies towards clericalism.

(3) Finally, on the basis of the antithesis between the layman and the master of a religious community (the layman is a non-religious), the negative character of the layman (the layman is non-clerical), through which he is co-responsible for the church in a non-official way, gains a positive content —not a generically positive content (because this is based on his membership of the church) but, as it were, a specifically positive content. This positive 'specific qualification' is the

layman's *christian relationship* with the secularity of the world. The setting in order of temporal society, as the characteristically lay form of looking for the kingdom of God, is thus included in the typological definition of the christian layman of the second Vatican Council. It is in this way that the council clearly formulated the *christian* place of the layman both in the church and in the world or, to put this differently, the council has thus clarified the specifically lay participation of lay people in the mission which the people of God have in the church and the world ('Laici ... pro parte sua missionem totius populi christiani in ecclesia et in mundo exercent"; Constitution on the church, 4, 31).

One could therefore say that, in accordance with the tendency which was apparent from the pre-conciliar draft, through all the emendations and up to the final version of the constitution, this typological definition of the christian layman remained essentially the same and that the only difficulty was in finding a balanced formulation. A certain hesitation and uncertainty is discernible in this search for a balanced placing of the layman's 'relationship with the secularity of the world' in the definition of the christian laity, if the formulations of the successive schemas are compared with each other. I have, in passing, already indicated several of these differences in emphasis. If, however, the commentary of the pre-conciliar commission and those of the conciliar commission are weighed up against one another, then even more striking differences in emphasis emerge, even though the basic version is the same throughout. I should like to discuss briefly the most striking of these.

In the commentary of the pre-conciliar commission on the first schema, the following was said: 'lay people are not secularists, but members of the church in the secular world. They are therefore *distinguished* not by their secular activity, but by their active belonging to the church.'[33] The conciliar commission, on the other hand, commented rather differently in the same context on the new text of the second schema: 'lay people are not secularists, but members of the church in the profane world. They are therefore *above all characterised* not by their secular activity, but by their active participation in the activity of the church.'[34] These two texts, though obviously closely related, are nonetheless to be seen in a rather different perspective. In the first, the relationship with the secularity of the world is not regarded as distinctive for the layman and the negation obviously aims to contrast the christian layman with non-christian man. The second text, on the other hand, is more concerned with the specially lay characterisation of the layman *within* the church and the negation therefore contrasts the layman not with men generally but, at least implicitly, with members of the clergy and religious communities. The subtle difference in emphasis—between 'distinguished by' and 'above all characterised by'—may therefore be explained in this way. All the same, one feels a lingering uncertainty. In the second text, the commission wanted to affirm quite clearly that the layman above all, and precisely as a christian, had a specifically lay task within the church and not simply in the world—this was a clear tendency in the whole of the second schema. Taking this subtle difference in emphasis as its point of departure, the commentary on the amended second schema or third schema went a step further, in view of the fact that the relationship with the secularity of the world was, in this commentary, twice called the *nota specifica*, the specific element of the christian lay state ('Per notam quodammodo specificam', see *Schema constitutionis de ecclesia*, 1964, 4, *Relatio de* 30, p 126; the second case is: 'dignitas laicorum in eius nota specifica', *op cit*, *Relatio de* 32, p 128). For this reason, a sentence about the possible secular activities of members of the clergy and religious communities was inserted into the commentary on this schema to the effect that such activities were usually carried out 'in a supplementary manner', with the result that priests and religious were not able to replace lay people in this sphere.[35]

We may therefore say that the commission hesitated because it was not seen clearly from the very beginning that it was not, in this context, a question of 'the relationship with the world'—this relationship is, after all, specifically human and as such does not come within an ecclesiological definition of the layman—but rather a question of a 'christian relationship with secularity' and this qualification certainly can form the basis of an ecclesiological specification of the layman. The basis of this hesitation is to be found in the fact that the total mission of the church was referred to before demonstrating that this primary and exclusively religious and transcendent mission of the church has as a consequence a secondary mission, specifically of the church, in the world, that is the orientation of the process of humanising this world (which is a universally human task) towards salvation (which is the object of the church's mission in the world). It is not the process of humanising the world as such which is peculiar to the layman in the ecclesiological sense. On the contrary, lay people have a special function, precisely as christian lay people, in orientating this process of humanisation towards salvation—a secondary, but still essential aspect of the mission of the universal church—whereas the clergy have an official function within the church in this mission. This hesitation seems, however, to have been overcome in the third schema (that is, the amended second schema) and the fourth schema (that is, the final text). The third schema speaks about the active participation of lay people in 'the mission of the whole christian people in the church and in the world' (31) and the final version not only adopts this text, but also makes it explicit a little further on in the same passage (the same 31) that the specifically lay contribution to the mission of the church in the world is to be found in the search for the kingdom of God in and through the management of temporal matters and their setting in order in accordance with God's will.

The council's ecclesiological definition of the layman does not, then, contain any reference to 'the relationship with the secularity of the world', but it does refer to the 'christian

relationship with secularity' and this is an essential element
of the ecclesiological concept of the layman because it is, for
the church as such, co-essential. Not only, therefore, do both
the layman and the priest have their own tasks in the primary
mission of the church (that of evangelisation)—they also have
their tasks in the orientation of the process of humanising
the world towards salvation, the layman carrying out his task
in a specifically lay manner, that is, precisely insofar as he
is concerned from day to day with secular matters, so that he
can orientate the world towards salvation, not magisterially
or pastorally like the priest, but completely involved in it,
as it were from within.

We should not forget that this was the first time in the
history of the church that a council had concerned itself
with lay people as such and that, partly because of the revival of the christian consciousness of the church since the
nineteenth century, it was not until the twentieth century
that any thought was given to a 'theology of the laity'. It is
certainly only in the present century that this aspect of
theology has been considered in a totally new way and, despite the roots that it has in the theology of the past thirty
years, it forms quite a new chapter in ecclesiology. The
council did not examine all the many questions which are
still being debated among theologians, but it has certainly
sanctioned the common views that have emerged from all
that has been written about the christian laity in the past
thirty years and may be regarded as the achievements of the
christian consciousness of faith of today. On the other hand,
however, we may say that the council took the phenomenon
of the christian layman in the life of the church and the
world as its point of departure. Looking at the phenomenon
of the layman, the council recognised that he was situated
in the world as a believer and that he was conscious, especially since the rise of 'Catholic Action', of his responsibility
for the state of the church. The council further aimed to
define, in the dogmatic constitution on the church, in broad
outline and concisely, the implications of this phenomenon,

the believing member of the church who, as a non-office-bearer, participated in the life of the church and, as a non-religious, lived in the world. Because the council's aim was merely to provide a 'typological' definition of the christian layman, it should still be possible to penetrate a little more deeply and to look for a truly theological definition. After trying out various formulae, the constitution did in fact carefully select a number of clear expressions, but these are interspersed with less sharply formulated digressions and even repetitions which simply have something to say in a warm tone and a positive manner about the layman in the church and the world. The typological description of the layman is, however, without any doubt the central point of the fourth chapter of the constitution, 'The Laity'. It is in the light of this typological definition that the whole of this rather loosely worked out chapter should be read and interpreted.

III. A look at the past and at the future

A. A look at the past

(1) Apart from a large number of publications dealing with 'Catholic Action' and the 'general priesthood of the faithful',[36] little was written before the war, at least by catholic theologians, about the theology of the layman. In 1957, however, it was possible to compile a bibliography of some two thousand titles.[37] As I am, however, not concerned with the whole theology of the layman in this article, but only with the theological definition of the layman, I shall naturally enough confine myself to those books and articles which include some attempt to define theologically the concept of the layman. The first attempts of this kind were made immediately after the second world war and it was clear from the very beginning that the various authors were struggling with the correct placing of the 'secular character' of the layman. I will now try to situate these various attempts briefly in chronological order.[38]

In his first articles on this subject (1946–48), Congar (Y. Congar, 'Sacerdoce et laïcat dans l'Eglise', *La Vie intellectuelle* 14, 1946, pp 6–39; 'Pour une théologie du laïcat', *Etudes* 256, 1948, pp 42–54, 194–218) considered the christian laity in connection with the distinction between the church as an 'institution' of salvation and the church as a 'community' of salvation and emphasised the layman's active participation in the life of the church and in her priestly, prophetic and royal character; in other words, the first, generic element of the typological definition of the second Vatican Council. This was also the most striking element in the so-called 'lay movement', in comparison with the passive attitude which had characterised the laity in the past. Congar above all developed the layman's non-official participation in the primary, religious mission of the church. On the other hand, he also pointed, even in his first articles, to the layman's secular task, which he had to orientate towards salvation.

In 1949, the present writer affirmed in an article (E. Schillebeeckx, 'Theologische grondslagen van de lekenspiritualiteit', TGL 5/I, 1949, pp 45–166) that the common religious wealth shared by the laity, the clergy and religious communities had first of all to be analysed, so that the layman's membership of and active participation in the primary mission of the church might be emphasised, and that consequently the negative definition of the layman (as a non-office-bearer) should be positively supplemented by the layman's specifically lay relationship with the secularity of the world, through which he is also distinguished from the religious. This relationship was seen as the distinctive aspect of the layman, a special mark which characterised not only his membership of the church, but also his participation in the primary, religious mission of the church. The author certainly affirmed in this first article that he wrote on the subject that the christian task of the layman was primarily in the world, but that he could also, in addition to this, carry out an apostolate in the church, though he always did this as a layman.

The same year also saw the publication of H. Urs von Balthasar's view of the christian laity (H. Urs von Balthasar, *Der Laie und der Ordensstand*, Einsiedeln 1949). His principal argument was that the layman was contrasted with the cleric, but not with the religious. The (married) layman in the world was, he maintained, too fully occupied with the things of this world to be able to carry out an apostolate, which was not a free time pursuit, but a full-time undertaking. The members of Catholic Action were, in his opinion, clericalised lay people. The true lay apostolate, therefore, in which Urs von Balthasar stressed both the word 'lay' and the word 'apostolate', was carried out above all by the members of secular institutes, who were truly lay people and who at the same time devoted themselves fully to the apostolate.

Returning to this question in 1950, Congar (Y. Congar, 'Qu'est-ce qu'un laïc?', *Vie Spirituelle (Suppl)*, 15 Nov 1950, pp 363–92; later included in *Jalons pour une théologie du laïcat*, Paris 1953. See also the whole of this number of the *Supplement*) attempted to penetrate more deeply into the distinctive aspect of being a lay person. In this quest, he followed the modern trend, namely that the christian layman is a believer who takes the secular structures and the inner nature of things seriously and whose contribution to the kingdom of God is made in and through his commitment to the temporal, secular order.

In his first work (1952–53), G. Philips (G. Philips, *Le rôle du laicat dans l'Eglise*, Paris 1953) also stressed the layman's participation in the primary, religious mission of the church, but affirmed, on the other hand, that he had to experience his call to holiness in and through his work in the world. This lay activity above all applied to Catholic Action, which was, however, not identified with the lay apostolate.

In 1954, Karl Rahner (K. Rahner, 'Über das Laienapostolat', *Der Große Entschluß*, 9, 1954, pp 245–50, 278–82 and 318–24; later included in *Schriften zur Theologie*, pt 2, Einsiedeln 1958[3], pp 339–73) gave his attention to this question and from the very beginning placed the specific and distinctive element of the laity in its relationship with the world. The immediate basis of distinctively lay christian activity was, in Rahner's opinion, the layman's being a christian, but the extent of the lay apostolate was specifically determined by the specific place occupied by the layman in secular life. What primarily constituted the lay apostolate was, Rahner insisted, the layman's being a christian in ordinary human situations in the world, although, in addition to this, the layman was also able to perform an apostolate specifically within the church. Up to this point, Rahner's view runs parallel to that of the present writer but, unlike him, Rahner concludes that the layman who in one way or another carries out a full-time apostolate specifically within the church and in this way turns his back upon his ordinary lay activities ceases to be a layman. The present author, on the other hand, even de-clericalises the apostolic content of the minor orders and re-serves the hierarchical apostolate exclusively for deacons, priests and bishops (E. Schillebeeckx, 'Wijding', *Theologisch Woordenboek* III, Roermond and Maaseik 1958, col 4967–82).

C. Baumgartner (C. Baumgartner, 'Formes diverses de l'apostolat des laics', *Christus* 13, 1957, pp 9–33) developed his view in connection with the ideas of K. Rahner. The true christian apostolate was, in his opinion, concerned with the salvation of men and for lay people this was Catholic Action. The lay apostolate of christian life and example—what Rahner called the true lay apostolate—was, Baumgartner believed, strictly speaking not an apostolate, which was fundamentally an orientation of the things of this world towards salvation. Here too, we find the tendency to affirm that the layman's active participation in the primary, religious mission of the church makes him, as it were, a member of the clergy.

This concludes my very brief outline of the most characteristic attempts made round about the year 1950 to define the layman theologically. In contrast to the negative concept of the layman according to canon law,[39] that of the christian who does not hold office in the church and who has no share either in the jurisdictional power or in the power of ordination, a search was made at about this time for a positive content to the concept of layman. Two tendencies, in many cases overlapping, are noticeable—this positive content was gained either (both) from the layman's membership of the church or (and) from his involvement in the ordering of life in the world. Some theologians at this period based their argument on the fact that the word *laos*—from which the word *laicus*, layman, is derived—was not used in the bible for pagan peoples and therefore meant 'the people of God', with the result that the layman had, according to these theologians, to be defined in the light of his relationship with the church. Other theologians, on the other hand, pointed to the modern sense in which layman, *laicus*, is used and its connection with laicity and secularity. What emerged very soon, however, was that the central point which gave rise to so many differences of opinion was the 'relationship with the secularity of the world'. Is this relationship really typical of the layman and if so, in what way is it typical?

(2) In 1958, I. de Potterie published a semantic study of the concept of *laicus* and *laikos* in the ancient church,[40] in which he insisted, on the basis of very convincing textual material, that the word *laos* in Graeco-Roman society meant the people precisely as opposed to their leaders or rulers. In this sense, it was formally a functional concept, meaning 'not belonging to those in authority, or to the leading, intellectual class'. Although the word *laos* was only used in the bible for the people of God, it was also used with the Graeco-Roman shade of meaning. In other words, it meant that part of the people of God not belonging to the leadership of that people and thus distinct from the priests, levites and prophets. Furthermore, in secular Greek, the word *laikos* meant a member of the ordinary people, belonging to the people, as opposed to the leaders of the people. In this sense, the word is not met with in scripture. It does not occur either in the Greek translation of the old testament, the Septuagint, although it does occur in certain early christian translations of

111

the old testament books, where it meant non-sacral, not dedicated to God in worship. This distinction between 'lay' and 'sacral', however, only applied to things and, what is more, things used by the people of God. In the first writings of the church, however, the word *laikos* soon came to be applied—from the time of Clement of Rome—to people and it was in this way that the distinction between the two typical words *clericus* and *laicus* came about.

From the semantic point of view, then, the word 'layman' was used in the early church to mean firstly a member of the church as the people of God, secondly a member of the community of the church, but over and against the church's hierarchy, and thirdly a christian with a certain relationship to the secular world.

I do not believe, however, that a semantic study of a concept of *laikos*, which is in any case not strictly biblical, can provide a definitive answer to this question. But a view like that of the early church expressed in the ancient concept of *laikos* can have a stimulating effect. This semantic study did not change the views of theologians in any important way, but it did stimulate them to give a more subtle shade of meaning to their idea of the layman.

(3) This new shade of meaning which was, at least explicitly, introduced was the recognition of the *christian* relationship with the secularity of the world.[41] In other words, it became far more clearly and more widely understood that an ecclesiological definition of the layman could not include the layman's relationship with the secular world if this secularity was regarded simply in itself, purely as man's situation in the world. The relationship with the secularity of the world can only be included in the theological concept of the layman if the church herself includes a relationship with the world which is specifically of the church in her own mission, in view of the fact that the *theologically* distinctive aspect of the layman must be found in a relationship with the church. If this were not so, we should be introducing a foreign element into the ecclesiological definition. In these most recent of

past attempts to define theologically the concept of the layman, then, the twofold mission of the church as the whole people of God has been more clearly emphasised. The first aspect of this one but twofold mission is concerned with the order of salvation itself, whereas the second aspect, which is the inner consequence of the first, is concerned with the orientation of the secularity of the world towards salvation. Both aspects of this one mission of the church—evangelisation and the permeation of secular society with the leaven of christianity—must therefore be found in all active believers, whether they are lay people or members of the clergy, but each according to official or non-official aspects.

A christian relationship with the secularity of the world, not the simple fact of being situated in the world was therefore becoming increasingly recognised as the specific qualification of being a layman in the church.

B. A look at the future

The three elements which we have found in the writings of those theologians who have been looking for a theological definition of the layman during the past fifteen or so years have in fact been included in the council's dogmatic constitution on the church. The first of these is universal and positive—the layman's membership of the church as the people of God. The second is negative, or rather related to the layman's function in the church as a non-office-bearer. The third element is specifically positive and is at the same time illuminated by contrast with the members of a religious community —the layman's relationship with the secularity of the world as the typically lay form of the search for the kingdom of God. The council's 'definition' reflects all the modern theological ideas that are common to the authors I have discussed in my 'look at the past', but not one of these theologians' own views has, as it were, been consecrated by the council. A great number of questions have therefore been left open. What the council has clearly affirmed, however, is that it is not only in the world that the layman has his own distinctively lay task to fulfil, but also in the church. This affirmation has eliminated certain one-sided emphases.

Nonetheless, the council has not defined the relationships between the three elements more precisely. What it has, correctly, pointed out is that the layman, as a member of the people of God, has a direct contribution to make to the primary mission of the church (the task of evangelisation), although he does this as a non-office-bearer, and that, as a christian, he also has a task in the world. Whether or not the specific qualification of the layman—his christian relationship with the secular world—also plays a part in his participation in the primary, religious mission of the church (in other words, not simply as a non-official member of the church, but precisely as a layman in the world) has not, generally speaking, been discussed in the theological debates. The consequence of this is that some theologians have been inclined to call the first form of lay apostolate—the layman's contribution as a non-office-bearer to the primary, religious mission of the church—a camouflaged clericalisation, whereas others have felt that this form of apostolate deprives the layman of his own lay state, at least if he carries out this apostolate full time, and makes him formally a member of the clergy. In my opinion, this alternative is inevitable—these authors have been quite consistent in this—if the specific qualification of the layman (his christian relationship with the secular world) is one aspect *alongside* the other two aspects (his membership of the church and his being a non-office-bearer). This alternative can only be avoided if this 'third aspect' is not simply regarded as pointing to one of the many forms of lay apostolate, but precisely as something that specifies the whole life of the layman—as a qualification of his membership of the church and therefore also of his active contribution as a non-office-bearer to the primary, religious mission of the church (this aspect has been analysed briefly by the author in 'The Layman in the Church', *loc cit,* note 41 below). The fact is, however, that theologians who, rightly, stress the layman's task in the church alongside his christian task in the world tend to regard the layman in the first case as 'neutral', that is, as an apostolic member of the church who is a non-office-bearer. In this sense, the typifying christian relationship with the secularity of the world suddenly seems no longer to play any part, so that some theologians are bound to have the impression that a disguised clericalisation is at work here. What should be made clear, however, is that the layman's christian relationship with the world colours his whole (active) being as a christian—his life of prayer, his forms of faith, love and hope, his contribution as a non-office-bearer to the primary, religious mission of the church and even his specifically lay collaboration with the hierarchy in their apostolate (either in an organised form or not). After all, the present situation has made it abundantly clear that the hierarchy cannot carry out even its own apostolate any more unless lay people contribute their own specifically lay experience.

If we do not accept the consequence of this insight, we shall ultimately introduce a remarkable division into the life of the christian layman between a sphere in which he devotes his best energies as a neutral, non-office-bearing member of the church to the primary, religious mission of the church, but in which his own specifically lay experience and contribution hardly comes into play, and a sphere in which he, as a christian, assumes the full lay state in the world. In fact, two views have not really been combined—the earlier view of the layman as a non-office-bearer and the modern idea that he has something to do with laicity or secularity. The fact that the layman (as a member of the people of God) has a positive relationship with the secularity of the world because he is not a member of the clergy, even if he carries out a purely primary, religious apostolate, does not seem to have been thought out consistently. The consequence of this is that the layman's specifically lay contribution in the task of evangelisation is in fact not fully effective and, even where it is to some extent effective, it tends to take on 'clerical' forms which diminish it considerably. The three elements which the council included in its typological definition of the layman should not therefore be regarded as the end of a turbulent process that has taken place in the past, but rather as a breathing space which will act as a stimulus for further development in the future.

6
A NEW TYPE OF LAYMAN[42]

There is certainly food for thought in the fact that the question about the real place of the layman in the church did not arise until modern times, when man discovered the world precisely as the world, an event which is usually known by the name of secularisation. This term, however, has a long heritage. During the *Ancien Régime*, the church was more or less identified with the 'christian society' and for this reason any recognition of the ordering of life within this world according to its own values, that is, as a sector of life determined by values directly relating to the world, was regarded as desacralisation, as a separation of the world from the church. This process, however, is fundamentally nothing but a loyal recognition of secularity, of the special value of the world as world, and it is only against the historical background of the situation that preceded it that this secularity can be called secularisation, that is, the legitimate emancipation of the world from the tutelage of the church.

It should not cause any surprise that it was only as a result of man's new experience of the world that there was any growth in the christian consciousness of the real task of the layman. In its various expressions, faith never anticipates man's experience of his own existence. It may therefore be useful to begin with a short historical outline.

I. The historical background to the problem

Christians in the very early church were aware that the church was non-world, that the church was, in other words, the beginning of the eschatological kingdom of God. 'The world' was, on the contrary, the kingdom of sin, the unredeemed world. The church and the world were opposed to each other as the redeemed world to the unredeemed world.

In this world, christians regarded themselves as *paroikoi*, that is as strangers in a world which was hostile to them as christians and persecuted them. On the basis of this, both the laity and the clergy spontaneously regarded themselves as the people of God unanimous in its opposition to the world. In this way, the unity of the christian community of laity and clergy was noticeably firm. There was not so much a difference between laity and clergy—although this was not denied—as between christians, both the laity and the clergy together, on the one hand, and the world on the other.

The first change occurred in the patristic period, especially after the peace of Constantine. Three factors encouraged this change in man's view of the church and the world once the persecutions of the church had come to an end.

In the first place, monastic life gave the world a new meaning for christians. The earlier distinction between the world and the church as non-world ceased to apply and the world, which no longer persecuted the church, but officially accepted her, gradually became a 'christian world'. The ancient biblical antithesis between the church and the world became an antithesis between 'being a christian in the world' and 'being a christian in the manner of a monk', that is, in the manner of non-world. The consequence of this was that the positive statements, which were previously applied to the whole of the christian church, were now increasingly applied only to monks and priests, whereas unfavourable biblical pronouncements were applied more and more to the life of christians in the world. It was in this way that the disparaging attitude towards christians in the world came about and that the original biblical antithesis between the church and the world gradually changed into an antithesis between the clergy and christian lay people who remained 'in the world'.

In the second place, after the peace of Constantine, the church was patronised by the secular powers and the clergy and the monks were granted all kinds of privileges and dispensations in society. This made the antithesis between lay people and the clergy even sharper.

Finally, the clear distinction in the early church between the priesthood and the monastic vocation gradually became blurred in the patristic period. Both ways of life influenced each other. Many monks were ordained priests and priests accepted many of the aspects of monastic spirituality, such as celibacy, the monastic habit and a tendency to live, like monks, in community. For their part, monks also demanded to be called clerics. In practice, then, the clergy included both those holding office in the church and the monks, and these two groups were sharply differentiated from the laity.

Furthermore, there was also a great change in the Western system of education at the end of the patristic period after the barbarian invasions. During the first centuries of christianity, christians did not feel the need to found their own schools and simply went to the 'official' schools. Very little was left, however, of this state educational system after the dislocation of the empire brought about by the barbarian invasions, and the church herself therefore began to found her own schools, which became, after the Carlovingian renaissance, the official 'state' schools. Education was thus taken over by the church and became an important cultural force in her hands. Education was enjoyed by the clergy, priests and monks, with the result that *clericus* became synonymous with 'literate' or intellectual and *laicus* with *illiteratus* or *idiota*, 'illiterate'. A social contrast thus increased the already very sharp contrast between the clergy and the laity. Lay people were, in fact, the ignorant people in the church.

The situation remained unchanged in the middle ages and indeed became even more deeply rooted. The laity was even referred to then as *laicorum genus bestiale* (see Curtius, *La littérature européenne et le moyen âge*, Paris 1956, p 261), a phrase which probably had a less coarse and unfavourable sound in the ears of medieval man than it does in ours today, but which nonetheless points to the fact that the scale of values was clearly inspired by monastic thinking in medieval society. Lay people were in fact illiterate and had not yet come of age at that time. They were simply the objects of the pastoral care of their priests in a society with extremely hierarchical structures which was controlled by the church. This church was above all thought of as an institution that was subject to the authority of its priests, who moreover enjoyed all kinds of favours and privileges, and was at the same time also synonymous with christianity.

This, however, obscured the antithesis between the church and the world, which had existed clearly in the early church, and even to some extent that between the church as monastic life and the world as the life of christians generally which had existed in the patristic period. A new antithesis began to emerge, that between the clergy and the laity in the narrower sense, the worldly rulers; in other words, between the *sacerdotium* and the *imperium*. The only lay people who counted in the middle ages were the emperor, the monarchs and the princes, with the result that Pope Boniface viii, for example, could say that 'the laity has always been hostile to the clergy; antiquity teaches us this and it is only too clear in our own times' (see the bull *Clericis laicos*, 25 February 1296; published in Friedberg, col 1062). This tension between the laity and the clergy was in fact a tension between the leaders of the church and the worldly rulers within the one christianity.

The real dimensions of the world were not discovered until the modern age. Although Thomas had formulated the principles in the middle ages, his ideas made little headway against the prevailing Augustinianism of his own times. Initially, this discovery of the world took place in the sphere of natural science, its chief exponent being Galileo, but gradually the process of secularisation began to affect the whole of human life. Today, this tendency has developed into a new anthropology, in which man regards himself as a being who attains human fulfilment in the world. Man and the world have been discovered in their directly secular dimensions, in their political, social, economic and other aspects. The ordering of life within this world is man's task, whether he believes in God and the christian revelation or not.

The result of this discovery of man and the world is that

lay people have come to occupy a very important place. It is they who have the task of building up the world. This has at the same time meant that the question of the place of the layman in the church has become an important theme in our thinking about faith.

It should therefore be clear from this very brief historical survey that the church only began to take the laity quite seriously when man and the world had come to be regarded as fundamentally lay or secular. Laicity in the anthropological sense of the word—the recognition of the secular dimensions of man and the world—opened the eyes of theologians to the laity in the christian, theological sense of the word. This historical bond between the discovery of the 'laicity of the world' and the discovery of the layman in the church determined the nature of the earliest theological approaches to the question of the layman and his place in the church. This approach was later abandoned, when doubt arose as to whether the link with secularity was theologically relevant. During recent years, however, there have been signs of a gradual return to the earlier position. Theologians remain convinced that the theological definition of the layman's place in the church must be ecclesiologically based, but— and this is the point of the synthesis—they also stress, and rightly, that the church, precisely as church, has in her laicity a distinctive, but real and meaningful relationship with the world.

On this basis, a purely ecclesiological definition can be given of the layman and, what is more, in such a way that the layman's relationship with laicity within the world is included precisely in this ecclesiological dimension. In other words, the anthropological and sociological concept of 'layman' is not alien to the ecclesiological concept of 'layman'.

II. The council and the layman
Although the second Vatican Council strove to dissociate itself from this historical background, which resulted in a clericalised view of the church, this nonetheless continued to

have an effect in many of the statements of the council. A laborious search was made for the layman's place in the church, as though this was the real subject for discussion. But, from the point of view of biblical theology, the problem is exactly the other way round—what is the place of the church's office in the people of God? From the biblical point of view, the negative definition of the layman as a non-office-bearer is bewildering. A definition of this kind can only be understood in the light of the past, when the church and the hierarchy were almost identified and when the layman was purely the object of pastoral care on the part of the clergy and thus, by definition, not a member of the clergy.

For a catholic, it will be clear that the general priesthood of all believers is not the same as the official priesthood. The official priesthood, in service of the general priesthood, has an irreducible character. This office is a specific service in the church performed by certain believers who are appointed to this task by the college of those holding office in the church and with the consent of the whole people of God. Viewed in this way, it is remarkable that the christian state of those believers who have a different service to perform in the church should be known as 'non-clerical'. If we were consistent, we should define a priest as a 'non-layman', an apostle as a 'non-evangelist', an evangelist as a 'non-presbyter', a teacher as a 'non-deacon' and so on.

It is understandable that the council, subject to the constant pressure of a very old tradition, was not able to define the christian layman theologically and therefore chose the easier—and theologically less relevant—way of defining the layman phenomenologically. The council did not in fact succeed in defining the layman positively—although it tried to do this, it only in fact succeeded in finding, via a negative definition (the layman as 'non-cleric' and 'non-religious'), a positive definition simply of the state of being a christian itself—something that applies to all members of the church, lay people, members of religious communities, deacons, priests or bishops.

The dogmatic constitution on the church has this to say about the laity:

> By the word 'lay people', we here mean all christian believers outside the members of the priesthood of holy orders and of the religious state recognised by the church; those christian believers namely who have been embodied into Christ by baptism and set up as the people of God, who participate in Christ's priestly, prophetic and royal office in their own way and who consequently for their part carry out the mission of the whole christian people in the church and in the world. A secular characteristic is peculiar to lay people. . . . The proper vocation of lay people is to be found in their search for the kingdom of God by taking care of and according to God's will setting in order temporal matters. It is in the world that they live, namely in all worldly professions and employments, in the ordinary circumstances of family and society—their very existence, as it were, interwoven with these. It is there that they are called by God, in order to contribute in the manner of leaven from within to the sanctification of the world by carrying out their own task . . . of throwing light on and setting in order all temporal matters with which they are often closely connected, so that all this constantly takes place and goes forward according to Christ and proclaims the praise of the creator and redeemer (4, 31).

If this conciliar description, which does not aim to be a definition in the strict sense of the word, is examined more closely, four elements of what 'layman' in the christian sense means emerge from it:

(1) The layman is generically defined by his active membership of the church as the people of God. He takes part in the total mission of the church, which is not directly interpreted here as a hierarchical mission. In this way, the positive christian wealth of membership of the church is firmly emphasised and what both the clergy and the laity have in common as christians is forcefully pointed out.

(2) Secondly, against this background, a more precise description is given by defining the limits of what characterises the layman negatively by comparison with the members of

the clergy—the layman is, in other words, defined as non-clerical, as a non-office-bearer. Taken in connection with the generic characteristic of the layman, then, this means that the layman participates in the total mission of the church in a non-hierarchical and non-official way.

(3) Thirdly, this manner of being a christian is also contrasted with the religious life. This is connected with a fourth characteristic.

(4) As a kind of positive 'specific qualification' ('per notam quodammodo specificam'; see the *Relatio de 30, Schema Constitutionis de Ecclesia*, 1964, 4, p 126; see also *Relatio de 32, ibid*, p 128) of the quasi-definition of the christian layman, his christian relationship with the secularity of the world is taken into account—he looks for the kingdom of God by taking care of temporal matters and by setting these in order in accordance with God's will.

The christian mission of the layman in the church and the world, then, was fully accepted by the council. This was certainly an advance on the purely negative definition of the layman provided by canon law. Nonetheless, a certain dualism still remains. This is expressed in all kinds of details which are discernible throughout the development of the constitution, from the first schema, through the various drafts and up to the final version. For example, the layman has a task '*also* in the world'; he has a task '*also* in the church'; he has a mission in the world '*also* through religious activity' and so on. In the final version, we read: 'in the church and in the world'. All the same, the earlier dualism recurs now and then in the definitive documents: 'the layman *also* participates in the church's apostolate'. Such statements were historically influenced by the ecclesiology which was still prevalent just before the council and according to which the church was more or less identified with the hierarchy. The church's mission was simply a hierarchical mission and the question then was how to involve the layman more actively in that mission. This is reflected in the repeated use of the word 'also' in this section of the various documents leading up to constitution on the church.

If the other conciliar documents are also considered in this context, then we find on the one hand texts which speak in a more positive way about the layman than the constitution on the church and others which fall behind. In the decree on the pastoral office of the bishops (*Christus Dominus*), for example, the list of the collaborators of the bishops (25–35) closes with a mention of the (exempt) religious, but there is no mention at all in these sections of the decree of the laity, although the decree does speak elsewhere of lay people in the pastoral advisory council of the diocese. In the decree *Ad Gentes Divinitus* on the church's missionary activity, lay people are not included among those who co-operate in the building up of the local church—with the single exception of lay catechists (15–18)—whereas lay people are discussed quite freely in the rest of the document.

The old tendency to regard the laity as in no way responsible for the church's mission, but purely as the object of the pastoral care of the clergy, is apparent here and there in some of the documents of the council, although this view does not characterise the council as a whole. The decree *Apostolicam Actuositatem* on the lay apostolate includes some formulae which go further than the constitution on the church. From the very beginning, it is clearly affirmed that every activity within the mystical body which is directed towards the building up of the kingdom of God should be called an apostolate and this apostolate is carried out by all members of the church, though in one way by the clergy and another by the laity (2). This statement, then, rejects in principle any inclination simply to regard the lay apostolate as a kind of participation—whether organised or not—in the apostolate of the hierarchy and affirms the direct participation of all christians in the apostolate of Christ himself, with the result that Catholic Action can no longer be regarded as the true form of lay apostolate (even though, in a later section, the decree strongly emphasises this form of lay apostolate, despite the protest made by many of the fathers of the council).

In the decree on the church's missionary activity, too, the essential function of lay people in the building up of the local church is ultimately recognised (21 and 41). The constitution on the liturgy may also be interpreted as a declericalisation of the liturgy, which was previously almost exclusively in the hands of the priest, the lay believers being his 'clientele'. In the constitution on the liturgy, however, the council has affirmed that not only the clergy, but also the whole christian community, the people of God, is the subject of the celebration of the liturgy, in which each has a hierarchically regulated function. The laity thus began once more to take an active part in the liturgy which had, almost of necessity, to be celebrated in the language of the people, while the discrimination between the priest's communion under two forms and the communion of the laity under one form was, at least in principle, removed.

The dogmatic constitution on revelation affirmed that the laity was, as subject, actively involved in the handing on of the deposit of faith and of the realities of salvation and was no longer to be regarded exclusively as made up of believers who received from and listened to the hierarchy. The decree on the office and the life of priests (*Presbyterorum Ordinis*) speaks, more strongly than the constitution on the church and even more strongly than the decree on the lay apostolate, about the rights of lay people with regard to their priests and about the dialogue and co-operation between priests and lay people (9). According to this decree, priests must leave a great deal of freedom of movement to lay people, must recognise their autonomy in the secular sphere and must entrust them with more offices in the service of the church. The pastoral constitution on the church in the modern world also points out that lay people have the right to the evangelical comfort of their priests, but warns priests that they were not sent to provide cut and dried answers to all kinds of prob-

lems connected with the world, for which lay people themselves must be responsible (1, 4, 43).

The whole of the second Vatican Council may in fact be
regarded as a declericalisation of the catholic church, although, once again looking at the council as a whole, this
attempt cannot be called 100% successful—the pressure of
a thousand years of tradition was too strong for this. Fundamentally, however, the attempt was successful, even though
echoes of the older clericalism are still discernible in all six-
teen of the council's documents. Because the documents were
compiled independently of each other by different commissions and were not, for example, conceived in the light of
one basic vision, that of the constitution on the church, and
also because the commissions worked alongside each other,
different emphases in the detailed appreciation of the laity
in the church in the different documents are not entirely
inexplicable. Some of the decrees, like the one on the means
of communication (*Inter Mirifica*), in which the part played
by the laity ought to have been central, remained outside the
beneficial influence of the change of attitude which took
place in the minds of so many of the fathers of the council
throughout its four years. It was therefore possible, in the
context of the typically lay material of the means of communication, for a recommendation of publicity for the work
of the church to conclude with a passage about the necessity
of training 'priests, religious *and lay people*' for this work (15).

We may certainly say that the council did not unquestioningly take as its point of departure the laicity of the people
of God, while conceding that the christian laity could not
dispense with the leadership and guidance of the hierarchy.
Most of the fathers of the council had unconsciously to overcome a great deal of inner resistance before they could give
lay people their rightful place in the church. The situation
was precisely the opposite in the early church. From the experience of Christ and the community of believers whom he
had gathered around him and who remained together after
he had left them, the explicit need to build up a hierarchical

leadership gradually arose and this was, as a result of the church's situation in society at the time, distributed among *episkopoi, presbyteroi* and deacons. The laicity of the people of God was in the first place unquestioningly accepted and it was only later that the question of the division of offices and *charismata* arose. The laity was therefore not related, in the beginning, to the hierarchy. The reverse was true, namely that the hierarchy was related to the laity, with the result that office in the church had to be justified on the basis of its service to the people of God. In the light of this, the qualification 'non-clerical' was irrelevant to the theological definition of the layman, although it is of course true that not all members of the church possess that office.

The biblical view was, however, restored to a position of honour in the council at the last moment. In the dogmatic constitution on the church the third chapter, in which the 'people of God and the laity' were originally discussed, following a discussion of the church's hierarchy, was divided into two and radically changed. The discussion of the 'people of God' became chapter 2 in the final version and this preceded the chapter on the hierarchy. The rest of the constitution was, unfortunately, not sufficiently adapted and rewritten to make it harmonise with this changed perspective. The biblical view was, however, certainly restored in principle and this meant an entirely new orientation for the positive possibilities of the laity within the church, namely that the church's hierarchical and official mission was no longer the only possibility and not even the primary and most obvious possibility. The decree on the lay apostolate was also changed in this sense, so that the final version stated that there was a variety of services in the people of God, but a unity of mission (2) and that there were many special gifts for the building up of the community of love (3), of which the hierarchical office was one. The hierarchy has a special and quite distinctive task, but this has to be supplemented by all kinds of other gifts and services. All these are mutually complementary, with the result that a division of the people of God into two blocs—laity and clergy—is difficult to justify from the biblical point of view, even though a specific distinction must be maintained between the general priesthood and the official priesthood. In addition to the services carried out by those who we call clergy, there are also many other services and offices carried out by believers whom we call lay people. This is, however, not a real division of the people of God into two blocs, since this would, of its nature, be an underrating of the many services performed in the church.

It is only on the basis of this view of the multiplicity of services in the church that any declericalisation of the church can be carried out consistently, without violating the irreducible and distinctive character of the one service that we call the clerical office, or causing its specific meaning to be misunderstood. This biblical perspective is in principle indicated in the second chapter of the constitution on the church and one of the first consequences to be drawn from it can be found in the fourth chapter, which deals with the laity:

> The church . . . shows in her institution and government a remarkable diversity. 'For as in one body we have many members, and all the members do not have the same function . . .' (Rom 12 : 4–5). Although there are some believers who are, by the will of Christ, appointed as teachers, distributors of the mysteries and shepherds over the others, there is still equality between all members of the church. . . . The very diversity of gifts of grace, services and expressions of power unify the children of God (32).

This biblical vision did not, however, penetrate completely into the council and elements of the older antithesis between the clergy and the laity are still discernible in the conciliar documents. For example, the priest is in the first place there for the church, even though he may *also* carry out activities in the world, whereas what characterises the layman, on the other hand, is his involvement in the world, although he may *also* have an essential function in the church. The relationship between the church and the world was clearly not fully thought out in all its consequences at the council and the 'definition' of the layman and, although less obviously, that of the office-bearer is consequently not entirely satisfactory. Every form of being a christian, in whatever kind of service or function in the church (either lay or clerical), is a manner of being a christian in the world. Even religious life cannot be interpreted in any other way than as a specific manner of being in the world. The church is the 'universal sacrament of salvation' (Pastoral constitution on the church in the modern world, I, IV, 45), the sign of salvation in and for the world. All christians are implicated in this sign, each according to his own service or function in the church. The laity must also be defined theologically in this perspective.

The initial movement in this direction, which was made by the second Vatican Council and is most clearly discernible in the conciliar documents mentioned in this article may, however, be regarded as a great step forward. These texts are bound to serve as the pont of departure for the bringing about of a new type of lay existence within the church and for a total equality and maturity on the part of the laity which will eventually be taken completely for granted. The paternalism of the clergy will disappear without any diminution of the special service or function performed by those in authority who guide the church, or any devaluation of the role of obedience in faith. After all, if the members of the clergy are also situated within the people of God as a community of love, for which they have a specific service to perform, the authority of the church, exercised for the benefit of all members of this community of love, naturally acquires the character of love and service. In this way, authority is not deprived of its content—on the contrary, it is radically changed, so that it becomes a christian exercise of authority which can really be experienced as a sign, given to the whole of the world, as to how authority ought to function. Lay people will then feel really at home in the church and not like foreign workers who have been 'taken on' because of overproduction to do work which is really 'priestly' work. Christianity —the church—is certainly no more priestly work than work for the laity. The priest and the lay person simply have, in their own work—work which concerns the whole world—different services, functions or 'spiritual gifts', all of which are very closely connected and which together help gradually to build up and extend the body of the church as a community of love, faith and eschatological hope in this world, until the time comes when the whole community of men has definitively become the 'communion of saints'.

7
RELIGIOUS LIFE IN A SECULARISED WORLD[43]

If I wanted to be unpleasant—or should I say optimistic?—
I would say that the notice 'closed for alterations' was displayed on the front doors of all religious houses in 1967. It
is useless to try to deny the fact that there is a feeling of
unease in religious communities today. To deny its existence
is to be unrealistic. The traditional form of religious life is no
longer accepted and this is not essentially for unchristian
reasons—the intention is rather to ensure a human, christian
and twentieth-century authenticity.

Is the christian *aggiornamento* of the religious life
primarily an adaptation to the world or a re-adaptation to the
gospel, a re-evangelisation of man and his institutions by way
of a return to the inspiration of the gospel? There are only
very few data in Vatican II's decree on the renewal of the
religious life concerning adaptation to man's contemporary
experience. According to this decree, the renewal should con-
sist primarily of re-adaptation to the gospel, and this is a
right emphasis. Renewal in this case would be, basically, a
regrafting of the existing religious life on to the 'norms of
Christ', in other words, a renewal with Christ himself as the
norm. It would, in other words, not primarily be a re-adaptation to the original inspiration of the various founders of the
religious orders or congregations—as the draft decree expressed it—but a re-adaptation to Christ's *gospel*. A renewal
on this basis would undoubtedly mean a fundamental change
in the religious life as we know it today.

We, of course, tend spontaneously to think of adapting the
religious life to the modern age rather than of adapting it to
the gospel, but the problem arises at once—what should function as the principle of adaptation? Should it be the modern

age itself or the gospel? My question, however, is this—is this a false dilemma?

Return to the inspiration of the gospel is, in any case, the right guiding principle. We have therefore to *question* the bible once again. But this questioning must come from our actual life here and now. What do we have in mind when we question the bible again? We do it because present-day religious life confronts us with problems. The religious way of life has become problematic for us and it is in the light of these special problems that we ask of the gospel a new question which could not be asked by previous generations of religious because they were not living in a secularised world. The gospel cannot provide an answer to questions that are not asked of it—it can only give an answer to those that are asked. Not every period is ready to ask every question—every generation asks its own questions of the gospel from the vantage-point of its own context in life. We, therefore, living at the present period ask a question of the gospel from the vantage-point of a secularised world. And this question is particularly cogent for members of religious communities. From its very beginning, the religious tradition has always stressed negation, detachment and the need to 'serve God exclusively', with the result that religious have tended to experience their way of life in the form of a flight from the world, however varied this experience has been.

Man's contemporary experience of his own existence is in sharp contrast to this negatively conceived way of life. Even before we ask about the evangelical basis of the religious life, we already have, as men, a view of life which is quite different from the view held in the past. In the light of our contemporary experience of our own life, we shall clearly ask different questions of the gospel from those asked by religious in the past, even by the founders of our own orders. We shall ask about the inspiration of the gospel for our own life, for our own experience here and now. This presupposes a readiness to allow our questioning to be criticised by scripture and a readiness to change, enlarge and correct that questioning if need be because of scripture. We must allow ourselves to be questioned by God's word. After all, it still remains to be seen whether we can accept the whole of our contemporary secularising experience simply as it is. Man has essentially a 'potentiality for good', but he has also—and this is perhaps only the other side of the coin—a 'potentiality for evil', and this will also be made actual and present in our contemporary experience in a secularised world.

It is therefore clear that an *aggiornamento* of the religious life cannot simply aim to be no more than an adaptation to the world of today. We have, after all, no real guarantee that the present age itself contains nothing but elements which are worthy of man.

What is more, it can hardly be affirmed that we christians are in a position to criticise man's contemporary experience of his own existence. That seems to me to be altogether too high a claim. I would prefer to say that, as christians, we too are part of the spirit of the present age—we are immersed in it, *critically*, but we do not move alongside it. It is only in this perspective that we can say that the re-evangelisation of the religious life, or rather of our way of life as members of a religious community, contains an essential confrontation with the contemporary secularised world which is characterised by a striving towards full humanity and with the values which are brought to light in this contemporary striving. The decree on the renewal of the religious life hardly indicated that the primary demand of renewal—the re-evangelisation of the religious life—could only be achieved in confrontation with our secularised world. Anyone asking about the inspiration of the gospel without reference to the content of man's own experience is simply asking a question that is devoid of content and can expect no more than an unsuitable answer which has nothing to do with him existentially.

I believe that it is important and even necessary to draw attention to this hermeneutical background because it is possible to discern two tendencies in the contemporary literature on the renewal of the religious life, both of which should be avoided. The first is a naturalising tendency which expects all salvation to come from examining man's existence and thus from adapting the religious life to the new and recently thematised human values. The second is a supernaturalising tendency which in turn expects all salvation to come from the call to 'return to the authentic gospel'. Both tendencies lead, I believe, to an impasse. On the one hand, man's experience of his own existence needs to be illuminated by the revelation of the word, by the gospel. On the other hand, this revelation of the word now, in the present age, can only be understood in the light of the prior understanding of our experience. The gospel only functions *in* man's understanding of himself in this world.

I. A brief characterisation of our contemporary secularised world

(1) Whereas nature was, in the past, experienced without any problem as God's creation, man now experiences it as the raw material from which he creates his human world. Nature was once a numinous subject pointing to God. It has now become devalued to the level of the object of man's mastery of nature. This changed view of nature and different way of associating with nature has also led to a changed view of man. Work, which is now largely governed by science, offers all men far greater possibilities for a life that is more worthy of man. We no longer detect the *vestigia Dei*—traces of God —in the world, but the *vestigia hominis*—the world has become humanised and points directly to man, who is humanising himself in the world and growing towards full humanity.

Man has thus, in his distinctive character as man, above all discovered his *freedom*, the task to give himself freely his special character by making this world, through meaningful work in society, humanly habitable and thus to build up a community of people in justice and love. Mankind as a whole is at this moment experiencing an almost irresistible desire to make this world a better place for all men to live in and to improve the welfare of all men so that everyone can thrive in a climate of solidarity, justice and love.

This concern for the distinctively secular dimensions of the living reality of contemporary western civilisation is, however, also a definite choice made on the basis of several possibilities. We should not overlook this tendency towards one-sided emphasis. The Western world has chosen, from several possibilities, in favour of a rationalised activity based on a scientific and technical process of making man's control of the world perfect. This is a genuinely human aspect of the problem, but in practice it is only by controlling nature that man would seem to be able to handle the reality of the world meaningfully.

Our view of the world and our view of man, however, are closely connected—the way in which man associates with nature in fact determines the way in which he experiences his being as man. If he only makes the world *technically* more habitable, he runs the risk of making it *humanly* inhabitable by this one-sided emphasis.[44] Human relationships within the 'great society' are now enclosed within technical structures which ultimately aim to make human life more worthy of man and these structures do possess, from the technical point of view, a social humanising value. At the same time, however, they also result in other human possibilities in the 'great society' as it were gasping for breath. Purely contemplative association with the reality is regarded as being without any value at all because it is not clearly 'effective'. It is, however, equally pernicious, in response to these one-sided technical structures, to seek refuge in a flight from the world. This is why there is a growing need among men today to find other ways of associating with the world and with their fellow-men, and one of these ways is the 'contemplative' way of being in the world. This is not in the first place thought of in the sense of a contemplation of divine things, but rather as a need for fellow-humanity—it is a contemplation which believes in one's fellow-man and refuses to treat this fellow-man like a thing which one can have in one's power. *Homo faber* runs a serious risk of coming to regard his fellow-man as a part of the world that can be controlled, as a thing that one can have in one's power, by technical means, just as one has the things of nature in one's power in this way. In one sense, of course, man can be manipulated, but this must form part of our respect for the human person and must serve to make him free to choose human possibilities.

Apart from man's technical control of nature, then, and his noble efforts, prompted by care for his fellow-men, to make the world socially, economically and politically a better place for man to live in, new needs do seem to be arising because man is threatening to choke under all these structures which serve him, it is true, but which are becoming increasingly depersonalised and objective. In one sense, the modern phenomenon of demonstrating youth is—apart from the excesses which unfortunately accompany these demonstrations so frequently—a legitimate protest against contemporary society which is in control of everything and is so impersonal in its complicated structures that it leaves man out in the cold. It is not the technical complication of these structures that is objectionable, because this is precisely a modern phenomenon of effective charity. These structures do, however, lead to a form of domination by an oligarchy of experts—a fact which has been pointed out by social philosophers. As soon as man believes that it is possible to solve all the problems of his life purely scientifically, by means of exclusively rationalising institutions and measures, his deepest and inmost being is at once placed in a difficult predicament.

However ambiguous and uncertain our new view of man and the world may be, its basic characteristics are defined clearly enough. What man wants to do is to build up a new world on this earth and this is above all a project for the future, in contrast to the view of man and the world that he had in the past, in which the norm was provided and the form determined by the past and the *status quo*. Now, however, the 'golden age' is no longer behind us, in the past, but ahead of us, in the future.

(2) Many christians find that this new view of man and the world causes a crisis in religious experience. This is so above all because this new image of man and the world has become a project for the future and the living force of tradition and of what has been inherited from the past is in danger.

Nonetheless, it is possible to point to an impasse here. The Copernican revolution in man's contemporary experience of his own existence—usually referred to by the name of 'secularisation'—is not, in the first place, a phenomenon which may be designated as religious or irreligious. It is rather a change in man's relationship with the world. Secularisation is primarily a social event and, as such, it is a datum that is confined purely to this world. It does not in any way necessarily imply a decline in religion. It does lead to the emergence of new relationships between man and the form of his existence on this earth. Man himself becomes the subject, the demiurge of the form of his existence on earth.

Secularisation therefore only concerns man in his relationship with the world. It is, however, not entirely irrelevant from the religious point of view, because his image of God also functions within the previously given image of man and the world. A change in man's understanding of himself is inevitably bound to lead to a change in his image of God. Thus, although the process of secularisation as such primarily only concerns man in his relationship with the world, it does certainly have a changing, purifying and demythologising influence on his image of God inherited from his antiquated view of man and the world. In this way, the process of secularisation is also of some importance from the point of view of religion. According to the earlier view of man and the world, God functioned as someone who intervened in the world and who directly protected nature, history and human society, via the church. This is why the process of secularisation—the discovery of man's function to give meaning to and to humanise this world—was also a process of desacralisation.[45] The contemporary christian can give his full consent to this secularisation and desacralisation.

The question is, however, not so uncomplicated as this. Partly as a result of conservative tendencies in the church, this process of secularisation and desacralisation took place in an anti-church and anti-religious atmosphere. The result of this historically very complicated process—the so-called 'secularised world' of today—is consequently to some extent ambiguous. The term 'secularised world' stands in fact for many different realities, which cannot be grouped easily under one single heading, but which at the same time also include both christian and unchristian elements. This is why the christian cannot have a completely undivided, impartial and uncritical attitude towards the secularised world, an attitude of complete optimism.

Apart from this 'pagan' element which cannot easily be pointed out, however, the christian is bound to give his full consent to the 'secularised world' precisely in the light of his faith as a christian. On the basis of our faith in creation and our faith in Jesus, the Christ, we are bound to let the world be world, non-divine—we are bound to regard the world as that which God has placed in a position of autonomy and secularity. Creation means that God sets into being something which is different from himself, which must be the non-divine, the human, the secular or worldly. By affirming the secularity of the world, we are also recognising God in accordance with his special being, in other words, as the non-secular, transcendent reality. A sacralising, numinous view of the world is an offence against the transcendence of God.

This is confirmed in Christ. The most intimate unity imaginable between a man and God—the unity in hypostasis—posits this man precisely in his being man and in secularity. God manifests his transcendence precisely in positing the non-divine. The divine acceptance of the secularised world—creation is, after all, giving consent in love—is an act of giving the world to itself and to man and of handing it over to itself. And the more the secularised world is accepted by God (Christ), the more 'secularised' it becomes and the more it is given to itself in free, created autonomy. Only a world that is accepted by God is truly secularised. The process of secularisation is therefore essentially a consequence of christianity, although it is true that it was brought about historically partly by values which were not christian in origin and that it did gain its present form in an anti-christian climate of thought. Christ is the revelation of the secularity of the world and at the same time the revelation of God's transcendence. Secularisation, which lets the world be world, is at the same time something which lets God be God. The secularity of the world, which is accepted with resolute commitment, but to which no attempt is made to give an ideological substructure,[46] may therefore imply, in the actuality of man's life, an unexpressed faith in God. Christianity, then, is not an increasing deification or christianisation of the secularised world, but a progressive demythologisation of that world— an increasing secularisation which assumes the form of a humanisation of the world and of man himself in the world. The first christians became martyrs because they attempted to demythologise the state and the emperor and to lead them back to their non-sacral secularity. Wherever christianity is established, the process of secularisation and desacralisation begins to take place and is quickly followed by the sanctification of the world.

On the basis of our christian faith, then, we must freely allow the world to be secular. This is precisely christian secularity, which is in contrast to a pagan, non-christian secularity. It is only in the secularised world that the possibility of paganism in the real sense of the word is revealed for the first time in human history. The older, pre-christian and non-christian paganism is rather a form of religiosity existing in a non-secularised, sacral world. The real secularity in which we are placed contains in the concrete both christian and pagan elements and cannot therefore simply be identified with the secularity of the world that is confirmed by the

christian faith. The christian act of giving the world freely
to its secularity and the non-christian act of emancipation
are therefore indissolubly interwoven in the one totality
which we call the modern secular reality. This secularity is,
however, essentially and fundamentally a confession of christian faith.[47] The world is the space in which we exist and
which has been set free by our faith. The christianisation of
the world—an essential part of the christian's task—therefore
means making the world secular, making it human and, in
the light of faith, letting it be world. This is made possible
for us by grace, but it is at the same time also disfigured by
sinfulness.

I have indicated a few basic outlines of man's present-day
experience of his own existence which form the basis of
the prior understanding in the light of which we can ask
questions of the gospel concerning the inspiration of the
religious mode of existence. Before asking these questions,
however, we need to situate the religious life itself within
the secularised world that I have just described. After all,
some christians regard secularity not as a radical change in
our attitude towards the world, but—wrongly—as a secularisation of religion itself. It hardly needs to be said, of course,
that an interpretation of this kind makes nonsense of the
religious life.

II. Contemporary religious experience and way of life

Unlike an earlier understanding of scripture, which was in
tune with the traditional forms of Western christianity and
religious life, our contemporary existential experience at
once calls into question all kinds of contrasts and dilemmas
which were accepted unquestioningly in the past. Examples
of these contrasts are—God or man, dedication to God or
dedication to man, flight from the world or participation in
the secularised world, contemplation or action, self-denial or
self-expression, human or christian, natural or supernatural.
In the past, whenever a choice had to be made in a dilemma

of this kind, the christian and in particular the christian belonging to a religious community almost instinctively decided in favour of God, flight from the world, contemplation, self-denial, the christian and the supernatural and attached a certain negative significance to the human, participation in the world, action and the natural.

For this reason, it is important to situate the new image of God which is connected with the new image of man and the world in the light of our new view of man and the world.

A. The new image of God

What characterises our new view of man and the world is not only the fact that we can no longer experience the earlier image of God as relevant precisely because it is so closely connected with the earlier image of man and the world, but also the even more striking fact that we are incapable, as the literature on the 'death of God' shows, of forming a new image of God. In the past, christians and especially christians living in contemplative religious communities were always very conscious of the fact that God was unapproachable and inexpressible and that man was radically incapable of speaking about and imagining God adequately. The great mystical theologians of the past were also able to accept the consequences of this 'negative' theology. In the average theology, the average spiritual life and ordinary preaching, however, God was in fact generally experienced as someone who intervened in the secular sphere and such categories were too often thought of as adequate concepts of God. Religious experience was authentic enough, but it was caught up in a social context which inwardly coloured it and is now completely superseded. Concepts like 'religious faith' are consequently extremely ambiguous, because they do not make enough distinction between faith and its essential function within a social context—which does not mean that faith was less authentic in the past than it is in our new social situation. Surely we should not presume that we believe genuinely and that faith is authentic only now, in the modern age, simply because we have a different relationship with the world?[48]

We have, in the modern age, become aware of the fact, not only theoretically but also practically, that we have no concepts of God, and that every alleged concept of God is in fact 'godless', because it fails to appreciate God's transcendence. There is, however, a danger in this line of thinking in that God may now become a marginal concept, a 'void' (see, for example, C. Verhoeven, *Rondom de leegte*, Utrecht, third edn, 1966, p. 163). In the past, God was *also* thinkable —he moved the world, explained its mysteries and maintained moral and political order and even social stability. Now, he is no longer so. He has become a question, and there is no end to the discussion about the 'question' which God has become—among believers and non-believers in everyday conversation, in newspapers and books, and on the radio and television. Now that people are no longer secure in their thought about God, God himself has become the subject of conversation at every level. Whatever answer is given to the question of God and whether the point of view taken is that of theism, atheism, post-theism ('God after the death of God') or even post-christianity, the question itself continues to haunt us nowadays. Some thinkers have concluded that it is not enough simply to eliminate illusions, false ideas and antiquated images in order to come to a more pure form of truth about God. 'The image of God is not made in any way clearer and faith in God is not made in any sense easier by unmasking the idols. The aim is to make faith tidier by turning it away from idols, but no one knows whether it can then still turn towards God' (*ibid* p 165). What is really important, however, is that we should not forget our human predicament in the new question of God. Anyone looking for the truth must risk finding an element of untruth and anyone looking for God must risk finding an element of 'idolatry', a false idea of God. As C. Verhoeven has correctly said: 'The emaciated form of faith which is directed purely towards God lands in a vacuum and dies convulsively of suffocation. God is not obtainable separately from the world and separately from idols' (*ibid*).

This provides our question with a perspective. The life that is directed exclusively towards God or dedicated directly to God has no concrete content and is therefore in danger of pursuing a void. To describe a christian way of life (religious life) as an 'exclusive and direct dedication to God' is to expose it to disqualification by man's contemporary experience, as a utopian impossibility, an unintelligible absurdity in which God is lost together with our humanity. Even Thomas Aquinas, for example, said that our ideas of God were derived from our experiences in the world and the history of salvation (ST 1, 1, 7 ad 1). This has become even clearer in the light of our contemporary experience of our own existence. The only place where the truth of God can be found is man himself, with his actual environment and his history. Whenever God speaks, he does so through man with this world and history, and it is in this that we have to hear and listen to the voice of his revelation. It is precisely for this reason that there is no contrast between the word of God which reaches us via the speaking of believers in scripture and the word of God which comes to us via our contemporary experience. Scripture provides us with the norm by which we can hear God's word faithfully and truly in the appeal made by our contemporary experience. It is even possible to say that the bible only really comes to life when we have ourselves hit upon its essence somewhere in our own lives. On the other hand, we can also say that we only really get on the track of the gospel through our own authenticity (see H. Renckens, 'Geloof en religie in het Oude Testament', *Bijdragen*, 27, 1966, pp 412–42). Man has always given content to his picture of God in the light of his existential experience in history. Our life in the world as it were nourishes our understanding of God—the essential meaning of the christian faith is that our concrete existence is a divine promise of salvation. It is only in the light of human life in the world that God acquires real content for man. If this fact is overlooked, the consequences for the religious life especially can be fatal. In the past, this attitude was usually marked by a strong tendency towards isolation from the world and there is therefore still a danger that members of a religious community especially will turn not to the living God, but to a notional God—a God whose form is derived from a human experience in the past, which no doubt had a real content, adapted to that particular period, but which has become purely notional for us today, existentially a meaningless label and entirely without content as a result of our changed image of man and the world.

It will by now have become obvious that the various contrasts and dilemmas mentioned at the beginning of this section are in fact false dilemmas. All these contrasting choices—God or man, man or christian, flight from the world or commitment to the world, indirect or direct relationships with God—they are all unchristian contrasts. Thus, a life 'exclusively and directly dedicated to God', without any human or worldly intermediary, is simply an unchristian illusion. Despite all good intentions, it very often only leads to a lack of realism with regard to the inner structures of man's existence, the result of which is frequently a special kind of infantilism. But, thank God, human life in the service of men in many different spheres of activity generally contradicts in practice what is formulated in theory.

This also means that the christian cannot and should not identify the secularisation of the world—a historical process which also includes desacralisation—with a secularisation of religion. For the christian, a secularisation which might exclude religion as a human existential possibility is a misconception, a form of paganism. But assuming this essential difference between christian and pagan secularisation, we must continue to realise that it is only our life in the world with our fellow-men that is capable of giving real content to our experience of the living God. This means that we christians can certainly accept an immediate and personal relationship with the living God, but that we may also be convinced that this relationship with God is, as far as its actual content is concerned, mediated by human and secular realities. Precisely because this relationship is divine, it cannot be reduced, in its immediacy, to a dilemma, or be contrasted with this mediation by the world, by man and our fellow-men and ultimately also by the church. This is most clearly revealed in man's relationship with Jesus, the Christ. This interpersonal relationship is also an immediate relationship with God, experienced in faith, because this man is God in a perfect human form. He wishes to be God-for-us in a fully human manner. Immediacy and indirectness are not mutually exclusive in the relationship between God and man—it is in this that God reveals his transcendence.

From this position and against this background of man's contemporary religious experience, we can now go on to question the gospel about the inspiration that it gives to a way of life which is also rooted in this experience—the religious life.

B. The inspiration of the religious way of life

Properly speaking, we should begin now by investigating scripture in the light of certain questions which are based on our contemporary experience. This would lead us too far, however, and I am consequently going to follow a shorter course and simply present the result of this investigation and make some observations on it.

Scripture contains numerous evangelical counsels and it would be impossible to reduce all of them to the three classical counsels which give rise in the middle ages to the three so-called religious vows. Furthermore, it is, strictly speaking, only possible to indicate one evangelical counsel in the gospel itself ('unmarriageable for the sake of the kingdom of heaven', Mt 19:10–12), of which it is said explicitly that no divine commandment is given about it ('Concerning the unmarried, I have no command of the Lord', 1 Cor 7:25). Whoever does not follow this counsel can certainly attain 'perfection in love', but all the other 'evangelical counsels' are indispensable to all christians if they are to realise *de facto* the universal vocation which is to be found in this perfection in love. Both the christian commandments and the so-called evangelical counsels are necessary to all christians, and not only to members of religious communities, if they are to attain perfection in love. Only 'celibacy for the sake of the kingdom of God' is an evangelical counsel which is not necessary for the attainment of perfection in love. That is why christian celibacy is the real evangelical counsel which is left completely to the free choice and will of the christian. It is the evangelical source of what can later on grow into the 'religious life'. What is more, it has, in its deepest essence, an inner affinity with the other evangelical counsels, even though these may also be directed towards all christians, whatever the situation may be in which they are placed.

The essence and the evangelical inspiration of the religious life are, then, the christian way of life in the situation of celibacy for the sake of the kingdom of God. The religious life is essentially christian celibacy. According to this way of life, the gospel is seen as a (possible) christian mode of existence which is meaningful on the authority of the gospel. The personal choice to plan one's life in accordance with this christian possibility goes back to a commitment inspired by the gospel, insofar as the gospel proclaims this plan to be meaningful in the christian sense. The fact that a particular person is motivated in precisely this way by the gospel, in other words, that he is so powerfully addressed by the religious motive that he is impelled to plan his whole life and give it concrete form in the light of this appeal, is ultimately based on a personal sensitivity which is a repercussion from God's activity in him. In this sense, it is a very personal call by God and a personal response to that call, making him experience this religious motive very strongly. Viewed in this way, God is at the source of the religious life.

The religious life itself, however—that is, the whole of varied, but basically very uniform shape given in the concrete to this evangelical inspiration—is, as such, a human project and human handiwork, which has come about in and as a result of history and which is therefore, like everything historical, relative. The form which man gives to the religious life is, moreover, always being faced with crises because it is always being challenged by changing value-judgements and constantly altering ideas about man and the world.

Before I go on to discuss this problem, however, I must define the significance of this evangelical inspiration a little more precisely. We should be basically misunderstanding the existential possibility of celibacy, which has been guaranteed by the gospel, if we were to regard it as a choice, made possible by revolution, between a 'natural good' (marriage) and a 'supernatural good' (which, in this case, would have to be remaining unmarried for the sake of the kingdom of God). I have already shown that living for God takes place both immediately and mediately without any tension or conflict having to exist between the two aspects. Living for God also calls for a point of contact that is finite, human and secular, because it is only in the light of our life in the world and with our fellow-men that we can give God a real content without running the risk of pursuing a void. This means therefore that we could not experience celibacy as meaningful in the christian sense if it were not at the same time a meaningful possibility in the human and secular sense. Our so-called religious and supernatural motives would, in that case, certainly hang in the air. Both marriage and celibacy are humanly meaningful possibilities and both can be experienced for the sake of the kingdom of God and therefore meaningfully in the christian sense.

This means, then, that celibacy is not, first and foremost, a renunciation of a natural value (marriage) for the sake of a supernatural value. First and foremost, christian celibacy is not a 'supernatural value', but a human possibility which aims at a special dedication to a particular value. It is not a question of choosing between God and a possible partner in life. God and the partner in marriage are after all not in competition for our religious love. They do not confront our love with a choice, as though authentic and pure love of God were only possible if a human partner in life were renounced. Christian marriage and christian celibacy are both values which are based firmly on a natural, human foundation, but which belong to the supernatural, christian order of salvation when they are experienced in the religious sense. Christian celibacy, then, is a positive choice of a way of life which is, in itself, naturally and humanly meaningful and which, because of the inner suitability which it possesses, is chosen for religious motives and for the sake of religious values. By 'religious motives' in this sense, I do not return to the idea of a competition between God and his creature, but I understand them as an extremely radical attitude towards God and man and the world. By 'religious values', I do not mean a God 'outside the world' (who does not, in any case, exist), but the living God *and* man in his most profound reality— that is, after all, the kingdom of God.

The real suitability of human celibacy is that it expresses the fact that the celibate wishes to concentrate on one particular value in life which merits the dedication of his whole life. Freely chosen celibacy implies that the celibate is so fascinated by a particular value that he wishes to make the whole of his life subject to its invitation and to its service. This possibility, which is not necessary but is quite meaningful, gives rise, in a very special way, to an attitude of being totally available and of realising a particular value as a 'specialist' and in a concentrated form. It is, moreover, a value which is fundamental to all men. If the christian puts himself at the service of this value to such an extent that he wishes to remain unmarried because of it, his freely accepted celibacy makes him the exponent of a sensitivity to a fundamental value which is common to all mankind. A celibate of this kind does not claim to have a monopoly of this fundamental value. On the contrary, he becomes the active sign and the exponent of something that is common to all men.

He keeps this universal sensitivity to a fundamental value alive and activates it for the benefit of all men.

A similar relationship exists between celibacy and religious values. 'Celibacy for the sake of the kingdom of God', as a christian possibility guaranteed by the gospel, points to the pronounced power of attraction possessed by religious values, under the invitation, call and protection of which the celibate wishes to place his whole life to such an extent that he wishes to remain unmarried for the sake of them. He wishes to concentrate on serving these values in order to be the sign in the church and the world (not necessarily explicitly—the fact alone is sufficient) of that sensitivity which mankind should have to religious values. In this way, christian celibacy, which is based on a human foundation, has both a personal significance and a meaning within the church, where it acts as a concentrated *sacramentum salutis mundi*, a striking and intelligible sign that calls upon all men to be open to religious values.

We may even say, therefore, that the so-called evangelical guarantee of christian celibacy is nothing other than the fact that christianity itself has, from the very beginning, since the first, constitutive period of the church, experienced celibacy from within, on the basis of a profoundly human datum, as a meaningful possibility for a christian. The evangelical guarantee is contained in this christian understanding that, in view of the special nature of celibacy as a human possibility, christian life can be meaningfully experienced in celibacy and, what is more, for the sake of the kingdom of God, that is to say, in the service of religious humanity and thus in the service of God, the founder of the kingdom of God.

Seen in this light, not only marriage, but also the religious life and its evangelical inspiration are, on the one hand, demythologised or detached from their sacral modes of expression and, on the other, disclosed in their full authenticity with its power to appeal both humanly and in the christian sense. The purely human basis of the religious life therefore comes to stand, within the christian faith, in a much clearer light and can, from this vantage-point, make a renewed appeal to modern man.

Nonetheless, the fact remains that christian celibacy is still a charisma. Inwardly and directly, it represents a religious choice. Celibacy for the sake of other secular values—for example, for the sake of a political career, work in underdeveloped countries, science or art—are above all conditioned by these non-religious values, even though a christian would experience a celibacy of this kind in a christian way, orientate it towards the kingdom of God and thus give it a religious dimension. It is, however, not this that is meant when we refer to 'celibacy for the sake of the kingdom of God'. Unlike these other forms of 'christian celibacy', the directly religious form of celibacy is above all specified by religious values as such. In this sense, it is possible to speak of a *factual* surrender of a human value for the sake of a religious value accompanying this religious celibacy, just as, for example, celibacy for the sake of an effective activity in the social sphere also clearly implies a surrender of a human value. All the same, we tend to speak about this question quite differently from in the past and we certainly do not come into contact with the false dilemma of 'God or man'. Since the value that we have in mind when we surrender a human possibility is religious, this christian celibacy is given a transcendent element—the transcendence of the religious value itself.

In our time a new emphasis has been given to the religious life above all because we have a better sense of what I have called the indirect aspects of our immediate experience of God than we had in the past. It is, of course, correct that the implicitly religious value of the secular life of the christian should be stressed, but there is at the same time a danger that this secularity will be experienced as a pagan secularity rather than as a christian one and thus without any eschatological perspective. In this context, a way of life which presents a striking sign of the religious dimension of existence of all men is more urgently needed than ever before. Religious life can therefore also be regarded as a protest against a form of secularisation which is pagan rather than christian. Now that christianity is also becoming 'secular', the religious motivation of the church's service to the world is also being more clearly presented as a sign, and it is precisely in the religious life that this religious motivation is made strikingly visible within the church.

It is, however, true to say that the religious life has no immediate relationship with God without a secular mediation via fellow humanity. It is with very good reason that it is also fundamentally a life in community with one's fellowmen. It is also, however, above all, a way of life which clearly shows that the inspiration of this community, its work and the work of all its members has its roots in its religious motivation. What is, so to speak, less explicitly present in the secular life of all christians and is only made fully explicit from time to time in prayer, meditation and the celebration of the eucharist, is made constantly explicit and strikingly visible in the whole way of life of members of religious communities, despite the fact that the prayer and the 'withdrawn' aspect of this life is not as great quantitatively as it was in the past. In the concrete, it is a question of giving form to both the immediate and the indirect aspects of every christian life. In the church, in reciprocal help and admonition, the emphasis falls, in one group—that of the religious—on immediacy (without denying indirectness), whereas, in the case of the other group, that of non-religious, the emphasis is on indirectness (without denying immediacy). In our contemporary secularised world, there is even more need for christianity to show that these two possibilities are mutually complementary. Taking them together, they are a sign in the world and at the same time a protest against both naturalising and supernaturalising tendencies in the church and in the world.

Celibacy, then, is a human possibility which can be experienced meaningfully in a christian sense on the basis of a special motivation by religious values (in the sense of 'not being able to do otherwise'). Furthermore, the christian way of life does not acknowledge the false dilemma of 'God or man' or of 'contemplation or action' (it does acknowledge a difference in proportion, of course). In this case, it should cause no surprise if the christian who chooses celibacy should wish to conform fully to the deepest message of the gospel and to live a life of prayer and service to his fellow-men in their most distressed circumstances, according to the demands of contemporary society and man's conscience today. The religious is therefore especially touched by the gospel to care for the poor. Regrettably, the vow of poverty has, as far as its juridical structure is concerned, become almost a caricature of this impulse. Although, from the purely juridical point of view, this interpretation can be vindicated, the gospel invites the member of the religious community to form a real community with the poor and underprivileged, who are, of course, specially privileged to Christ's love and care. This evangelical call may result in his living in the same way as the poor whom he cares for. It may even impel him to live with them, sharing their way of life fully. It may, on the other hand, lead him to work towards improving their situation in society by undertaking social work, by studying the social sciences or by working for the developing countries.[49] Without this positive human content, the vow of poverty is nothing but a pious illusion. It must result in a real poverty corresponding to the general economic situation in the society in which the religious institution is placed, a poverty which takes the level of prevailing human poverty into account. (This may sometimes mean, of course, that the religious community strives to raise the level of its environment.) It also implies a very special sobriety in such matters as food, clothing and relaxation, a special sense of efficacy of work and finally a careful balancing of the relationship between the means and the end of the religious institution.

This concentration on religious value will also lead to a different experience of obedience. When religious communities were still structurised according to feudal concepts,

obedience implied a blind surrender to the will of one man
—the abbot, prior or guardian; this man even had all the
attributes of a prince of the church with mitre and staff in
some monasteries and was an object of secret jealousy among
the bishops of the period, who were equally princes of the
church. Nowadays, of course, it would be hopeless to expect
anyone to hear an evangelical call in this. But there must be
authority even in christian community of love, in which all
the members are inspired by the gospel and are striving to
be of one mind, and there must also be obedience to that
authority. The myth that religious authority in all things
imposes commandments on us 'in the name of God' stems, of
course, from a past age. It is undoubtedly true that the ethos
of the religious community is called, and rightly so, religious
—in other words, the 'will of God' for the believer. After all,
we are not atheists in a religious community. But this ethos
—what should be done—is not addressed to us only by the
superior of our community, but also by our situation in life.
What is more, it also appeals to our own consciences. One of
the most objective guarantees that we are doing God's will is
that we respect the reality, the inner structures and what the
matter itself calls on us to do. In the past, this listening to
God's will was often narrowed down to a blind carrying out
of what the superior called on us to do. It was not so very
long ago that deliberately meaningless orders were given the
members of religious communities simply in order to put
them to the test. This sometimes resulted, unfortunately, in
producing immature and even infantile people, all in the
name of 'holy obedience'. This obedience may only have been
required perhaps once or twice in their lives, in the case of
some of them. On the other hand, however, a religious who
tried, day after day, to listen attentively to what God was
calling to him to do and to experience obedience in all the
circumstances of his life in the light of the inner structures
of the reality itself, but was never given an order or even
heard the superior express a wish was often called a bad
religious. No, obedience is imposed on us by the whole

community in which we live, by our life together, by love, friendship and dialogue, by the general well-being of the community and finally also and formally by the superior of the house, as its leader.

The three religious vows, which I have just outlined in accordance with their content, thus have a positively human content within a way of life which concentrates in a special way, but without excessive tension, on serving religious values, the most fundamental dimension of human life. They are above all not characterised by negating or disregarding human values for the sake of emphasising religious or supernatural ones. This would clearly be a diminution of the religious value of the believer's life in the world. It does nonetheless imply a choice of a certain possibility that is meaningful in the christian sense and the consequent exclusion of other meaningful possibilities, perhaps even those which offer to most christians the most obvious and even the best opportunities in life. This means that this choice in fact includes a severe sacrifice. But it is not in the first place a question of this sacrifice, of the exclusion of other, apparently better opportunities. What is above all at stake is the christian's happy and positive choice of this particular way of life—the religious way of life. When he found the treasure hidden in the field . . . he went out in his joy, sold all that he had and bought the field (Mt 13 : 44). The man who decides to become a religious does not positively choose the sacrifice—he chooses a valuable, fruitful and christian way of life, knowing that sacrifice will be involved in this choice. Christ's *kenosis* or emptying of himself was similarly not a question of disregarding human values for the sake of supernatural ones. On the contrary, it was a positive choice made from many meaningful messianic possibilities. Christ chose the way, not of secular power and domination, but of human impotence. He chose to live and die quietly in a fully human situation and experienced this, because of his religious mission, in the meaningful possibility of celibacy so as to keep his hands, as it were, completely free and available for the kingdom of God.

Thus the inspiration of the religious life is not characterised primarily by negation or a flight from the world, but by a positive choice—a decision to fly, with the world, towards a future, to the future of man, to God himself as the promise of salvation for man in history. In dedicating ourselves in this way to a religious value which far transcends all that we can do ourselves, and in faithfully serving this transcendent value, we shall no doubt be required to make many sacrifices. The first of these is, of course, the choice itself, which at the same time means an exclusion. But even more important as a source of sacrifice is the gift of ourselves to the value that is constantly served—in other words, to God and our fellow-men—because this unconditional service of love is also constantly contradicted by human selfishness, both in ourselves and in others. The emptying of himself by a religious, following Christ's example, is the very essence of his religious life insofar as love is also the essence of that life—a love which does not seek itself, but goes outside itself and forward to encounter others. Especially in its positive value as a gift and in its positive commitment to God, man and the world, love means that man, who is finite and whose being has been distorted by sin, must continually correct, sacrifice and empty himself. But this often painful process is certainly quite different from a flight from the world or from what many people mean by asceticism or mortification in the sense of 'dying to the world'.

(2) The religious life is therefore a real possibility. It is not a question of an isolated action, but a choice in life, in the sense of a permanent state of life. Nowadays, it is difficult for us to regard as meaningful a possibility which is binding for the whole of a man's life. Our deeper understanding of human behaviour has enabled us to appreciate more clearly the reasons for this difficulty. We realise now that all kinds of conscious and unconscious factors underlie an action by which a man commits himself for the whole of his life. Although this is acknowledged to be, in itself, a deeply human act (*actus graviter humanus*), it is, in fact, be-

cause of the very complicated nature of human psychology, often an unjustified decision, taken sometimes lightly and not always fully consciously. It should, of course, be a plan for the whole of one's life, expressing a fundamental will to live in this particular way. If it is to be a fully meaningful and valid decision, the person making it should normally be morally capable of overcoming all temporary failures and of realising this plan in christian hope. If this moral capacity is lacking, any lasting commitment to the religious life would be inwardly contradictory. In fact, of course, it is often extremely difficult to judge the extent to which a man possesses this moral capacity. The simple fact that he wants to commit himself for life is certainly not a sufficiently decisive indication. 'Human action' has in the past too often been seen in the abstract and sometimes purely juridically as a 'free, conscious act' and its concrete aspect has too frequently been overlooked. The spirit of the modern age tends to stress the latter and we are bound to support this.

On the other hand, however, it seems to me that we should be guilty of misunderstanding the structure of our being as men if we were to regard a definite choice to commit ourselves for the rest of our life as humanly meaningless. The possibility of a wrong choice should not make us forget that denial of a humanly meaningful commitment for the whole of one's life is one of the less attractive features of the spirit of the modern age. One of the essential aspects of man's integrity as man is that he should recognise the existence of values which transcend the situation in which he is placed here and now and which are in themselves worthy of his dedication, not simply because he appreciates them and gives his approval to them here and now in his present situation, but because they possess an inner power to invite and even to demand. There are thus values which are valid in themselves and which do not become valid simply because we give them validity. A value of this kind is acknowledged in a free, moral decision and man, the subject who freely chooses to accept it, thus *de facto* accepts it as valid in itself. But this validity is not derived from the man who chooses to accept the value—he gives his consent to it. Man is a free subject and an important part is, of course, played by the extent to which he is free. I do not deny this, but maintain that, even if this aspect is taken fully into account, there are still basic ethical values which are absolutely binding on man, in whatever particular situation he may be placed. None of us would, for example, acquit from guilt a man who, under the pressure exerted by the Nazi régime, freely and consciously chose to take part in the work of exterminating his fellow-men. There are, I insist, values which are absolute and which are therefore valid in all circumstances and always apply to man as a free subject. A man's moral plan of life is therefore at the same time also a commitment on his part for the whole of his life. There is always, of course, the possibility that he may be weak and fail, but this plan of life would be meaningless if he were to accept it as only temporarily valid and not as a commitment to moral values for the whole of his life. To put it very crudely, to view it in this way is to regard taking part in work at Buchenwald and Dachau, for example, as a temporary impossibility here and now, but as a meaningful possibility in the future.

The situation is, however, rather different in the case of an existential possibility which is not necessary and is therefore not ethically obligatory, but meaningful. This, for example, explains the possibility of a dispensation from religious vows. But why and on what basis would it be possible for a choice of a plan of life which is meaningful in the christian sense to become meaningless simply because there is not any obligation to make this particular choice? Because he is free, man can in principle pull down today what he built yesterday. The deepest meaning of his freedom is not to be found in the fact that he is thereby not engaged. On the contrary, it is situated in his faithfulness to the value to which he has freely dedicated his life. If a value is worthy of man's dedication to it for the whole of his life, a positive commitment for the rest of his life to this value is not only possible, but also meaningful. Even though failure is part of man's state of being man, he is always greater than his failure.

The choice of this particular possibility, the religious life, implies both a decision and a firm resolve—it is a free self-determination, a choice between various possibilities all of which are meaningful. A man may decide to live in christian celibacy for a period and this is also a meaningful possibility, but it is not a decision for the whole of his life like a decision to enter the religious life. This essentially includes an act of definitive self-determination which is given its full form in historicity. It is not simply an action, but a decision for the rest of one's life which is justified because the meaning of the value transcends the temporary situation in which one is placed here and now and is worthy of a dedication for the whole of one's life.

Despite the reality of human failure, then, a commitment for the whole of man's life is not only possible but also positively meaningful both from the point of view of the value itself and from the point of view of man who determines himself in history and gives form to his life also in history. In other words, faithfulness is a basic human possibility. Anyone who denies this is inevitably overlooking the finest aspect of man's life. Is man's definite will to be faithful simply meaningless? Is faithfulness only something that simply happens to be there or not? Does the matter of factness of faithfulness not point to a resolute will 'once and for all time'? The possibility of being faithful means that, however much he may be involved in history, man can to some extent transcend the purely temporary aspect of his existence, thanks to his consciousness of time. It also means that he can, with his will here and now, influence the future and even the past— this is clear from a re-interpretative reading of the bible and other ancient documents. Is it therefore also meaningless to affirm this will to faithfulness in the presence of the community? Being open to all possibilities means, in fact, committing oneself to nothing and refusing to let oneself be genuinely touched by any value. This may be justified, of course, during the period before any decision has been made, while the person concerned is still trying out various values to see which invites and attracts him most of all, but this period cannot be regarded as a final way of life, unless it is not realised that every choice implies a limitation, the inevitable result of our human predicament and also the condition for the genuine realisation of anything at all. A man needs the whole of his life if he is to be able totally to realise the one, limited possibility that he has chosen. The very essence of the human person is formed by a fundamental option or definitive choice which is to be realised in historicity. What is more, being a person is being faithful and, as christians, we know that this faithful resolution for the whole of life is simply our response to God's faithfulness, his gift which he never regrets bestowing on us. Despite our failure, human faithfulness is possible in God—which is why a man's decision to enter a religious community for life is also a supplication, an act of hope in God. We respond to God's love not only with an act, but with ourselves, with the whole of our lives.

The fact that this choice to follow the religious way of life is in principle indissoluble is not in the first place to be found in the public vow which may accompany the decision; in other words, it is not situated in the institutionalisation of the religious life, but in its very nature as a fundamental option. A man will naturally give consent to himself in faithfulness in this choice, that is, in his life-long commitment to and service of this value. On the other hand, however, being directed towards the community forms an essential part of being a human person and the religious way of life in particular is essentially related to the real meaning and value of the church as a community. For this reason, it is possible to affirm it in the presence of this community and to let it be in turn confirmed by the community, because the very meaning of this community is involved in this. Within the christian community of the church, the claim that is made to a way of life in christian celibacy is at the same time also a claim made to all christians to respect and not to violate this way of life. It is moreover also an appeal to the community to help those who have chosen this life to be both human and christian according to their openly professed fundamental option. In this, it is similar to marriage, which is also a claim made to the community to respect the exclusiveness of the bond of marriage.

The whole of this personal background is presupposed before the vows are taken and the juridical order comes into operation. The religious vows are meaningless without this personal faithfulness. It is from personal faithfulness that the vows derive their deepest meaning. If this faithfulness becomes separated from the legal order, tension may, of course, arise. A way out of the difficulty may be provided by a juridical dispensation, but this does not resolve the problem of faithfulness or loss of faithfulness and cannot therefore be the last word. The essence of the religious vow is the promise to God to be faithful to one's decision to follow this particular way of life, with the result that the vow is, from the christian point of view, a resolution based on the christian hope that God's power will prevail in man's impotence.

There is, of course, a difference between the public vow, which also involves the community of the church, and a so-called conscientious promise, which is purely private in character. It would be an inner contradiction to commit oneself to a way of life in christian celibacy and at the same time to leave one's fellow-christians completely free not to acknowledge this or else not to take it into account. Because they are publicly made in the presence of members of the community of the church, religious vows therefore also commit other christians to a certain extent to help to make this way of life possible, both in the negative sense—by not courting a member of a religious community—and in the positive sense—by caring for every one of one's fellow-christians in accordance with his or her way of life. It would be better to analyse more fully the personal and social significance of these 'public vows' rather than to concentrate on—and be scandalised by—the juridical factors which they also include. The immediate and personal relationship with God contained in the vow is indissolubly linked with the mediation of the community. The vow is directed towards God, but it takes the form of an agreement made in the presence of and with the human community of the church. In the person of its representatives, this community accepts the vows together with the involvement that they contain for the community itself.[50] In these publicly made vows, there is an essential element of reciprocity between the person making the vows and the whole community of the church, represented in the first place by the religious community which the person concerned is joining. A religious community which makes the freely chosen religious way of life of its members either very difficult or else impossible by its structure, its lack of communication or its absence of genuine human relationships or of a suitable environment is—leaving aside, of course, the juridical implications—bringing about, as it were, a one-sided dissolution of the involvement to which it had agreed at the time of the vows made by its members. The community may therefore be the guilty party in the case of failure on the part of one of its members. This brings me to my last consideration.

III. The religious way of life and the actual forms of it

Planning one's life in the light of such concentration on the religious value that celibacy, which is meaningful even in the purely human sense, is fully accepted as a real possibility in the christian sense and as a sign which will keep the sensitivity of all christians alive to this religious value—this is the essence of the religious life, both in the human and the christian sense. All the rest—including all the actual forms of this religious life—is the work of men. These forms of the religious life no doubt came about under the inspiration of the gospel, but they all go back to historical experiences with their own distinctive social patterns. This is, of course, inevitable. The historical character of all these forms of the religious life is indisputable. No eternal value of any kind can be ascribed to them. They can be radically questioned in the light of new experience. In this sense, then, the religious life is simply the handiwork of men. In view of the inviolability of the human and christian evangelical inspiration, the psychologists, sociologists, managers, group hygienists and practical men should all have the last word, not the theologians, in assessing the actual form that the religious life should take and, indeed, those who belong to religious communities have always to some extent been conscious of this. In the general meetings and chapters that take place from time to time, the constitutions of the religious orders have been regularly adapted to the new demands made by changing circumstances and these periodic adaptations were usually sufficient when the pattern of society was fairly uniform and man's view of the world more or less unchanging. The situation is quite different, however, when a complete social revolution takes place, as at the present time—minor adjustments are no longer sufficient and radical changes have to be introduced. The whole way of life has to be subjected to criticism because the traditional form is so characterised by an out of date view of man and the world and is therefore the expression of an image of God which has become antiquated and alien to us today. The actual form of the religious way of life is in conflict now with our present religious experience and is thus depriving the evangelical inspiration of its character as a sign which addresses and encourages us and others. To judge by our present form—if this is still in accordance with the rules and constitutions which are still in principle valid—we are the living relics of an earlier pattern of society. Yet we are living people who are experiencing the modern pattern of human existence and breathing it in with every breath we take. We can probably also give clearer expression to the contemporary experience because we are able to contrast it with the traditional forms with which we, as religious, are still living. This is precisely why we are all so conscious of the critical situation in the religious life today and are so convinced that this crisis can only be cured with drastic remedies and certainly not with a plaster here and a bandage there. Our way of life may still be human and evangelical in its essence, but we must radically restructurise the forms that it takes if we are to prevent our religious houses from becoming empty—it is, after all, an indisputable fact that many are leaving and few are taking their place. A radical renewal of the forms of the religious way of life is necessary if we are to ensure that it will once again represent the prophetic charisma—and this is, after all, what it fundamentally is—in the church.

A religious institution which is unable or which refuses to adapt itself to contemporary existential experiences must inevitably accept the consequences of this and prepare for its own funeral service. It is certainly not laid down anywhere that the orders and congregations in existence at present are bound to continue into eternity. It is, on the other hand, an evangelical necessity that the religious way of life should continue to be a present reality in the church. It may indeed happen that some of the older orders and congregations—and all of them are, of course, 'old' compared with the new situation in human society—will not re-evangelise and rehumanise their own forms to adapt them to the standards of contemporary experience, as interpreted and, if necessary, corrected, in the christian sense. If so, there will undoubtedly be other orders or congregations which will understand more fully the evangelical charisma and give it a form whch will be a living and attractive sign to the present age. New orders and congregations, after all, have always been a living criticism—perhaps a concealed criticism—of the shortcomings and faults of the older orders and congregations, their diminution of the evangelical experience or of their failure to hear the invitation of new situations. It has always been so in the course of history in the case of all religious institutions and it is so today. Once again we are 'in the dock', and now even before any new institutions have been set up which may seize hold of modern man with fresh evangelical charisma.

On the other hand, however, the older houses are buzzing with new plans which certainly do not seem as though they will fit into the existing structures of their present way of life and which may well result in rejection or perhaps a massive exodus.

There is usually a period of satiation in every kind of institution, after which it is impossible to reactivate the traditional structures, even with the best will in the world. The present crisis of the religious life has arisen after twenty years of strenuous efforts made to save the situation in our orders by a genuine attempt to give new meaning to old practices, observances and patterns of life. This attempt is clear evidence of the strong inner will that is present among the members of our religious institutions, who refused to lose heart. A call went through all our religious houses—certain observances had to be dropped, while others had to be inspired with the 'contemporary' spirit. Giving new psychological, phenomenological and speculative meaning to older structures in this way certainly evoked a response in very many of the members of religious communities who were open and of good will and, what was more, brought about—at least in the initial stages—a certain revival. In the long run, however, even the finest plans failed because the objective structures were like old bottles which could not hold the new wine and all the good will which had gone into these plans rebounded, as it were, on itself. It became quite clear that the point had been reached where the traditional structures had to be questioned quite radically. Although it was generally agreed that the tension between charisma and institution should be preserved, a complete structural reform could no longer be delayed.

My analysis of the situation may seem to be to some extent one-sided, but this is because I have only just mentioned that the various institutions have been active, during the past ten or so years, in abolishing all kinds of older observances. In my opinion, this has only resulted in making the crisis all the more acute. The renewals which have been carried out so far really amount to no more than a gradual throwing out of old ballast. There has been no attempt to re-evangelise and no new forms have been given to the monastic life. Life has been made rather more sociable than it was in the past within the same old or less old walls, but it is a life which is undirected and lacking in any new style and which strikes some religious as so empty and so lacking in real content that they eventually leave. These people, after all, expected to find something more profound and real when they entered religion, not what is offered to them now—a reality that has been stripped bare and pumped dry.

It is only against this twofold background—on the one hand, an antiquated form which still persists and, on the other, a framework deprived of all its style and energy—that the real urgency of the crisis in the religious life can be seen and at the same time the great need for a radical re-evangelisation in a new form which has developed from within. This can only be the task of the community itself and especially of its younger members. Unlike the older members, who so often experience man's present pattern of existence as something that is completely new, these younger religious feel that the forms of their life today are hopelessly alien to everything that they themselves normally experience. They, after all, accept what is 'new' almost without question, because they have grown up with it since the time they were born. The young men who are now offering themselves as novices were not even alive during the second world war, which was, for us older religious, the beginning of the breakthrough of the new existential experience. So, as I have said, the renewal can only be the task of the whole community, with special emphasis on the contribution that the younger members can make. I do not mean this in the sense that all the older members have to do while their younger colleagues are looking for new forms is to watch carefully to see that the 'essence' of faith is not infringed. It is, after all, quite possible to ask whether the younger people are not more sensitive to this 'essence' of faith, especially in the contemporary world, than the older ones. A discussion in which the younger members of a community had the right to speak in their creative search for new forms, while the older ones took part in the conversation as 'guardians of orthodoxy' would be bound to fail because there would be so many impasses. On the other hand, a dialogue in which either the younger or the older members were denied the right to speak on a certain subject would be no dialogue at all. In the meantime, however, all of us, both young and old, must be patient. We must put up with the discomforts and hardships of a period of search, and experience them above all as the religious sacrifice that is demanded of us in our present circumstances. Above all, we must also keep to the rules, if we want our community to remain open to life, because life goes on in the meantime. To appeal to patience in this way should not, however, act as an alibi for allowing the discussion to go on for ever without coming to any conclusions and remaining completely uncommitted. If we do this, our religious houses will simply become places where a new peripatetic reflectiveness is practised. There will be no time left to live the religious life because we shall be reflecting all day long about what it is or should be. We shall have no time left to love because we shall be reflecting all day long about the nature of God's love. We shall no longer be able to live simply and genuinely for our fellow-men because the whole day will be taken up with discussion about the nature of this love for our fellow-men. On the basis of an already existing religious understanding, it is often far better simply to say 'act first and think later'—orthopraxis is a source of orthodoxy. A way of life is first lived on the basis of a pre-reflective understanding and only then, on the basis of this experience, thematised or rationally justified. New forms of the religious life are not born in commissions or studies—they have their origin in an inspiration which looks tentatively in practice for an expressive embodiment.

I personally believe that the solution will only be found in officially approved experimentation inside—not outside—the orders or congregations themselves which must be broad enough not simply to 'tolerate' these experiments, but to support them enthusiastically. It should moreover be assumed from the very beginning that those who embark on any process of experimentation will be loyal and completely at the disposal of their superiors. On the other hand, of course, we can hardly expect the older members of the community who feel at home, both in the human and in the christian sense, in the 'older' style of life and who have very often reached a very high level of spirituality there to want their old age—during which they should be granted, even in the purely human sense, a little peace—to be made more difficult by being obliged to take part in all kinds of experiment. At their age, they are less adaptable and inevitably to some extent inflexible in their preference for the older forms. They must be allowed to enjoy God and his gifts in their own way. On the other hand, if they were to take part, of their own accord and in their own way, in this religious adventure, it would undoubtedly be a great blessing, because we very much need their religious experience as well—'fellow-humanity' is, after all, a cry which cannot be regarded entirely as a word of God. Experiments of such dimensions can, however, only take place satisfactorily in special houses when the superior expressly gives the order for them to be carried out and bears ultimate responsibility for them.

This brings me to one last point, for which some of you must have been waiting—the question of the return to the original tradition of the order or congregation.

In the decree on the renewal of the religious life, the theme of the need to return to the basic inspiration of the institution was stressed more than the need to adapt to contemporary experience. This was, in my view, a mistaken emphasis because it did not do sufficient justice to the original inspiration of the order or congregation.

After all, what was this original inspiration in the first place? It was really nothing more than an attempt to experience anew the appeal of the gospel in the context of new existential needs of the church and the world. Our founders, who were often saints, gave form to the evangelical inspiration in a definite, historically conditioned context in which they made a special appeal to people. Faithfulness to the inspiration of our founders should not take the form of a desire to return to the first years of our institution. I would even go so far as to say that it should not even take this form if the founder laid down that certain details should never be changed. If he did stipulate this, he did so on the basis of the context in life in which he was placed and which he thought, lacking, as a complete child of his time, any real consciousness of history, would always remain the same. If we cling to directives of this kind, we are attributing greater authority to our founder than we attribute to Christ himself. If, for example, there are no more slaves, what use is a religious institution for the purpose of ransoming slaves? Faithfulness to the original inspiration of the order would mean that the members of the community would turn to modern ways of helping people in the underdeveloped countries, with the aim of working towards the abolition of modern forms of 'slavery'.

I certainly believe that a monastic order or religious congregation can and must preserve its original charismatic appearance even at a later period which inevitably makes different demands. It may happen, of course, that a religious institution is founded for the purpose of alleviating a temporary need and for no other reason. As soon as that particular need has been satisfied, it is better for the community to dissolve itself or to join another, rather than to continue to vegetate without an aim in life. Such institutions do not usually have a distinctive spirituality, nor do they even look for this. But basic evangelical elements which never cease to be important in any age, such as the evangelical love of the poor which was, for example, expressed in the Franciscan order during the middle ages, calls for a special commitment to the task of giving a specific, contemporary form to this charisma which will appeal to all men. Otherwise, there is, in my opinion, a real danger of unfaithfulness to the original inspiration. Institutions with a strongly marked and universally christian spirituality often suceed, when their structures are radically changed, in extending the original features of their special charisma. But I sometimes wonder whether the so-called 'charismatic appearance' of an institution is not partly determined by a historical context in life which already belongs to the past—in which case, our faithfulness to the original inspiration would also mean that we have to have a critical attitude towards the image which the history of this 'original appearance' gives. (By 'critical' here, I mean not critical in the historical sense, but in the sense of asking whether this original image ought to continue to act as a norm for us now and in the future.) We must also be very careful to discern the extent to which our faithfulness to the original inspiration of our order is identified with faithfulness to the past and to merely traditional patterns of living.

Finally, I have to say, with all respect for the great work done by the fathers of the second Vatican Council, that these fathers were to some extent at fault with regard to those christians who are members of religious orders. They appealed perhaps rather too readily to the principle of exemption and left the religious to their own fate. This means in fact that they left them to the fatal destiny of patterns of society codified over the centuries, which superiors now have to try to advocate in the name of the constitutions of their particular orders. But the renewal of the forms of the religious way of life is above all not purely a matter for religious. It is a matter for the universal church, because the well-being of the whole church benefits from or is harmed by these forms. The council might have been able to accomplish by vigorous measures what is now in danger of becoming a very laborious process of 'give and take'. This is certainly what it will be if the central organs of the various orders, supported by all the members of the orders and the Congregation of Religious, do not really let the wind blow where God wishes it to blow.

8
COMMUNICATION BETWEEN PRIESTS AND LAY PEOPLE[51]

In this section I shall discuss the question of communication between the hierarchy and the laity, not from the psychological or the sociological but from the theological point of view. I shall therefore try to show that this kind of contact is necessary in the ecclesiological sense for the life of the church because, if there is no communication of this type, the full effects of what bishops and priests do on the one hand, and laity on the other, will not be felt.

I. Preliminary remarks
(1) In all that follows, the idea that christians cannot and should not be divided into two groups—clergy and laity—is central. There is a communal basis, which can be defined as 'being in Christ' or the 'people of God on the way to the land of God's promise', to which the terms clergy and laity are not applicable. There is, of course, a difference in function, service or ministry within this one people of God and the ministry which governs the community, the hierarchy, is one of these functions. It would not have a beneficial effect on the organic growth of the community if everyone tried to do everything and for this reason each member of the community has his own task or service to perform and this distinction between functions must be respected. What is more, the official ministry has something special which cannot be found elsewhere. The charisma of office can also be traced back to a gift of God and therefore forms the basis of an undeniable difference between the people of God and those holding office, who act 'in the name of Christ' and are placed 'over and against' the people of God. 'Clergy' and 'laity' can therefore be called words indicating a function in the church.

(2) Because of their different functions within the one people of God, the lay person and the priest will experience christianity differently. Each occupies a special situation in the church and will therefore have a special and indeed one-sided experience of christianity, which will have to be supplemented by the experience of the other. The layman, for example, can not only contribute his expert professional experience to the life of the church, but can also draw on his typical experience of faith as a layman, which the priest cannot do. The leaders of the church are therefore bound to listen to him, not only because he can give them expert technical device, but also because of the special contribution that he can make to the communal consciousness of faith in the church as a lay person.

There is, however, an essential link between the experiences of faith of the people of God and the consciousness of the hierarchy, which is not primarily a creative organ, but a function which leads and guides, directs and judges the life of the church. Obviously, the hierarchy cannot do without living material which has to be guided, directed and judged in this way and therefore needs the initiative provided by the whole of the people of God and the contribution made by the life of the laity. It is precisely because of this structure that there is a great need for organs of contact between the laity and the national or diocesan episcopate.

I believe that ordinary priests are, because of the nature of their particular office, the most suitable 'organs of contact' or links between the episcopate and the laity. They must have the trust and confidence both of the bishops and of the laity and they are in fact among the people of God in their everyday lives, while at the same time having a natural bond with the episcopate. It goes without saying that there should be no 'one-way traffic' here—the priests are not only the voice of the bishop among the people, but also the voice of the people in the presence of the bishop.

I do not wish to deny the need for direct communication between the episcopate and the laity by stressing the importance of priests as a link between the two. Bishops should without doubt be freed from much of the administrative work that occupies so much of their time now, and appear more clearly as shepherds and pastors in the local parishes and centres. The people of God itself is calling for a re-assessment of the pastoral functions of the episcopal office—the bishop should be less of a 'prince of the church' (which is still emphasised by the distance between him and the people) and more of a good shepherd, to whom everyone can appeal. On the other hand, however, we must be realistic here. A bishop cannot be everywhere at the same time and he cannot answer all the telephone calls made by people in his diocese who ring him up about every trifle.

Lay representatives might, of course, be a possibility here, but the most obvious links between the bishop and the laity are clearly provided by ordinary priests—they form a natural college gathered around the bishop and are at the same time dispersed among the people. Close contact between the priest and the people committed to his charge and his bishop seems to me to be the most suitable means of communication. I do, however, sometimes have the impression that, in re-assessing the functions of the episcopate and the laity, we have lost sight of the distinctive role of ordinary priests as a suitable means of communication. This is regrettable, because these ordinary priests, both secular and regular, are so often the best sounding-board for what is afoot among the laity and they fulfil this task in a very varied and sometimes even contradictory way, so that what they say is, in fact, mutually complementary. I should like to make a special plea for greater contact between the bishops and their priests on condition that the priests are really at one with all the hopeful, perhaps surprising and even painful questions that are being asked by the christians committed to their care.

(3) Although great improvements still have to be made at the level of the bishop's presence in his diocese as a pastor, I still believe that the focal point of the problem of communi-

cation is to be found in contact between ordinary priests and lay christians.

A distinction has to be made in the concrete expectations which lay christians have of their priests between, in the first place, expectations arising from faith in the essence of the priesthood itself and, in the second place, expectations which, partly rightly and partly wrongly, lay christians have of the priest on the basis of the actual part he plays in contemporary society. These expectations therefore clearly contain, on the one hand, essentially unchanging elements and, on the other, elements which are always changing according to time and place. What is more, these elements are also bound to change if the real, revealed function of the priest is to play an efficient and effective part.

The priest therefore has a status in the church which has been assigned to him by Christ via the church. This is the deepest meaning of his ordination, by which he is appointed by Christ himself, together with his companions in office, as a status-bearer, one having status in the church.

In the concrete, then, the complex of expectations which christians have of the priest is a synthesis of human, historically conditioned expectations on the one hand and of christian expectations determined by the essence of the priesthood itself on the other. This means that it is the task of the theologian, for the benefit of specifically christian expectations, to examine critically the total expectations that the christian community has of the priest. A priori, it is, after all, not absolutely certain whether this factual pattern of expectations is really in accordance, in all its parts, with the saving significance of the office of the priest.

This does not mean that all initiatives taken by lay people in connection with these expectations are necessarily pernicious and that only priests themselves can determine the way in which they should view their priestly apostolate. The priestly apostolate is a datum of revelation and is as such bound to live in the faith of all christians, not simply christian priests. All christians have also to reflect about this faith. Lay

christians will also, on the basis of their experience as believers, have expectations of the priest and of the nature of
his work which might have escaped the attention of the
priests themselves. The answer which lay christians themselves give to the question concerning their expectations of
priests is extremely important because it partly expresses the
expectation that Christ himself has of his priests. The Spirit
of Christ is active not only in the hierarchy and the priests,
but also in the lay believers who have their special contribution to make to the task of establishing the real significance
of the priest in the life of the community of the church.
Nonetheless, like every charismatic expression in the church,
these expectations which lay christians have of priests have
also to be examined critically by theologians—and ultimately
and indeed definitively, on the basis of this theological investigation, also by the church's teaching and governing authority—so that their authenticity and value to faith may be
judged.

II. The office of the priesthood

I should like, therefore, to analyse in broad outline the content of the church's office of the priesthood before going on
to other aspects of the problem. From the point of view of
the church, the priesthood is an office, a mandate or mission
to carry out certain cultic, prophetic and pastoral and governing tasks in the service of the community of the church. In
his cultic role the priest is the one who directs the liturgy
and presides over the sacramental life of the community. In
his prophetic role he administers the word; that is to say he
proclaims the good news. In his pastoral and governing role,
he is appointed to care pastorally for and lead the christians
entrusted to him. These three elements form a meaningful
unity and the one implies the other. They have a lasting
quality in the church—they are 'indefectible' because the
church is founded on completed redemption, an eschatological reality which cannot be superseded. Like the church herself, the church's office, as a service to Christ and the people

of God, is also borne up by the Spirit of Christ. It is also a permanent function in the church. From the sociological point of view, this means that the priest comes within the category of 'status-bearer'. A status in the community of believers is assigned to the priest. This is done, however, via the church by Christ himself, so that the sociological concept of 'status' is not really adequate as an expression of the reality of the priesthood.

The church is institutionalised grace, in other words, this visible community is a sign charged with the reality that it signifies. When the church bestows office on one of her members, then, she is at the same time bestowing grace on him—his solidarity with Christ and with the community of believers is the fruit of his ordination, in other words, of his reception of office in the church in and through a sacrament. The effect of ordination is not simply an office, a status in the community of the church. It is also a special, inward and existential orientation towards Christ and towards the community of believers, a charismatic ministry of the people of God. That is why the formulae of ordination say not only that the priest is appointed to an office, but also that he must also be the *forma gregis*, that is to say, he must be a living example of christian life for his people. In a very special way, he must bear witness with the whole of his life to being a christian, that is, especially to the love of God and of his fellow-man. It is not only in administering the sacraments and in proclaiming the word of God that he has to bear witness to being a christian—he has to do this with the whole of his life, that is, above all in his encounters with other men. The priest's inter-personal relationships must also be a sacrament of grace, a transference of the love of God into service of his fellow-men and, in particular, with the members of his own community. His specifically sacramental actions are no more than a very striking climax of this.

The concept of office or status can therefore quite certainly be applied to the priesthood, but indicates only one aspect— the formal aspect—of the priesthood. I would say that the

priesthood, precisely as an office, includes both status relationships and personal or 'face to face' relationships. In other
words, the remarkable tension that is present in the priesthood comes from the fact that the personal relationships of
the priest are also status relationships. This is to some extent
a breakdown of the sociological concept of 'status'. On the
other hand, however, there is a danger of a degree of un-
authenticity in the priest's personal relationships—if he begins, in the literal sense of the phrase, to 'play a part' in personal relationships there is always the chance that genuinely
spontaneous personal relationships will never develop and
that these are simply 'acted out'. This, of course, has precisely
the effect of undermining their very essence.

If, then, we say that personal relationships with lay christians in the course of pastoral work come within the priest's
official duties and are thus status relationships in this sense,
what must be kept in mind here is the special character of
the priestly office as one which can only be experienced fully
in personal holiness. It is only a priest who, on the basis of
this personal holiness, is impelled by the need to work for
the salvation of others and is therefore motivated by priestly
love who can, as a priest, experience personal relationships
in a purely spontaneous manner and without playing a part,
even though he may appear to others in those personal relationships as a status-bearer. This is only possible if the priest
has completely grown into his priesthood, to such an extent
that his spontaneous appearance as a man is at the same time
an official appearance as a priest and a bearing witness to
faith, hope and love.

In the most obvious sense of the word, then, the priest is,
as one having status in the church, or 'status-bearer', one
who proclaims the word of God, who administers the sacraments and who is the leader of the parish or the community
of believers entrusted to his care. He is, however, also a
status-bearer in the less obvious sense of the word, when he
has personal, face to face relationships in the course of his
pastoral work with lay christians. Then too, he is 'chosen

from among men ... to act on behalf of men in relation to God' (Heb 5:1)—a man among other men, but one who has been appointed, via the church, by Christ to devote himself to the care of others and to work for their salvation. The priest also has other status roles and face to face relationships in addition to these essential features of his office but, although they are not in any sense separate from his task as a priest, they are certainly historically conditioned.

On appointment as parish priest, for example, he will not only have to do all that I have outlined so far, but will also find that he has to perform the function of chairman of the parish council and many other parish organisations. Furthermore, in view of the present-day stratification of society, he will automatically have to assume a definite social position because of his status as a priest. In this way, he will, within the total structure of society, give rise to various expectations —and aversions—which are strictly speaking outside the expectations which lay people have of their priests as men having status in the church. This social position thus in fact constitutes an undivided unity which gives the priest—seen from the human point of view—a special 'total society position' (which he, as an individual, can hardly ever or never break through). This 'total society position' unfortunately often works to the disadvantage of his activities as a priest proper. All this is, of course, closely connected with his priestly office, but as such it is purely historically conditioned. All these status relationships are secondary but, especially if the society in which the priest is placed has reached a high level of sophistication, they may do harm to the primary status relationships. In the past, on the other hand, this secondary social position often tended to further the primary status relationships of the priest. It has frequently been observed that the prestige enjoyed by a priest is often dependent, not on his being a priest, but on his 'total society position'. It is most important that we should begin soon to clean out this Augean stable to enable the priest to fulfil his primary, priestly status functions properly.

In addition to these secondary status functions, the priest also has face to face relationships which are not of a directly pastoral character. These could be called his private personal relationships—with his fellow-priests, personal friends and relatives. In these private relationships too he is still a priest, although he does not appear formally as a status-bearer in them, but as a private person. It is, of course, true to say that christians still treat him as a priest even in these private personal relationships, and even though there is sometimes a tendency towards mystification in this attitude, it is nonetheless a real one—in everything that he does and in all his relationships, he continues to bear witness to another world—the religious world. If he is at fault here in his private relationships, a certain harm is done to his power to bear witness at the altar, in the pulpit or in pastoral work with his fellow-men.

III. The function of a priest

This, then, is the status function of the priest in broad outline, both according to its unchanging and essential elements in the life of the church and according to its secondary forms which are historically and socially conditioned and therefore changing.

The essence of the problem is that the priest's task is religious and it is this and not the secular as such which determines his appearance and activity as a priest. It is, of course, true that the moral and religious aspects of man cannot be separated from all his other relationships. The religious element is transcendent, but it embraces and penetrates the whole of man's life. In this sense, then, the priest is not a sacristy official. He is at the service of the members of his community in all the aspects of their religious lives—at the altar, in the pulpit, in the presbytery and in personal relationships in the course of his pastoral activity.

Since his office is carried out in a very special field, then, he will recognise and respect the special legitimate forms of secular life. He does not have to give meaning to his pastoral work by being present in every sphere in which lay people are active for the sake of maintaining communication with lay christians. This would be a misunderstanding of the special nature of the lay apostolate. Through their baptism, which has enabled them to share in the universal priesthood of all christians, lay people too have the task of bearing witness to their being christians wherever they are. A transference of value has to take place between christians. The lay apostolate is conditioned by the secular situations in which lay people are placed, whereas the priest renounces the secular situation to some extent in order to be free to carry out his distinctively priestly activities. The apostolate in face to face relationships is therefore above all a lay apostolate. In this, lay people carry out their apostolic work in informal relationships—for example, in a circle of friends, in the neighbourhood in which they live, in their leisure-time activities with others or in their sphere of work. Lay christians are the obvious people to conduct this apostolate in the closed but informal relationships that come about spontaneously in the sort of sphere that I have described. Officially at least, the priest is out of place in this kind of relationship. In tending to take over the part played by lay people, he would be misunderstanding their special apostolic power and witness. Taking over from the layman in a sociological situation in which he is so frequently treated as an 'outsider' by a homogeneous group of lay people inevitably means that his priestly task is handicapped and made ineffectual. This is, I believe, what happened in the case of the worker-priest movement in France. The basic inspiration of this experiment was the conviction that it was necessary to communicate with the workers through the 'apostolate of presence' among them— by sharing their condition, the priests could bear witness to christian love in informal relationships within industry. The priests, however, did this work anonymously—they did not appear as priests. What they did, then, as anonymous priests, was purely supplementary apostolic work—the work that christian lay people ought to have done but did not in fact do. In other words, they replaced laymen in what was strictly speaking a lay apostolate. I think that this may, of course, be necessary from time to time, especially in order to stimulate lay people to take part in an essential activity of the lay apostolate, but in itself it is a substitute apostolate for the priest.

The course followed by the worker-priest experiment is, I believe, characteristic for all forms of apostolate in which the priest plays the part of layman. This situation is indicative of the fact that the distinctively lay apostolate has not yet completely and explicitly penetrated into the minds of christians. The priest, it should be remembered, does not occupy an all-embracing place in the lives of christians—he does not have to be present everywhere. Both at the personal and at the social level, there is a sphere of mutual solidarity among christians which does not as such form a part of the social organisation of the church. Even though the priest may not, as a man, be excluded from circles of this kind, the part that he plays in them is not that of a priest as such.

The pastoral aspect of the priest's activity, insofar as it takes place in face to face relationships, is therefore very delicate. In any case, the priest should never intrude into natural or purely secular relationships, not even when he is visiting his parishioners' homes. He must respect the natural basis of family life—in marriage it is the husband and wife who should, in the first place, care for each other in the pastoral sense. The priest should not intervene here as an 'alien' factor. He is bound to respect the natural structure of marriage and help both the husband and the wife, if necessary, in their moral and religious interests. But there has been more than one case of priests, in their so-called apostolate, unwittingly driving a wedge between man and wife. The same situation applies too to all kinds of natural groups, communities and societies. The priestly apostolate is not furthered, in principle at least, by the priest joining in, as priest, these groups or communities.

The real difficulty is that the priest as a status-bearer is also forced, in modern society, into a social position. This social position makes him a stranger when confronted with others in different social positions. The priest is no longer 'among us' as 'one of us'. He will not, moreover, succeed in building a permanent bridge between himself and others if, as a priest and remaining within his social position, he tries to break through the impasse by spending his free time with lay people and doing what they do during their leisure—going to or playing football with them, for example, or with young people to their favourite haunts.

A person with whom one has confidential relationships is not always the person whom one sees most frequently. So it is with the priest. We should not exaggerate the importance of the modern concept of 'communion', at least not in the sense of the priest's becoming entirely absorbed in this 'communion' with others. Even though he may still be 'one of us', despite his social position, he is nonetheless the *segregatus*, the one set apart whom we visit if we have a real need to, if something important happens in our lives, not if we are troubled by some everyday trifle which we can just as easily sort out for ourselves.

It should therefore be clear from this that the distinctive task of the priest is not to be found, in principle, in purely secular functional relationships, in the informal relationships which often accompany these or in the face to face relationships of various closed groups. On the other hand, however, it should also be clear that all these relationships, insofar as they are a partial expression of a moral and religious attitude, do come within the sphere of the priest's pastoral activity. This in turn points clearly to the fact that one of the most important tasks of the priest in the pastoral sphere—in addition to his sacramental and kerygmatical activities—is to establish circles of trained christian lay people so that a transference of value can take place via the christian life of and witness borne by the laity to all these spheres in which the priest inevitably remains a stranger.

It has, however, to be stated explicitly that what I have

said so far does not in any sense mean that priests should not, by virtue of a special charismatic call, be apostolically active in, as it were, a non-conformist manner in sectors where they do not, 'according to the book', really belong. What is more, these charisms may, at certain times, have to become institutions. It is, for example, possible to ask whether the time has not come for certain 'natural group leaders' to be ordained priests in some circumstances (without making them follow the normal pattern of conventional training for the priesthood) and allowing them to remain in the same sphere of activity. The revealed essence of the priestly function is an 'unchanging' datum, but the way in which this is carried out can change according to historical circumstances. People are nowadays much more sensitive to the universal and immanent presence of grace in all people and consequently to the importance of their own personal decisions than, for example, to the concentrated presence of grace in the church. In the past, priests spoke almost exclusively about the sacraments—baptism, confessions, the mass and solemnising marriages. Now, people are much more open to the less institutional aspects of God's activity, with the result that the dialogue between the priest and the lay person will be more concerned with the personal insights and decisions of christians and with the perspective that these open in the direction of the ecclesial character of grace. In my opinion, communication between priests and lay people should take place far more at this personal level. The priest will continue to bear witness to the orthodoxy of the church and to proclaim the law of the gospel and the sacraments, but he must learn to shed his dogmatic self-sufficiency and his frequently brusque and authoritative way of speaking. If he does this, he will be able, as a man of God and at the same time a sympathetic person, to go along boldly with lay christians in the search, without making discussion impossible by speaking too soon or too brusquely about the sacraments and Sunday mass. The priest has, in the past, too often identified himself with orthodoxy. Now, however, he must learn to look more carefully for the essential and immanent presence of grace in the christians committed to his pastoral care, for the authenticity that is present in their personal lives in order to direct this more and more towards the church. There is no doubt that priests tended to deal too brusquely with people in the past by telling them to practise their religious duties and frequent the sacraments. In doing this, priests offered no solution to the problems of the laity and no orientation in their search. They must look, together with the laity, for an answer and not think that they already possess the truth and only have to apply it to whatever case arises. We can readily agree with Karl Jaspers' comment that mankind has 'lost its naivety'— man is no longer a child and will no longer be put off with transcendent solutions which often do no more than simply cover up his difficulties.

I know, of course, that it is fashionable to talk nowadays of 'horizontalism'—the transference of all religious experience to the purely secular level. According to this view, which undoubtedly contains an element of truth, authentic religion is nothing other than the service of one's fellow-men. Love of one's fellow-men has replaced the experience of God, which is called a mystification that injures true religion. People who do not acknowledge the revelation of the word can in fact, in and through their genuine love of their fellow-men, be implicitly christian,[52] even more so sometimes than those who explicitly profess to be christians. Christians themselves, however, are not required to revert to a kind of pre-christian 'implicit' faith! There is, as I have said, an essential element of truth in this reaction, which does, however, incline, as a reaction, towards *hairesis*. It is this element of truth which makes this very widespread tendency so dynamic in its influence. After all, it is true that we had too often mystified religion, turning it into an empty love of God which could not be measured against any real commitment on the part of believers to actual men. We had so much to say about our love of God and covered up the problems of our fellow-men, leaving them to their fate. But man has now become fully conscious of himself and has the impression that religion in this form is simply a mystification because the gap between the love of God and the love of men is too great. We can therefore say that communication between priests and lay people will be restored, at least to some extent, when priests, without entirely neglecting the real dimensions of the God-centred sphere, also take the horizontal dimension seriously and integrate it into their religious attitude. If they do this, they will really be in touch with what is happening among lay christians.

This is why I do not think that all kinds of new 'organs of contact' or links between the clergy and the laity have to be established; I do think, however, that the priest needs a new inner organ of contact, a new feeling for the problems confronting men today. Whenever he in fact has this feeling, there is almost always frequent and intense dialogue between the priest and the layman. To open and maintain good communications between priest and layman is not so much a question of new organisations, then, but rather of a new feeling between the two parties.

Many christians will inevitably ask whether, in this new spiritual contact with lay people, the priest will not of necessity get his hands dirty. Does his solidarity with his fellow-men not mean that he will inevitably be separated from his bonds with God's word, the law of God and the church?

This is a serious question and one which is not always dealt with seriously. There is certainly a real danger that people are becoming indifferent to the value of truth in human life. They are tending to regard man's subjective conscience as the norm and are not even asking what is the norm of conscience itself. Man's ethos of truth is bound to suffer by this. It is forgotten that man's salvation can be endangered if he does not live according to the truth, even if his conscience, though in error, is not guilty. It is precisely because the man who is in error does not come into contact with reality—and it is reality which constitutes his salvation—that his error is a fundamental threat to his existence as a christian.[53] The danger exists, even if his error was made in good faith. Of course, in contrast to this, there is also the datum that innocent errors do not endanger man's salvation. These apparently opposing views can only be reconciled by the affirmation that, in the last case, man's knowledge attains to what is necessary for his salvation, which implies that, wherever this is not the case—that is, wherever the knowledge that is necessary for salvation is not in fact attained in the case of error—this error cannot be entirely without existential guilt. The psychologist may perhaps be able to have non-directive discussions with his partner in dialogue, but more is required of the priest, the 'steward of God's mysteries' (1 Cor 4:1)—he has to bear witness to the word of God, which has appeared among us as human truth. He is 'set apart for the gospel of God' (Rom 1:1).

A problem of communication here, however, is that the priest must not simply bear witness, as it were, in a vacuum —he has to bear witness in such a way that people will be able to listen to it properly, not so that it will just be heard in the material sense. The word of God must not be thrown at people like a brick. It must be experienced by those who listen to it as a value. In order to bear witness in this way, the priest must first be able to listen to the people to whom he wants to address the message. He should not treat them as something that he knows all about and can easily fit into previously existing categories, but as people asking special and original questions motivated by a desire for grace, even though their questions may seem to take the form, from time to time, of a radical refusal of grace. A refusal may sometimes be a real question, an unconscious openness to the authentic and liberating force of God's truth. The priest has above all to know how to touch this nerve-centre in his conversations with lay people and his testimony to the word of God.

Priests also have the duty to listen to what they themselves think are rash or wild ideas. Such ideas often contain echoes of what is in fact in the minds of many christians, and priests who are committed to the pastoral care of their fellow-christians surely have no right to close their ears to what is being thought and discussed in lay circles, whether it is orthodox or not. If some of the ideas that are going the rounds are 'way out', priests must not simply brush them aside with a disdainful gesture, but take them seriously and try to analyse them. Surely experience has taught us that there is almost always an element of truth even in the most rash sounding views and priests should not take an immediately defensive attitude towards them, but make use of the germ of truth they contain. In a word, they must first learn to listen before getting others to listen to them.

The priest always has to move in two directions at the same time in discussion—he has to care pastorally both for the weak and those without problems and also for the 'progressives', to whom he must give some latitude. Christ's hidden life, after all, lasted for thirty years. His apostolate and proclamation of the word as high priest, on the other hand, occupied only a few years. I believe that this demonstrates Christ's concern to listen first for years to his people and to the word of God in scripture before addressing the people himself and taking his message to them. In other words, this was a question of 'communication'. If the new possibility of communication is present, the need to look for new 'organs of contact'—and therefore to reorganise pastoral practice—becomes of secondary importance, a problem which can be solved by sociologists and psychologists and, ultimately, by pastoral theologians. The new readiness on the part of priests to listen means that this secondary problem will be solved more easily. But above all it should not be forgotten that this new 'spiritual' communication is not simply communication between people, but is also—both within and above this level of communication—a communion with the living God in Christ.

9
COLLABORATION OF RELIGIOUS WITH THE EPISCOPATE, WITH THE SECULAR CLERGY AND WITH EACH OTHER[54]

A tendency began with the second Vatican Council which can be called, in the widest possible sense, a 'decentralising' movement in the church. Underlying this movement is a genuine desire to take the church's interest away from herself and to enable her to become more of a servant of Christ and of religious and secular mankind. In this context, what is said is that the church wants to leave her 'triumphalism' behind, especially at the level of the leadership of the church. In the past, the hierarchy tended to stress too much that it was the centre of the church, as though the whole of the people of God were at the service of the hierarchy, instead of its being at the service of the people. In this, the hierarchy presented itself as a static and unchangeable factor, a massive rock past which the changing world had continued to flow during the centuries, but which had itself remained fixed, unchanged and unchanging, unaffected by the passage of time. The hierarchy thus pointed far too little away from itself towards Christ and the people of God.

This really contains, in a condensed form, essentially all that I want to discuss concerning the relationship between the secular and regular clergy, between religious themselves and between brothers and sisters in religious orders, both among themselves and with the hierarchy, within the framework of the living church, the people of God in all its variety which is, as such, the universal sacrament of salvation for the world. It is unfortunately true to say that we are still inclined to think at once of the hierarchy as soon as the word 'church' is mentioned. The bible and the fathers of the

188

church, however, have bequeathed us, in the words *ekklesia* and *convocatio,* a very different concept. According to these sources, the church is the great hand of the assembled people of God, chosen by him and saved by him, dedicated by him and set apart as a whole to serve and bear witness to him in order to be, in the world and for the sake of the world, the sacrament of the salvation that he offers to the world, even in its material aspects.

In the first place, the people of God is the medium of God's salvation, placed for ever by Christ in the world and subject to the unceasing help of the Holy Spirit. It is precisely for this reason that the office—the authority which is, in the name of Christ, present within the people of God—of the church must be, at least in certain decisive aspects, infallible and 'indefectible'. Otherwise, this office might, in a peremptory and proclamatory way, separate the church from her abiding subjection to Christ. It is therefore impossible to separate the church's office from the community of the church. This brings us back clearly to Paul's letter to the christians of Ephesus: 'for the equipment of the saints (that is, christians), for the *work of the ministry,* for the building up of the body of Christ' (Eph 4 : 12). Every christian, then, has a special and inalienable task to fulfil in the 'work of the ministry'; all that the hierarchy has is a responsibility as an authority. This too should not become an argument for centralisation—it is above all a question of leadership and guidance. Modern society is emancipated and the people of God have achieved a genuine christian maturity. For this reason, too, more emphasis must be placed on the direct guidance and co-ordinating activity of the episcopate than on its strict and centralised leadership. In modern society, to stress leadership would be to give rise at once to resistance, because the word 'leadership'—and even more the underlying reality implied in the word—meant in the past an attitude on the part of the hierarchy, according to which members of the church were primarily regarded as 'subordinates' and objects of pastoral care and not as people who were co-responsible for the 'work of the ministry'.

I. The place of members of religious communities in the people of God

As members of the people of God, the members of religious communities also share in the 'work of the ministry' and, what is more, share in this work in a special way. At the second Vatican Council, the bishops opposed Cardinal Ruffini's assertion that the charisma only occurred in the apostolic church and had no place in the modern framework of the church, in which it would only serve to disrupt the order and discipline of the church. The generally prevailing conviction that the charismatic and prophetic element had to be regarded as essential to the modern church as well was interpreted by Cardinal Suenens, Mgr Florit of Florence and Mgr Sarrain of Chile.

The religious life is a striking expression of this charismatic and prophetic element in the church. A religious institution is basically a charisma in the church which has become an institution. A group of believers who have been seized and inspired by the Spirit has given this charisma a suitable institutional form so as to ensure that it will continue to be active in the church in a lasting and effective way. I am speaking here of those institutions which are known as mixed or active, as opposed to purely contemplative, and can therefore say more precisely that a definite or universal apostolic charisma is institutionalised in a religious order or congregation, which is then, as a 'crystallised' charisma, at the church's disposal, in order to help the church in carrying out her apostolate effectively. This, then, is a special case of the charismatic element breaking through here and there and from time to time in the people of God, not from above, but from below. The hierarchy, as the principle of leadership and guidance, naturally has to supervise this kind of charismatic expression as it has to supervise all expressions of the life of the church insofar as they become public.

In approving a given apostolic institution, the church is at the same time accepting the existence and the active effect of a universal or clearly orientated apostolic charisma and recognising the ecclesial character of the special contribution that this religious institution makes to the 'work of the ministry'. The first task of the local hierarchy in connection with an institutionalised charisma which has been approved by the church—that is, in connection with an active religious order or congregation—is therefore bound to be, firstly, to respect fully its special inspiration and orientation, secondly, to give it latitude and scope to work and function properly, and thirdly to enable this work to be fully geared to the total government of the church.[55] Because this special contribution made by religious institutions is so important to the life of the church, these institutions have been guaranteed the freedom and the right to take apostolic initiatives (which is, after all, the task of the whole people of God under the supervision of the hierarchy) by the church's leaving this to the discretion of religious superiors. These are, of course, in turn bound to ensure that the charismatic inspiration of the order or congregation is preserved in its original soundness. This 'relative autonomy' is simply an expression at the juridical level of the church's recognition and respect of the special charisma of this particular religious institution. It therefore forms an essential part of the charismatic character of the whole people of God. The so-called 'exemption' with regard to individual bishops is one of its historical forms and not the only possible form. If, however, this form eventually disappeared, another juridical form would certainly have to be sought in order to safeguard the special contribution made by the apostolic charisma of a religious order or congregation and recognised as such by the church. Otherwise the church would in fact either misinterpret this charisma or else not give it full scope to express itself, to the detriment of the 'work of the ministry'. The fact that the episcopate is itself to some extent bound by a charisma born in the bosom of the church should not cause any surprise or be regarded as presumption on the part of members of religious orders or congregations. It is simply a concrete case of the universal and fundamental bond which ties the bishops to the deposit of faith present in the whole people of God. The church's office is certainly an authority, but it is an authority that is an instrument of the Lord and subject to him. As a teaching office, this authority even acts *ex sese*, 'of itself', that is by virtue of the presence of the Spirit of God in the office and not by virtue of a delegation of the people of God, although it does determine and direct what is active and present in the unanimous faith of the people of God. The hierarchical office therefore has the mystery of Christ as its norm, not in the abstract, but by virtue of the Spirit who is active and present in the church and who evokes many different charismas in the life of the church.

From the purely human point of view, of course, it is not difficult to understand why some christians deny the existence of these charismas. They are afraid that these charismas may endanger church order and discipline. These charismas do not introduce an alien datum into the church, but what they do bring in is something that has not arisen as a direct result of an insight or of the leadership of the hierarchy (unless, of course, they are charismas originating from office-bearers themselves).

The charisma often arises quite independently of the hierarchy. The christian who thinks in purely hierarchical terms, then, and not in terms of the whole people of God, is bound to regard those charismas which do not originate from the hierarchy itself, but under the impulse of the Holy Spirit from below, from the people of God themselves, with a certain caution and even fear. What is more, the charisma is in itself often an element of unrest and renewal in the church. The christian who thinks of the hierarchy exclusively as an 'establishment' which centralises and controls everything and strengthens the existing order in the church, and who regards the believing people simply as obedient subjects and not as members of the church who can themselves take initiatives, will inevitably view the charisma as an uninvited and unwelcome guest. He has only to take one step further in this direction and he will simply deny the existence of charisma in the church. The charismatic character of the church is always very difficult to digest for the christian who sees the hierarchical office as an autarchy. A person holding authority in the church, especially, can only fully accept the presence of the charisma if his attitude is one of selfless service.

It is, of course, indisputable that all kinds of secondary phenomena accompany an institutionalised charisma of this kind and that there is a strong tendency towards ossification, especially if it lasts for centuries. As Léon Moulin rightly observed, 'The drama of the avant-gardistes is that they include a few saints, several geniuses and a large number of fanatics' (*Le monde vivant des religieux*, Paris 1964, p 94). I cannot, however, discuss these secondary phenomena here. The respect shown in the church for authentic, living charisma, in this case, the religious life, is sufficient proof that the church's hierarchy is not a high-handed authority, but one which is bound to the norm of Christ and subject to him as well as to the work performed by his Spirit in the life of the church. The hierarchy, as the authority which is ultimately responsible for the whole 'work of the ministry', must be able to co-ordinate the special apostolic contribution made by the religious institutions with the other apostolic activities which are taking place within the province of the church. It is for this reason precisely that the conciliar decree on the pastoral office of bishops in the church expresses the desirability of involving provincials in the overall planning of, for example, a province of the church—in this apostolic planning, of course, the episcopate may not be exclusively responsible for everything that takes place, but it is certainly ultimately responsible. To involve the provincials of religious institutions in this way, in the first place as witnesses to the presence of a definite apostolic charisma in the province, is, from the ecclesiological point of view, the inevitable result of the historical change in emphasis in the concept of 'exemption'. It is very characteristic of this tendency that it was officially announced in the Netherlands that a national pastoral institution was to be established in the name of the episcopate and the council of provincials. The official document was signed by Cardinal Alfrink in the name of the episcopate and Father van Waesberge as chairman of the council of provincials. Symptoms of this kind seem to be very promising. In the past, the concept of 'exemption' and everything to do with it was approached from an exclusively juridical standpoint. In our present search for new forms which are better suited to the contemporary age, we should above all be guided by ecclesiological insights and our first question should be concerned with the problem of co-ordinating the charismatic element with the bishops' responsibility. The question, therefore, should be: How can we, in the contemporary framework of the church, co-ordinate and combine the inalienable right of the apostolic charisma—this is, after all, what the active religious institution is by definition—to exist and therefore the inalienable right of members of such institutions to take apostolic initiatives, with the equally established fact that the bishops alone, as the successors of the apostolic college, are responsible, in the mode of authority, for all the apostolate that takes place in the church or in a province of the church? The juridical regulation of this is secondary and may change with changing circumstances but, whatever happens, it must do justice to both poles of the problem. Otherwise, either the charismatic and prophetic element in the people of God or else the principle of hierarchical authority which is entrusted to the college of bishops will not be respected.

There is not an antithesis, but there is inevitably a tension in this structure and this tension should not be released for the sake of what might be called rest in the church. The unrest which is sought by the charismatic element is quite essential to the life of the church. If the hierarchy, for the sake of having everything in the church within its control (and this is imaginable, for purely human motives), were to fetter the charisma or allow it only very limited scope, the very being of the church would be placed in a very serious predicament, because the church would be identified with the hierarchy in a disguised manner. Those in authority in the church must above all trust the special dynamism of the people of God, or the place of honour accorded to that people in the constitution on the church will be no more than a verbal concession, not a consistently accepted datum of faith.

In addition to this, the pope, as the head of the college of bishops and in this sense therefore also that college itself, in principle gave his approval to the apostolic charisma of the canonically sanctioned religious institutions; in other words he recognised the authenticity of that charisma in the church, with the result that these institutions have been given a real canonical mission. This is a new title, on the basis of which the individual bishop who is, after all, bound to the college of bishops is, from the eschatological point of view, obliged to take positively into account the presence in fact of apostolic communities in his diocese. The bishop who does not take this into account in his apostolic planning for his diocese (or province) will not only be acting in a short-sighted way from the ecclesiological point of view, but will also be giving rise to fragmentation and wastage of his forces. The bishops should therefore regard what is done efficiently and well by religious and others as the work of the local community of the church and thus as their own work, not as the work of strangers which must be carried out as soon as possible by their 'own' people—in other words, the secular priests. The members of religious orders and congregations, priests, brothers and sisters, have a different juridical relationship with the episcopate from that of the secular priests, but they are no less the bishop's 'own' people.

On the other hand, however, religious must also be careful not to regard their bishop as a 'stranger' who intervenes from outside. He is as much one of their 'own' people and, as the *pastor animarum* or 'pastor of souls', he respects the specially religious apostolic charisma and tries to gear it actively to the whole 'work of the ministry' in the diocese (or province). It is unfortunately the case that a policy of string-pulling for positions of apostolic power which is quite contrary to the mind of the church and seriously impairs the efficacy of the apostolate is all too frequently followed on both sides here. I would myself regard it as a very unhealthy development if there were to be a marked increase in the number of apostolic activities advertised as taking place 'under the guidance of the hierarchy'. In this case, any other apostolic work, undertaken on the initiative of the people of God—either lay people or religious—would be in danger of being devalued to the level of an apostolate of secondary importance and of being announced as such in the presence of all believers. Far be it from me to deny the right of the bishops to initiate themselves all kinds of apostolic undertakings and to carry these out themselves or have them carried out directly under their guidance. In this context, however, direct or indirect insinuations, of the kind which are certainly heard in the church and which qualify other apostolic work as inferior and as less valuable to the life of the church, should most emphatically be eliminated. The simple reason for this is that it is, from the ecclesiological point of view, quite wrong, and implies a failure to appreciate the true ecclesial nature of the people of God as a whole.

II. The relationship between the episcopate and the presbyterate

So far I have especially discussed apostolic religious institution as such, and have not considered at all the clerical character of many of them. The situation is, of course, made much more complicated and tense by the problem of regular priests. Before examining this question, however, it is important to consider the relationship between bishops and the priests or, more exactly, the relationship between the episcopate and the presbyterate.

The priest proper is the bishop and this priesthood is by definition collegial—it forms the college of the bishops under the leadership of the pope. The presbyterate or derived priesthood is a participation in some of the tasks which are peculiar to the college of bishops. Although the term is already used in a somewhat different sense, the priests are therefore, in a very real sense of the word, 'auxiliary bishops', that is, 'coadjutors' or 'helpers' of the college of bishops. In the church the presbyterate is inwardly orientated towards the task of assisting the episcopate in its service of men. Everything that the priest does as such takes place in the name of and in submission to and in aid of the episcopate. All presbyters, both secular and regular priests, are therefore men who work in collaboration with the whole of the college of bishops. Dogmatically speaking, no special relationship with any individual bishop is established by ordination to the presbyterate, whether the bishop administering the ordination is the local ordinary or an auxiliary bishop (in the usual sense in which the term is used). What is established is a relationship with the world episcopate. This also applies, without any reservation at all, to religious who are ordained priests. The concrete manner in which the presbyters are employed in the service of the world episcopate will depend, of course, on this college of bishops, in community of faith with the pope. It can take many forms. One very usual form is that of the so-called secular priesthood, in which the presbyter is bound to a local ordinary and therefore to a definite diocese. (Even this link with a diocese is, however, still relative, because a bishop in residence is bound to care directly for the world church—for example, in the missions—and has therefore to hand priests over to other dioceses.) A second very common form is that of the regular priesthood. These priests, who are also members of religious communities, possess a greater measure of independence with regard to the individual bishop, for the purpose of perpetuating the special charisma of their order or congregation, which often entails a definite apostolic specialisation. They are therefore able to provide, with even greater efficiency, the dynamic and apostolic element for the whole of the world episcopate, and it is for this reason that they also have a separate relationship with the co-ordinating principle of unity of the world college of bishops—the pope. They carry out the priestly apostolate in the explicit form of the *vita apostolica*—the evangelical way of life of the apostles. In other words, what here specially enters into the office of the church in the apostolic way of life of regular priests is the charismatic element.[56]

Those members of religious institutions who are at the same time carrying out a priestly apostolate are, of course, much more dependent on the episcopate than those whose apostolate is not also priestly. The universally christian apostolic way of life is, after all, not a participation in the episcopate—it is the one christian mission of the whole people of God. The priestly apostolate as such, on the other hand, is certainly a participation in the hierarchical apostolate of the bishops, or at least in that of the whole college of bishops. In the sphere of the administration of the sacraments, of the proclamation of the word of God and of priestly pastoral care, the leadership of the episcopate and indeed of the local bishop in residence, who is the representative of the universal college of bishops in the diocese or local community of the church, is therefore indisputable. On the other hand, the pope, as the head of this college, has approved the special apostolic charisma of priestly religious institutions and, to safeguard this charisma, has placed these priests directly under their own superiors. For this reason, the leadership exercised by the individual bishops takes place, in the case of the apostolate of regular priests, via the provincials of the various communities who are, so to speak, the juridical exponents of the inalienable right of the apostolic charisma of these regular priests to exist. Real recognition of and respect for both the presbyterate as a participation in the episcopate and the special apostolic charisma of regular priests inevitably leads to a dialectical movement between the bishops and the provincials and this of course means a state of tension which can only remain healthy as long as each partner is open to the views of the other and takes them fully into account. Here, too, failure to appreciate the attitude of the partner would inevitably upset the essential dialectical structure of balance between office and charisma. Either the office of the church itself would be stressed without regard to the specialised apostolic charisma available to it via the regular priesthood, or the essentially ecclesial *diakonia* or service provided by this charisma would be disregarded by too much emphasis being placed on the importance of the group.

What is more, because the presbyterate is by its very nature a participation in the saving mission of the college of bishops, the apostolate of both secular and regular priests is bound to be collegial. The priestly apostolate is bound to take place in collegial collaboration not only with the episcopate but also between priests themselves. At the present time, especially, there is a great need for the collegiality of the work of priests to be re-assessed. This means that there is also a great need for dialogue between the provincials themselves and between the provincials and the bishops.

At the present time, there is intensive circulation of ideas and experiences between parishes, dioceses, countries and even parts of the world. In such circumstances, a haphazard apostolate can only be fruitless. It is also no longer possible to justify the placing of the apostolate in the hands of one order or congregation. Not only is co-ordination necessary: there is also a growing need for specialised centres which will be at the service both of the bishops and of the provincials of religious institutions and in which the religious and pastoral situation of the diocese and province will be examined scientifically and advice will be given to the bishops and superiors. The time has passed when it was possible for one particular religious order, for example, to carry out its own apostolate completely autonomously. This autonomy is no longer possible, nor is it desirable now. It is, of course, still necessary for an order or congregation to think carefully about its own apostolic task, but this process of reflection is only meaningful and effective as long as the conclusions reached by specialised centres consisting of representatives from the diocese and from all the religious institutions are taken fully into account. Each institution will have to consider for itself which objectively necessary apostolate within the actual religious situation, insofar as this has been, if I may use the phrase, 'mapped out' in the province, is most in accordance with its own special apostolic charisma. In addition, both on the part of the bishops and on that of the various religious superiors among themselves, there must be sufficient respect for the special feeling in the different religious orders for particular forms of apostolic work. This is necessary to prevent one person (or group) from greedily and selfishly taking the largest slices of the cake for himself and leaving the unappetising crumbs for others or even compelling them in this way to renounce their special apostolic charisma. One has the impression certainly that everyone wants to do everything nowadays. Ordinary common sense tells us that this is inefficient. The tendency on the part of secular priests to forsake the traditional apostolate of parish work in order to go in for an apostolate on a 'grander' scale is, I believe, regrettable. The *paroikia* is the diocese of the bishop. Because it is impossible for him to be everywhere at the same time, he divides this district or 'parish' into subdepartments where he, the local bishop, is represented by the presbyters, who are, after all, his collaborators. In this way, the local community of the church is founded in faith, worship and fraternal love as the condition for the missionary impetus of the people of God. This implies complete dependence on the local bishop—this work is therefore primarily the task of the secular, that is, the locally incardinated priests. These men can, of course, also perform other apostolic work, but this should not be to the detriment of the work of the *paroikia*—or should this be left to members of religious institutions who, on the basis of their special apostolic charisma, are not really equipped for it?[57]

On the other hand, however, I am bound to point out the

danger that members of religious institutions often tend, wrongly, to identify their own special apostolic charisma with certain forms of apostolate which have come about in the course of time and which they perhaps, in view of the needs of the particular period, have taken care of from the very beginning. Faithfulness to the original apostolic charisma may, however, sometimes mean that it is necessary to break radically with certain apostolic forms or with the practice of furthering devotions that are no longer suitable for the times we are living in. I do not want to conduct an examination of conscience for other orders and congregations, so I will simply give an example from my own order. According to the Dominican tradition, we are bound to propagate the sodality of the Holy Name of Jesus. In some provinces abroad, Dominicans do this zealously and with success, but this devotion would no longer be in accordance with the Dominican image in Northern Europe, with the result that very few Dominicans further it any longer. Examples of this could be found in most orders, and members of each should therefore ask themselves seriously whether they are not wasting apostolic energy in continuing to promote such traditional and especially devotional practices which are so much tied to a past period. They should ask whether they should not give up certain practices altogether and perhaps not ban others which have proved their worth, but certainly renew them radically. To cling uncritically to such practices in the name of the tradition of the order or the congregation may—viewed within the framework of the whole apostolate of the church—be a form of unfaithfulness to the original inspiration of the special apostolic charisma of the order or congregation. We should, in that case, be giving the people of God stones instead of the bread they are asking for. It cannot be denied that some congregations have continued to propagate pastoral and devotional practices which are, at least to some extent, tied to the historical past and which are not in accordance with the present life of the church. This sometimes leads to the bishops and secular priests gaining the impression that members of religious institutions form a kind of separate church with different objectives from those required by the times we are living in. This impression—which is not always a false one—can also result in all kinds of tension which make universal, collegial collaboration extremely difficult.

Comparing for example the apostolic activity of Belgium with that of the Netherlands, I have the impression that the apostolate in Belgium has a very collective and individualistic structure. In the Netherlands, on the other hand, the structure of the apostolate is different and, in my opinion, much more effective. The bishops there have, for example, set up a national pastoral institution and have appointed a religious as chairman, with secular priests serving under him. A similar organisation has been established by religious with a secular priest as chairman. Parochial and diocesan activities are supervised by a committee containing both secular and regular priests as members. There is hardly a single institute which would think nowadays of setting up something specifically Franciscan, for example, or Dominican. The national president of Catholic Action has, for years, been a layman with very extensive powers. I think that Belgium is very much less advanced than the Netherlands in these fields. Many structures are completely out of date and not only every order and congregation, but also every diocese, is confronted with serious apostolic tasks, but each behaves as though there are no other orders and congregations and no secular or regular priests.

Of course, I am aware of the fact that your coming together in this way for the past ten years as provincials contradicts what I have just said about the situation in Belgium. It is clear proof of your conviction that something has to be done to correct that situation. I am personally of the opinion that the orders and congregations should be less energetic in revitalising their own apostolic activities. In view of the diminishing number of members in each institution, such activities carried out separately may not be able to last very long. Rather than do this, each institution ought perhaps to provide people to give guidance to mixed apostolic undertakings; by 'mixed', here, I mean activities in which both secular and regular priests of all kinds collaborate. At the same time, each institution should also be humble enough to supply members who would play a subordinate part in these mixed undertakings. At present, what so often happens is that every member of every order or congregation wants to have his own special apostolic task, of which he is the chairman, secretary, treasurer and general factotum. It hardly needs to be said that this is not to the advantage of apostolic efficiency! It sometimes even seems as though apostolic work has to be specially created to provide work for religious who are ordained to the priesthood. A religious is not, in other words, ordained priest because there is a need in the church which requires a priest, but rather the reverse seems sometimes to be the case—a priest is freshly ordained and a search has to be made for an activity for him! I am, of course, putting it rather strongly, but I do feel that some younger priests think about it in this way. This does point to a lack of co-ordination and of apostolic planning on a large scale. And this should be possible in a country with so many secular and regular priests and with its own catholic university. If this university aims to be worthy of the name of 'catholic', it must have a part to play in the task of thinking seriously and scientifically about the apostolic and pastoral situation in Belgium, a country in which so many secular and religious priests are trained sociologically and psychologically at a high academic level, to name only one or two of the advantages that they enjoy. Everything is available here in Belgium for it to be possible to co-ordinate and guide pastoral activity on a large scale and in an expert manner. There is, of course, still the problem of control, and that is the affair of the bishops and provincials, who should in any case have a carefully and scientifically thought out pastoral guidance at their disposal. As long as this is not available, many priests will continue to do valuable apostolic work, often silently and unseen, and to be a sacrament of faith, hope and love for many unknown people. Many others, on the other hand, will just muddle along for a while until they eventually become blasé, lose all confidence in their apostolate and even leave the priesthood itself—men who have lost their initial enthusiasm and look back on their lives in the ministry as a mistake.

I think that as provincials you, together with the bishops, have a great, but also an inspiring responsibility here, not so much individually (although your first and immediate responsibility is to your own order or congregation) but collectively. After all, the individual, even if he has the whole order or congregation behind him, cannot nowadays solve the problems of the apostolate. The pastoral situation is too complicated for this—or rather, it is too difficult to penetrate.

This, then, is what I felt that I had to say to you, reverend fathers and brothers, and I have kept it general and basic in tone because I believe that it is ultimately a question of christian practice. Nonetheless, if the apostolate is to be practised meaningfully, it must be understood fundamentally and in principle and illuminated by dogmatic insight.

10
THE CATHOLIC UNDERSTANDING
OF OFFICE IN THE CHURCH[58]

Any historical and theological consideration of the past in the church always implies the questions of today. The origin and past of the church are, of course, always normative for the church, but only in dialogue with the present. The present questions concerning the priesthood are therefore bound to play an explicit part if we look in the origin and past of the church for the normative criteria which must be taken into account in any attempt to give a new structure to the office of the priesthood. On the other hand, however, it would be incorrect to think of the past—and especially the origin and past of the church—simply as an aspect of our contemporary understanding of the church and the world. If we do this, any appeal that we may make to the past will simply be an attempt to strengthen our own conservative or progressive views and our own conservative or progressive positions. A historical and theological examination of the origin and past of the church must always be a critical event. It confronts not only us and our present, but also our ideas of origin and past with the difference, the alien aspect of a historical situation. In this way, the past calls in question our contemporary understanding of the church and the world. Moreover, it would be dishonest to question the past in the light of our contemporary experience of the world and the church without critically questioning this modern understanding and without allowing it to be subjected to the scrutiny of the past. Every period in the history of the church is subject to the criticism of the period that follows it and this period in its turn must be open to correction from every preceding period.

I. Office in the 'apostolic church'

We shall have especially to consider, hermeneutically and dogmatically, the traditionally catholic statements, in particular when formulated in ecumenical councils, about the priesthood. These can be set out schematically in the following way. The *sacerdotium*, which is subdivided into episcopate, presbyterate and diaconate, was instituted by Christ as one of the seven sacraments, and this sacrament of ordination, which is guaranteed by the 'apostolic succession', imposes—only in the case of a 'valid ordination'—a 'character' or special mark. Despite the universal priesthood of all believers, this 'official' priesthood is, in its correlation to the community, nonetheless 'essentially distinct' from the services rendered by the laity, although these are equally of the church.

In the formulations of this survey the actual form of the priestly office during a previous period of history is so closely interwoven with the understanding of this same period that, without a historical and hermeneutical approach, all kinds of premature theological and pastoral conclusions might be deduced from it, conclusions which could completely inhibit any attempt to bring the pastoral office up to date or at least limit such an *aggiornamento* to minor adjustments. A hermeneutical and dogmatic reconsideration of the *sacerdotium* in the church is urgently necessary, both in view of the present crisis in the priesthood and also in the light of ecumenical concern. In this reconsideration, the claims and the prestige of experts in every field, which have made the 'investiture to sacral authority' incredible in our modern desacralised world, must also be borne in mind.

I shall confine myself here to the 'offices of the church', which I see in the following light. The offices of the church, which certainly emerged from the community of the church according to sociological laws, nonetheless owe their emergence to the community of the church as set in order by the apostles, in other words, to the community of the church as authoritatively guided by the apostles from the very origin of that community. What, then, is at the origin of the sociological process of growth (in which the Spirit of God is active) is not a community that was initially guided without authority, but the apostolic community itself.

There is no direct link between the contemporary offices of the church (the episcopate, the presbyterate and the diaconate) and an act of institution on the part of Jesus while he was on earth. It is clear from historical analysis that already existing models in the Jewish and hellenistic world and demands made by the historical situation of the church influenced the factual structure of the leadership of the community. Even seen from the sociological point of view, a social group such as the church would be unthinkable without official ministries. The sociological process within the church which caused the episcopate, the presbyterate and the diaconate to emerge from an originally greater number of offices in the church (many of which disappeared later or merged with others) is, however, correctly interpreted on ecclesiological grounds (the church is after all the 'temple of the Holy Spirit') as the work of the Holy Spirit, the Spirit of the exalted Christ. Even though these offices do not go back to a historical act of foundation by Jesus, they are, by virtue of the nature of the apostolically ordered church, themselves the fruit of the Spirit and not simply the result of a sociological process of growth. In this sense, it can be said that these church offices are based on a *ius divinum*. Such a 'divine dispensation' can, however, be so understood that it includes and at the same time makes possible a historical growth of various forms and divisions.[59] So long as the church is able to distinguish the sign of the Holy Spirit in it restructuration is possible, not only in the past (this is quite clear from history), but also in the future. Having regard to the unique aspect of the apostolate, the apostolic leadership of the primitive church clearly functions as a model if a criterion is sought by which the Spirit-guided character of a proposed restructuration can be recognised.

The 'office of the church' thus forms an essential part of the apostolically ordered church as this is apparent from scripture, and therefore an essential part of the church as the 'church of Christ', but the church herself can regulate the concrete forms, division and powers of this office. In accordance with the example of what has been done in modern society, it is possible to divide the offices of the church into legislative, administrative and corrective (or 'penal') authorities. Furthermore, even an episcopal or presbyterial structure of the leadership of the church is not dogmatically inviolate, although the collegial unity of all the 'shepherds' of the church, with the office-bearer who has the function of Peter in their midst, is. It is therefore possible to divide and regulate all the powers of those who are now called bishops, priests and deacons differently, so long as this is done in a way that really enables the church to function as the church that was founded on the apostles and prophets with Christ as the corner-stone. It is clear from the *acta* of the second Vatican Council that even the statement that the episcopate is the 'fullness of the priesthood', that is, of the office of the church, is not a dogmatic statement, not only because the council had no intention of laying down 'dogmas', but also because this statement is concerned with the *present-day* order of the church, which can never be defined since different orders of the church are dogmatically possible. (It is clear from earlier practice in the church that ordinary priests, for example, could have the same powers within the church and even the same sacramental powers as bishops; there have, moreover, also been times when the powers of deacons were greater than those of presbyters or priests.) The threefold division of the one office, with the familiar demarcation of their special ministries and powers is, from the dogmatic point of view, subject to change and restructuration, within the fundamental college of those bearing office in the church with the one who has the function of Peter among them. Whether or not they will have to be re-adapted in the future to the modern situation and to what extent they may have to be adapted is a question of pastoral policy in the church. This has, in the first place, to be seen in the light of the needs of the community of the church, in which at the moment the question of a new division of functions in the office of the church is unmistakably present. Even without 'dogmatising' it is, however, possible to say in general that, on the basis of their real content, a threefold division between episcopate (in the original sense of supervision over the various communities within the church and their priests), pastorate and diaconate is a pastorally suitable formula and that it is still an open question as to how the pastorate should be differentiated or how it can be subdivided into specialised functions.

What, then, emerges in the concrete from the foregoing is that there is a real need for the leadership of the church to consult the behavioural sciences and in particular religious sociology in order to conduct a suitable pastoral policy, especially in changed cultural circumstances. What must emerge from pastoral experience, illuminated by sociological investigation and research undertaken among groups, and seen against the background of dogmatic possibilities, is what new divisions are necessary within the office of the church in order to ensure that it will function meaningfully in the future, not only in the light of the situation in the west, but also in the light of the situation in the east and the third world, with the meaningful models that already exist there. Within the apostolic criteria, meaningful development and pastoral suitability must be the guiding principle in any such restructuration, that is to say, the guiding principle for a *ius condendum*, since the apostolic criteria do not bind the church to a definitive structure of her offices, which might crystallise out into a rigidly fixed and unchangeable *ius conditum*. It is, for example, evident from scientific research that there is a lack of 'vertical' lines in the structures of the church between the summit, which is in fact formed by the bishop, and the very broad base, formed by the priests and the people. Between these two there are no intermediary structures, that is, offices with real powers sanctioned by the order of the church. This, however, is a pastoral conclusion and here I wish to confine myself to the dogmatic possibilities.

In any attempt to give the church new structures, the ecclesiological foundation must be borne in mind. This is that (a) the universal church is made fully present in every local church, so that the local church has, in accordance with its own needs, a right to its own special appearance and its own order and (b) every local church, in making the universal church fully present in this way, has at the same time to be 'in communion' with other local churches and with that church in which the one who bears the office of Peter resides. The result of this is pluralism, but a pluralism within a necessary unity of church order.

II. The meaning and validity of the office of the church

The content of the office of the church and of its validity or authenticity within the church must also be apparent from the essence and mission of the apostolically ordered (local and universal) church as the church of Christ or the 'community of God'.

A. The church's office of leadership

The content and meaning of this office (here I am disregarding the manner in which these functions can or should be divided among various 'offices' so that the church can perform her pastoral task suitably) are, by their very nature, determined by the essence and mission of the whole church. Our ideas of the content of the office are therefore partly determined by a more explicit and more subtle understanding of the church which may even include a correction of the past. We can therefore provide the following schematic outline of the lines of force in the church's office of leadership in the light of the church's earlier and present understanding of herself. These lines of force include leadership and guidance of the christian life of the community of believers so that Christ may really be the only Lord of that community, directing the ministry of the word in faithfulness to the apostolic confession of faith, conducting the sacramental services of the community and taking care of the 'consolation of the gospel' in admonition, exhortation and so on. The church's office of leadership also implies leading in the love that desires and seeks to attain justice for all men, in other words, being responsible for the evangelical care which the community must have for man in his historical situation. This task also includes not only a critique of society as a whole but also a critical attitude towards the community of the church. Finally, one of the normal tasks of the leadership of the community is that of receiving new candidates into the office of the church. In a word, it is a special, official care which will ensure that Christ is really the only Lord of the living community that is to be founded or perpetuated. All these tasks do not, moreover, have to be carried out in a purely formal manner, but in a way which is really credible within our contemporary society and which can function suitably, understandably and meaningfully. The behavioural sciences have their own special contribution to make to the furtherance of these tasks of the church's office.

The spirit-filled character of the church's office means that it always has a twofold dimension. Those bearing office are at the same time both (a) representatives of the community of believers in the presence of the world and (b) representatives of Christ in the presence of the community. This implies that (a) what is living in the community will crystallise out in their person, because this community itself is the bearer of the good news to the world and may, on the basis of the gospel, express itself in a 'critical no' to the world. It also implies, however, that (b) the office-bearer has a special, that is, an official mission, brought about by the Spirit, over and against the community and for the benefit of the world. His authoritative function, which is purely service to the full power which the Lord has over the community, also gives the office-bearer a critical function towards the community, in which he nonetheless remains tied to the apostolic confession of faith. This does not mean that the church is divided into two blocks, the college of those who bear office and the believing people. This is not so, in the first place because faith and the life of the church are not in any sense made the exclusive property of the clergy by this function which is set over and against the community. If it were, the clergy would then have the task of handing on to the community the property entrusted to them. The treasures of faith belong, on the contrary, to the whole of the believing community, which is, as a whole, the 'temple of the Holy Spirit'. Those holding office in the community serve that community which is guided by the Spirit and any authority invested in this leadership is derived from the apostolic message and confession of faith and directly from the exalted Lord. This authority is therefore, as far as its content is concerned, bound to a norm and is simply formal or jurisdictional, so that it appears as authority purely on the basis of jurisdiction. *Id quod traditur*, the apostolic inheritance (and everything that may appear to be necessary to maintain this inheritance dynamically in every historical situation) is always the basis, the fertile soil and the limitation of 'formal' authority. Furthermore, the exercise of authority is also determined in the church by the church's character as a community of love. The leadership and guidance of the church must, on ecclesial grounds, have the characteristic of serving love, which brings authority in the church within the sphere of a special service of love.

B. *The validity of the office of the church*

This christian and ecclesial authenticity is determined on the basis of its function in the community which is faithful to the apostolic church and therefore above all on the basis of the *fides ecclesiae*, the apostolic faith. This applies not only to the validity of baptism, but also to that of the office of the church.[60] This has ecumenical consequences for the catholic church since and insofar as she recognised the apostolic and therefore the ecclesial character of other christian churches at the second Vatican Council. This means, of course, that she has implicitly accepted, to the same degree, the validity of the office in the other churches. The fact that the church order in the other churches has been again and again differently regulated in the various churches since the reformation does not detract from this in any way. Even if the universal collegiality and the office of Peter, which could really function in other church orders, are not taken into account, an episcopal or presbyterial church order should not in itself be regarded as a dogmatic factor leading to division. As such, then, these are not an obstacle to unity, but only different and dogmatically justified church orders.

C. Apostolic succession

In the limited sense of a historical 'apostolic succession' in the office of the church this is one of the means by which the apostolicity of the faith of the community can be embodied. It is, however, apparent from the practice of the church, as formulated in the *ecclesia supplet* of the western tradition and the idea of *oikonomia* of the eastern tradition (both of these being ultimately 'juridical' definitions of the 'charismatic' origin of the mission of the office of the primitive church), that, in the case of the sacraments and the office of the church, no dogmatic solution is provided by precise 'chemist's prescriptions'.

The foundation of the apostolic succession in the office of the church is in the first place the apostolicity of the community itself, because it is precisely in the apostolic church that the Holy Spirit is active. The apostolicity of a christian community implies the apostolic faith and an office which proceeds from the apostolic church. The Spirit-filled character of the apostolic community of the church is therefore also the primary basis of the apostolic succession and thus of the validity of the office of the church. The apostolicity of the community of the church, that is, its belonging to one of the empirical communities of the church which, in mutual 'ecclesial recognition', claim to be the 'church of Christ', is the basis of the apostolicity or validity of the office of the church.

In normal circumstances, this radical 'apostolic succession' of the church is accompanied by a historical or horizontal succession in the office of the church—the college of existing office-bearers (however this may be organised) visibly (that is, by the imposition of hands) receives the candidate, at the expressed desire of the community, and once this candidate has been accepted into the college under the invocation of the Holy Spirit. On the basis of the character of the apostolically ordered church, however, it is in principle possible for an office which is *praeter ordinem*, that is, outside the valid church order, but which is nonetheless valid in the church, to come about, namely under the charismatic impulse of an apostolically-founded community which finds itself in a state of emergency. This occurs especially in the missions.[61] This situation would appear to be even more strikingly justified if (as some historians maintain) there really was a distinction in the early church between the so-called Pauline church order (of the gentile christians) and the Palestinian church order (of the Jewish christian communities), which gradually merged together, the Palestinian church order becoming predominant. There is, in my opinion, not enough historical proof for us to say that these two church orders were set over and against each other as antitheses, but it is quite certain that, in the primitive church (and more conspicuously in the Palestinian communities with their hellenistic tone), leading services in the community arose alongside the normal offices of the church, offices which did not have their origin in an official transference (the imposition of hands), but in a charismatic inspiration, even though this always took place subject to the critical recognition of the apostolic authority (Paul) and with the approval of the community.

Offices of the church which arose freely and charismatically were thus in principle regarded as acceptable by the christian community, but they had to prove their right to exist in the light of the apostolic criteria and to establish this within the community by their authenticity and meaningfulness. These offices arose in difficult, or rather in special missionary situations. In this way, the 'first-born' of a newly founded community often appeared spontaneously as official leaders of the community and it is frequently impossible to find any historical evidence proving that an imposition of hands took place. This is a charismatic fact which Paul simply accepted (see especially 1 Cor 16 : 15–16; Rom 16 : 5 can also be seen in this perspective). These cases of leadership in the community, which arose charismatically and outside the normal order of the church, but were nonetheless within the one, but differentiated church order, were recognised by the later church in her canonisation of scripture, as possibilities in principle within the life of the church. In the light of this, we are bound to keep this possibility open now in principle and even take into account a realisation of this possibility in the case of apostolically founded communities which are in a situation of emergency. In this context, we are reminded of the unlawful and so-called officially invalid consecrations of bishops which took place in China during the persecutions, or of believers who have emerged as leaders of christian communities in mission countries where there have been no priests for years. This theological possibility is also especially important from the ecumenical point of view, since it may lead to a renewed assessment of the validity of the office in, for example, the anglican church and other churches of the reformation, as the apostolic and 'church' character of these churches is recognised, and in addition it can be affirmed that they are (from the Roman catholic point of view) in a situation of emergency as churches with regard to the apostolic succession in the office. In view of the intention of this section, however, I cannot now go further into this question. In the foregoing, I have, however, established the connection with what has to be considered next: reception into the office of the church or, as it is in fact called both in catholic terminology and in the present-day, valid order of the church, ordination to be bishop, priest or deacon.

III. Reception into the office of the church

A. Essential elements of the confirmation in office

On the basis of the Spirit-filled character of the community of the church as founded on the apostles, reception into the church's office includes the following essential elements, whatever actual form may be given to this reception in accordance with the valid order of the church (which is changeable).

(1) Since the one who bears office also represents the community, the community's consent to the leadership of a certain candidate must be expressed in one way or another. The question which occurs in the traditional liturgy, 'Do you know whether they are worthy?', is certainly a real expression of this consent, but it is in fact formal. On the other hand, the candidate's desire to accept office in the community is also necessary. The desire of the local community cannot, however, be regarded simply as the ultimate authority, because a narrow 'clan' mentality (both in the conservative and in the progressive sense) may effectively paralyse the function of the 'shepherd' (who is thus chosen in accordance with the people's wish) to criticise the community in the name of the Spirit of Christ. We have evidence of this in the case of certain American protestant communities, where the members of the community have the last word in the choice of their office-bearer. Nonetheless, a vote on the part of the community is indispensable to the proper functioning of the one who chooses to be the leader in a community. He has, after all, to bear witness to and guarantee the unity and the peace of his community in his own person. This means that the candidate must also be suitable for the task, and the aid of the behavioural sciences is indispensable nowadays in any attempt to assess his suitability. I would like to make two comments here. On the one hand, the suitability of a candidate must not be judged in accordance with an image of the 'priest' which is associated with a previous period in history and which is probably already out of date. If this standard is

used, the most suitable candidates might well fail the test and 'stereotyped' figures be chosen as the most suitable. On the other hand, however, there can be no justification for the practice of judging the suitability of a candidate by an image of the 'priest' which has been formed privately and which has not been subjected to the norm of the apostolic criteria for an office-bearer in the church (I am thinking here in particular of the aspect of being 'over and against' the community). For this reason, both 'dictatorial' tendencies and unsuitability for leadership must be considered very carefully. According to the new testament, candidates for office in the church were normally chosen from among those members of the community who had already given some indication of 'charismatic gifts' and who toiled for the community (see especially Ac 6:3 and the pastoral epistles). In modern terminology, this means that candidates would be chosen from among fully committed believers. It cannot be denied that testing is useful, but I feel that a better method of selection would be to take into account previous *service* as a layman in the community, of course with the powers entrusted to him, even though this would mean that his reception into the office of the church would have to take place much later.

(2) Reception normally takes place by the college of the already existing office-bearers under the imposition of hands and, as I have already said, with the approval of the community (see Ac 14:23; Tit 1:5; 1 Tim 5:22; also Ac 6:6, where this is expressed less clearly). The imposition of hands by the bishop with his priests is, in the present-day order of the church, a sign confirming this reception. All the same, there are special ministries in the church for which there is no evidence in scripture of an act of reception by the already existing office-bearers, for example, for prophets and teachers (Ac 13:1 ff) and the ministries referred to in 2 Cor 8:19. What I have already said above about the charismatic emergence of offices in the church also applies here. These special ministries do, however, ultimately require re-

cognition by the community and by the leadership of the church.

This reception into the office of the church (with the consent of the community and of the candidate himself, and normally by the college of the already existing office-bearers or, in the case of possibly charismatic emergence, at least subject to recognition by this college) is only the historical and ecclesial form in which God's special call by the Spirit who guides the church appears (see, among other places, Ac 1 : 24 ff and 20 : 28). The office-bearer is thus able to know that he has been called in faith by God and that his task is to perform a special service in the one mission of the whole church to the world.

(3) This reception takes place in the college of the already existing office-bearers. Organic membership of such a college, the ultimate seal of the collegiality of which is to be found in the one bearer of the office of Peter, points to the task of every office-bearer, not only to care for the inner unity and peace of his community under Christ, but also to care for peace between his community and those led by other leaders and ultimately also for peace between his community and the whole catholic church. 'Catholicity' originally referred to the mutual communion of all local churches, a unity for which every community, together with its leader, was responsible. That is why the reception of a believer into the office of the church is not only a matter which simply concerns the local community, but also essentially a collegial matter concerning all office-bearers, insofar as it can be suitably arranged. It is only in collegial unity with his brothers in office and together with them subject to the apostolic norm that the office-bearer can be a criterion for the community. The basis for this is to be found in the writings of the new testament, which have canonised the fact that diverse apostolic traditions in their complementary totality are the norm for the life of the church—no separate tradition, even though it may be apostolic, can be allowed to isolate itself or

become independent and thus be exempt from mutual criticism.[62]

(4) Reception into the office of the church takes place under the invocation of the Holy Spirit (*epiclesis*). In this invocation of the Holy Spirit (which is expressed by the laying on of hands), God is implored to send the charisma of office, by which the one who is called becomes the representative of Christ and is able, *in persona Christi*, to take the lead in the community—to perform official service in the name of Christ over and against but within (that is, as a member of) the community. This act is what makes it publicly legitimate for a member of the community who is usually already charismatically gifted, to act as a holder of office in the church and furthermore, in the form of prayerful supplication, it also equips him with the charisma of office by virtue of Christ's promises. Just as the word of God, of which the office-bearer is the minister in the community, is a 'power of God', so too is the office-bearer's special mission. That is why even a non-catholic theologian like J. Jeremias is able to say that the imposition of hands, as the expression of mission to the office, is not only a suitable symbolic act, but 'an act of the communication of the Spirit' (J. Jeremias, *Die Briefe an Timotheus und Titus* (*Das Neue Testament Deutsch*, 9, Göttingen 1953[6], on 1 Tim 4 : 14). It is not difficult, of course, to verify this from the bible. It is also why this 'ordination' contains a task as well: 'I remind you to rekindle the gift of God that is within you through the laying on of my hands' (2 Tim 1 : 6).

In view of the fact that the charisma of office which God is implored to send under the invocation of the Holy Spirit is not a 'parcel' which has been previously determined by *ius divinum*, but is something that is determined by the concretely situated church, the content of the *epiclesis* or prayer of supplication will be inwardly marked by the differentiation and specialisation which is in fact unavoidable in the one office of the church. In accordance with what has already been said, then, this prayer will in the concrete refer to, for example, the charisma of office for the supervision of all the communities and their leaders (the 'episcopate'), the charisma of the 'pastorate' or the charisma of the 'diaconate'. In this way, it would at the same time be 'established' that, below the *episkope* or ministry of the 'overseer', the functions of the 'pastor' and deacon would co-ordinate and include 'autonomous' ministries and 'powers'. What is more, it would only in this case be meaningful for a new ordination to be given (*epiclesis*) on the possible reception of a candidate into a different basic differentiation of the one office of the church —which does not mean that juridical difficulties about 'validity' have to be raised whenever, for example, the temporary situation in which the church is placed requires a deacon to take over the function of a pastor or a pastor to assume the task of an *episkopos*.

B. Ordination and sacrament?

Reception into the office of the church under the invocation of the Holy Spirit and made visible in the sacramental sign of the imposition of hands is known, in the traditional terminology of the catholic church, as 'ordination'. On the basis of the *epiclesis* or invocation of the Holy Spirit, one could continue to call the reception into the church office an ordination, in order to give emphasis to the fact that the charisma of office, with its characteristic task of appearing 'in the name of Christ over and against the community' and at the same time in adherence to the apostolic norm and in communion with the whole community of the church, is in fact bestowed.[63] This emphasis on the liturgical element is not only justified, but also necessary during a period of radical secularisation. On the other hand, many believers still associate such a 'consecration' with an anointing of the candidate's hands with oil and tend to interpret this to some extent magically. It is therefore understandable that some christians prefer not to stress the sacral aspect of 'ordination' any more so as to avoid false mystification and also for ecumenical reasons. An attempt is thus made to avoid the suggestion that non-catholic confirmation in the office of the church, which is not a 'sacrament' and, in our view, is ritually rather 'cool', is in itself a factor which divides the churches and has, by definition, to be regarded as invalid. Whether this is so or not has still to be seen after all. The above-mentioned essential elements contained in reception into the church's office are in fact accepted by the catholic church but also by, not all perhaps, but many of the other christian church communities, lutheran, calvinist and anglican. These essential elements are regarded by catholics as sufficient reason for calling reception into the office of the church a sacrament (*sacramentum ordinis*) whereas, although these essential elements of reception into the office of the church are fully accepted by the non-catholic communities, the name 'sacrament' is not ascribed to them. In view of the fact that they accept what is objectively the same, however, the use of the word 'sacrament', which is analogous and has many shades of meaning, is, in this context, secondary. The Tridentine confession, 'seven sacraments, neither less nor more', is a reply to a question which is different from the one that is asked nowadays. In our days one starts from an ecumenical appreciation of the ecclesial character of each others' churches—we realise now that it is possible to say and do, from the perspective of a different church order and with a different 'church language', what is objectively really the same, with the result that the Tridentine statement does not need to be opposed to the protestant churches' present-day understanding of themselves.

IV. Character: an apostolic factor, not one which divides the churches

According to the traditional teaching of the catholic church, reception into the college of already existing office-bearers has a consequence which is known as a character. I should like to show that this 'mark' adds nothing new to what I have already in substance said.

Augustine introduced the word 'character', not in the first

place in connection with reception into the office of the church, but in connection with baptism, mainly in order to illustrate that baptism was *inviolabilis,* in other words, that it had to be recognised if it was administered with the Trinitarian confession of faith, even if this took place unlawfully, that is, in a non-catholic christian community. The inviolable or indelible mark was for him simply the inviolable value of the Trinitarian confession of faith at baptism which was, in Augustine's opinion, an activity of faith on the part of an apostolically founded church, even if this were separated from the *catholica.* He regarded this inviolability of the apostolic faith as equally applicable to ordination. The effect of ordination was not therefore destroyed by later 'heresy'. He never called this effect itself, however, a mark or character. Whenever he wanted to refer to the effect of certain sacraments that was not violated by sin as opposed to their effect of grace, he used the terms *sacramentum manens, sanctitas* (in the sense of *sancitus*) and *consecratio* or *ordinatio.* Being given office, then, was being placed in an *ordo,* that is, in a 'college' or 'senate', being received into the college of those holding office in the church. The 'character' or mark was, for Augustine, the outward rite itself in which the triune God was invoked. The 'mark' thus consisted of the visible and audible expression of the apostolic 'faith of the church', which preserved its inviolable value in the separated churches as well. The effect of this inviolability was that the 'ordained' person was *de facto* placed as an office-bearer in the church and was received into the *ordo* of those bearing office.

Following the early scholastic theologians, Thomas based his teaching on this Augustinian datum and regarded character in the first place as the outward rite of ordination itself, which was valid in the church and by which everyone was able to recognise that the ordained person had been validly received into the college of office-bearers and that this was not nullified by his going over to a separated church. In the first place, then, the character was the rite which situated, not the fact of being situated.

It is, however, possible to discern, even among the early scholastic writers, a tendency to call the effect itself (that is, valid membership of the college of office-bearers) a character on the basis of the rite which bestowed this mark (that is, a rite in which the apostolicity of the community of the church could be recognised). Thomas took over this idea, but noted that the character could only signify the effect itself of the rite of ordination (that is, real membership of the college of office-bearers) in the second place, by analogy. Later, however, he lost sight of the original significance of the character to some extent and began to regard this analogical significance as the real one. This, however, was only a question of words, since it had never been denied in the church that the ordained person was (by the rite) situated in the 'order' of those bearing office—this effect had simply not been called a character. Furthermore, under the influence of the rather one-sided cultic interpretation of the office of the church in medieval theology,[64] reception into the office was called a *deputatio ad cultum*, that is, a reception into the college of those who led in liturgical worship, with the result that the character came to mean an official power in the sphere of worship. In this way, the stress was laid on the view that the official acts of the one holding office were independent of his personal merits or demerits, even though the rite of ordination was still considered to be an active prayer of supplication, so that the ordained person would carry out his official acts in holiness and with apostolic zeal.

In its second meaning, which was analogical but which had become traditional, the concept of character therefore had two essential characteristics: (a) it indicated that the office-bearer had been validly received into the college of those holding office and (b) that he was, in his office, placed in a special way on the side of the Lord over and against the community—his service with regard to Christ's unique priestly and pastoral care was simply subordinate. This being 'in the name of Christ over and against the community' was, for Thomas, the essential element of the character or of being received into the office of the church.[65] This was something that was frequently forgotten later. Anyone who considers these two essential elements objectively is bound to admit that they express a biblical datum which has, up to the present time, been regarded in tradition as essential to the office of the church, no more than this, but also no less. These two elements of the character were interpreted ontologically. Within the framework of medieval thought this is understandable, but it should not make us blind to the inviolable biblical inheritance that they contain. In addition, the scholastic theologians were, in their ontological extension of these two data of the primitive church, to some extent misled by a misunderstanding of what Augustine had in fact said. Viewed superficially, Augustine apparently spoke, in a comparison with the stigma branded on soldiers of his own time, not only of an 'outward mark' ('si characterem ... extra habeas'), but also of an 'inward mark' ('si characterem ... intus habeas'). This distinction does not, however, refer to the character. This is borne out by a more accurate reading of the passage, which is: 'Puta te esse militarem. Si characterem imperatoris intus habeas, securus militas. Si extra habeas, non solum tibi ad militiam non prodest character ille, sed etiam pro desertore punieris' (*In Joan tractatus*, VI, 15; PL, 35, 1432). The mark with which the soldier was branded (often bearing the image of the emperor) was practically impossible to remove from his body (perhaps his arm). If he bore this mark *intus*, that is, in the army, he was under the protection of the emperor. If he was seen with this mark *extra*, that is, outside the army, everyone would know that he was a deserter and that he would not escape punishment. Augustine's comparison, then, was this: being within or outside the true church made no difference at all to the validity of the office within the church, so long as this had been bestowed with the characteristic rite of an apostolic church. The question posed by the church fathers and especially by

224

Augustine[66] in connection with the inviolability or indelibility of the 'character'—the source of all medieval reflections about it—was therefore posed (in modern terms) from a specifically ecumenical and inter-church point of view. No direct answer to the modern problem whether it is possible to leave the office on the basis of the indelibility of the character can therefore be found in the traditional teaching of the church. There are, however, elements in patristic teaching which provide an answer to analogous questions—according to Augustine, a priest who had been removed from his office still continued to be a priest (*De bono coniugali*, 24, 32; CSEL, 41, 226), but other church fathers did not apparently take this view.

The Councils of Florence and Trent simply reproduced this teaching about the office of the church which had been associated with the character since the twelfth century together with its ontological interpretation: 'The character is some (*quoddam*) spiritual and indelible sign in the soul' (Trent: Denz 852 (1609); Florence: Denz 695 (1313). It was (according to the *acta* with some hesitation[67]) given as the reason for the fact that this sacrament could not be given more than once. The Tridentine formula was in fact a repetition of the Florentine statement, which came about, however, in very different circumstances. The *Decretus pro Armenis* of Florence, which, in addition to repetitions of earlier confessions of faith, also included a practical instruction about the sacraments (taken over almost word for word from Thomas's *De articulis fidei et sacramentis*), presented this instruction not as a dogmatic statement, but as an expression of the sacramental theology that was current at that period. The Tridentine fathers took over the essence of this decree, but because they were concerned with a new situation, the protestant teaching of their period, this theological doctrine was given a different emphasis. They made use of the theology of the character which had been formulated by the scholastic theologians and had become traditional since the twelfth century, but they wished at the same time to ensure that the office 'in the name of Christ over and against the community' was a reality, in reaction against the view which rejected all difference between the office of the church and the community. It is clear from the Tridentine documents that this is the essence of the council's teaching, expressed, of course, in the terminology of the period, but one cannot maintain that the ontological interpretation of the character that was current in the scholastic period was sanctioned by the church. This fact is borne out by various data. The Tridentine fathers accepted, for example, a proposal that the essence of the character should not be defined (*Conc Trid*, ed Goerresiana, Freiburg, 1901 ff, 5, p 903). There was, however, considerable divergence at the council between the views of the Scotists and those of the Thomists concerning this point. Finally, it is confirmed by later theological interpretations and especially the theory of L. Billot, which continued for many years to prevail in the 'Roman' theology and yet maintained the view that this 'reality in the soul' was only a sign of 'moral power of office'. It should also be noted that neither Thomas nor Trent taught that the character was 'eternal' and both confined it to the life of the church here on earth.[68]

The character is therefore only of immediate importance to the office-bearer's official activities, because it is an indication of his having been really received into the college of those holding office in the church (with all the powers of ministry that result from this—cf St Thomas, 4 *Sent* 4, 1, 1). It does not therefore in itself refer to the whole duration of the office-bearer's life and does not apply to everything that he does, even though a distinction cannot always be made, in the case of a full-time office, between official actions and everything that the office-bearer may in fact be able to do in addition to these official actions. The character cannot in any case be regarded as a reason for coming to a negative conclusion in the case of the modern problem of part-time priesthood—such a conclusion would be based on a misunderstanding of the fundamental significance of the character. If this is only directly aimed at the exercise of office in the name of Christ, the possibility of the temporary exercise of office in the church is not excluded and the realisation of this possibility has to be judged from the pastoral point of view in the light of the church's situation within a given society. A similar approach has also to be made to the problem of women in the church's office—a question which could, of course, never have arisen in an earlier, predominantly male society, the remnants of which are still present in our own age. In this context, however, it should be noted that there was a strong tendency in the primitive church, on the basis of her conviction that there was 'neither Jew nor Greek' and 'neither male nor female' (Gal 3 : 28) in Christ and that no discrimination could be made between these, to anticipate the emancipation of women, especially in the to some extent already emancipated female society of the hellenistic communities. The prevailing situation in society, however, and less fortunate experiences (which resulted from this) inhibited the church for centuries.[69]

Finally, the essence of the character cannot as such be regarded as a reason for rejecting the validity of the office in the other christian churches. The traditional view that the character, as opposed to the grace, is not bestowed outside the sacrament and that a 'sacrament of desire' (*in voto*) is excluded in the case of the office of the church is to some extent the consequence of the ontological interpretation of the character, but not of the essence of faith, an attempt to express which is made in the character, namely that the office of the church functions in the name of Christ over and against, but within the community.

'Demystifying' the character, while at the same time preserving its inviolable essence, seems to have points of contact in the consciousness of the whole tradition of the church, in which one partial tradition throws light on another. This is especially evident in Trent and less evident in the 'spirituality' of the priesthood which has prevailed in recent centuries. The essence of theological teaching about the office of the church, which became overgrown in the course of time, does however give sufficient scope for a deep and personal experience of the office. The office-bearer is able to give, in the name of Christ, a real, valid and special (leading) service, both in the name of and over and against the community. This places him in a situation which appeals to his enhanced sense of responsibility, his humility and his personal and existential involvement with the mystery of salvation in the world. On the basis of the meaning of the charisma of office, it also means that he must 'dwell in the things of the Father'.

Finally, we may ask explicitly to what extent the teaching about the character is, in its authentic essence, a factor which divides the churches. The essential content of this teaching, as understood by the whole tradition of the catholic church—as a totality in which partial traditions have a critical function towards other partial traditions—is in fact accepted by many protestant churches, even though they reject the term character. In such questions, it is important to distinguish between a difference in the language used by the various churches and the basic conviction that is common to all christians. In this case, the affirmation that there is no difference between the members of the community and the one who holds office in the church is a factor leading to division among the churches. Any church which accepts this difference between the members of the community and the office-bearer with the qualification that the office-bearer is subject to the norm of the apostolic authority with its scripture and derives his own authority and leadership from this authority, and therefore maintains that the pastor's function is carried out in the name of Christ as a service to the community is, on the other hand, in fact affirming the same reality that the catholic church attempts to express in the concept of the character.

NOTES

The Mission of the Church is a translation of *Zending van de Kerk* with the omission of ch II, §§ 1–4, ch III, §§ 1–3, and ch V. The present ch 10 did not appear in the Dutch volume. The original publication of the articles which make up this collection is given in the first note to each chapter.

[1] First published in *Ex auditu verbi* (collection in honour of Prof G. C. Berkouwer), Kampen (1965), pp 216–32, and entitled 'Ecclesia semper purificanda'.

[2] G. C. Berkouwer, *Vaticaans concilie en nieuwe theologie*, Kampen (1964). (ET *The second Vatican Council and the new catholicism*, Grand Rapids US 1965.) This book was written before the ecclesiological questions were given their final form in definitive conciliar documents. Much of what Berkouwer wrote in his book about new possibilities for the catholic church has since become official in the promulgation of the dogmatic constitution on the church.

[3] The meaning of this is not primarily 'is *in fact* found' in the catholic church, but is even stronger, namely 'is *de iure* found'; see the justification for the rejection of an amendment: 'quod spectat ad additionem *iure divino*, ex contextu paragraphi patet sermonem esse de institutione Christi' (*Modi*, op cit, p 6).

[4] The choice of the word *purificanda* in preference to all other words or expressions which might suggest the same meaning was determined by the liturgical use of the formula *purificatio ecclesiae* in the Roman missal, among other places, on the first Sunday in Lent and on the fifteenth Sunday after Pentecost (see the *Schema constitutionis de ecclesia*, *op cit*, and the *Relationes de singulis numeris*, *Relatio in 8*, p 25).

[5] 'Alii . . . volunt apertiorem distinctionem inter Ecclesiam medium salutis et Ecclesiam fructum salutis. Quae distinctio iam satis videtur clara in textu' (*Relatio in 8*, *op cit*, p. 24).

[6] 'Munus autem illud, quod Dominus pastoribus populi sui commisit verum est servitium quod in sacris Litteris *diakonia* seu ministerium significanter nuncupatur' (*op cit*, 3, 24).

[7] The constitution completely abandons the idea that the bishop of *Rome* as pope (together with the world episcopate) guides the church. On the contrary, it bases itself on the formal reason, that is, the 'successor of Peter', so that the qualification *romana* in the formula *ecclesia romana* has a purely material significance: 'Dicitur *successor Petri* pro *Romano Pontifice* (which was the phrase used in the preceding schemes), ut appareat ratio formalis successionis' (*Schema constitutionis de ecclesia*, *op cit*, 1964, *Relationes de singulis numeris*, *Relatio in 8*, p 25).

[8] In the schema of the dogmatic constitution on revelation as it existed when this article was first written, it was stated: 'All the church's preaching, like the christian religion itself, must be nourished by holy scripture (6, 21).' Because of an amendment introduced into this text, this was unfortunately weaker than the previous text, which stated: 'All the church's preaching and the whole of the christian religion must always look up towards scrip-

ture as to their *norma* and *auctoritas*, by which they are both guided and judged' (*textus prior*, 6, 21). The final version, however, reads: 'All the church's preaching and the christian religion itself must therefore be nourished *and controlled* (*regatur*) by holy scripture.'

[9] 'De kerk als volk Gods', *Concilium* 1 (1965), 1, pp 11–34; E. Schillebeeckx, 'Kerk en mensdom', *ibid*, pp 63–86, also published under the title of 'The Church and Mankind' in *World and Church*, London (1971), pp 115–39, see also K. Rahner, 'Kirche und Parusia Christi', *Catholica* 17 (1963), pp 113–28.

[10] See also Y. Congar, *Sainte Eglise* (*Unam Sanctam* 41), Paris (1963), pp 131–54.

[11] Jn 7:39; see also 14:26; 16:7; Lk 24:49; Ac 1:5, 8. See E. C. Hoskyns, *The Fourth Gospel*, London (1947[2]), p 323.

[12] The constitution on the church attributes the 'perpetual renewal' of the church to the Holy Spirit (I, 4).

[13] In *Christ the Sacrament*, London (1963), pp 87–8, I called the cultic praise of God in Christ by the church the primary aspect of all sacramental saving power—whether it is expressed in a separate liturgical act or not, the *epiclesis* is essential for the sacramentality of the church. In other words, the sacraments have power within the plan of salvation on the basis of God's free grace to which consent is given. Thanksgiving, praise and petition are the bed along which God allows his grace to flow, via the sacraments, into the church.

[14] First published in *Tijdschrift voor Geestelijk Leven* 22 (1966), pp 533–554.

[15] See G. Baum, 'Doctrinal Renewal', *Journal of Ecumenical Studies* 2 (1965), pp 377–8.

[16] 'Never say God is *on our side*, rather pray that we may be found *on God's side*' (quoted by H. Cox, *God's Revolution and Man's Responsibility*, Valley Forge 1965, p 27).

[17] A *communicatio* given at the international congress of theologians held at Rome, 26 September–1 October 1966; see the *Acta congressus internationalis de theologia concilii vaticani* II, Vatican City 1968, pp 48–53.

[18] It is for this reason that this idea of the church as sacrament was expressed with a certain reserve in at least one conciliar text ('*as it were* the sacrament'; see constitution on the church, 1), because of pressure exerted by the minority group at the council.

[19] The church as the sign 'of herself'—we should not forget that the church is not the kingdom of God or ultimate salvation. She is subject to the promise of the kingdom which is to come. 'Sign of herself' thus means the sign which foreshadows the kingdom of God that is present in Christ.

[20] First published in *De kerk in de wereld van deze tijd*, Hilversum and Antwerp 1967, pp 78–109.

[21] 'Simul' (38 and 41) '*in* ipsa revelatione mysterii Patris . . . , hominem ipsi homini manifestat' (22). See also 11: '*religious*, therefore humanising'.

[22] This is clearly the meaning of 33: 'The church . . . wishes to combine the light of *revelation* (by which is meant the revelation of the word here) with the *experience of all*, in order to *illuminate* the way that mankind has been following.'

[23] Some of the fathers of the council objected to this sharp division between man's process of humanisation and the growth of the kingdom of God. Insofar as this process is an aspect of man's care for his fellow-men and an

expression of charity, they argued, commitment to a better future for mankind on earth cannot be adequately distinguished from commitment to the only necessary thing. In order to meet this objection, the clause 'insofar as this process of humanising the world contributes to a better regulation of the human community' was inserted into the final version of the text (see *Expensio modorum*, 3, 1, p 236).

[24] First published in *De kerk van Vaticanum* II. *Commentaren op de concilieconstitutie over de kerk*, edited by G. Baraúna, Bilthoven 1966, pt II, pp 285–304.

[25] Sacrosancta Synodus hic sub nomine laicorum intelligit fideles, qui baptismate ad populum Dei appositi, attamen in saeculo commorantes, solis communibus normis vitae christianae reguntur. Animum scilicet dirigit ad fideles illos, qui neque ad hierarchiam ordinis neque ad statum religiosum, ab Ecclesia sancitum, ex populo Dei vocati sunt, sed peculiari modo per opera quoque saecularia sanctitatem christianam ad gloriam Dei prosequi debent. In laboribus saeculi partes agunt, sed spiritu evangelico ducti, malitiae mundi valide opponuntur, immo vocatione sua christiana mundum velut ab intra sanctificant; *op cit*, (footnote 1, 1962), 6, 22, 37.

[26] Sacrosancta Synodus nomine laicorum intelligit fideles, qui baptismate in populum Dei cooptati in communi christifidelium statu Deo serviunt, et pro parte sua missionem totius populi christiani in munda exercent, etiam per actionem religiosam, sed neque ad ordinem hierarchicum, neque ad statum religiosum ab Ecclesia sanctitum pertinent. Animum scilicet convertit ad illos qui in laboribus huius mundi partes agunt, sed spiritu evangelico ducti, concupiscentiis saeculi valide opponuntur, immo vocatione sua christiana mundum velut ab intra sanctificant; *op cit* (footnote 3, 1963), 3, 23, 6.

[27] *Schema constitutionis de ecclesia*, 1964, 4, 31, pp 117–18. I do not give the Latin text here, because this version is so similar—with the exception of a passage which is dealt with later on—to the definitive text. In the omitted sections, at the beginning of the second half of the text, the distinctive characteristics of members of the clergy and religious communities are briefly outlined and after the sentence 'it is in the world that they live', this life in the world is concisely described. (See the definitive text, in which all these passages were preserved unaltered.)

Another striking aspect of this third schema is that the general title no longer contained the word 'dogmatic'—it was called *Schema constitutionis de ecclesia*, unlike both the earlier texts and the later and the definitive texts, which all had the title *Schema constitutionis dogmaticae de ecclesia*. None of the official documents give any explanation for this omission. It cannot have been a printing error, in view of the fact that the eight *Relationes* which were read before the vote on the *modi* of the eight chapters were also called *Relatio super caput . . . textus emendati schematis constitutionis de ecclesia*. This must have been noticed by the time the eighth *Relatio* was reached and this was given the evasive title of *Relatio super caput* VIII *schematis de ecclesia*.

[28] *Relatio super caput* IV, *textus emendati schematis constitutionis de ecclesia*, 1964, p 5: 'Notetur caput nostrum . . . non proponere *definitionem* "ontologicam" laici, sed potius descriptionem "typologicam", ut quaestiones et difficultates secundariae evitentur et propter alias rationes prolatas in notis typis mandatis in pagina centum trigesima tertia.' The last-mentioned

reference is concerned with the *Schema constitutionis de ecclesia*, 1964, p 133.

[29] *Schema constitutionis de ecclesia*, 1964, *Relatio de* 31, p 127. This is the reason why the word *hic* ('here', 'in this context') which appeared in the first schema was once again included in the third schema. See H. Urs von Balthasar, *Der Laie und der Ordensstand*, Einsiedeln 1949, in which the author defended the full lay character of these institutes, and K. Rahner, 'Über des Laienapostolat', *Schriften zur Theologie* ii, Einsiedeln 1958[3], pp 339–73, in which the author maintains that these institutes cannot be regarded as lay.

[30] 'Additur *religiosos*, quia definitio, vel potius circumscriptio typologica laicorum eos (=laicos) contradistinguit non solum a clericis, sed etiam a religiosis, per *notam quodammodo specificam* indolis saecularis'; *op cit*, *Relatio de* 30, p 127.

[31] The schema says *praecipuus locus* (4, 36). The *Notae* comment in this context that religious and lay people can also perform this task but, when they do it, it is usually accidental! See *Relatio de* 36, pp 132–3.

[32] See the constitution on the church, 4, 32, in which a great deal of use is made of Paul's idea of the difference between the members of the one body, each of which has an irreplaceable part to play in the whole body.

[33] 'Laici enim non sunt profani, sed membra Ecclesiae in mundo profano; unde non per opera saecularia, sed per suam pertinentiam activam ad Ecclesiam distinguuntur' (see Pre-conciliar schema, footnote 1, 1962, p 44). *Distinguuntur* is used here in an independent or absolute sense—the distinctive aspect of the layman is to be found in his relationship not with secularity, but with the church.

[34] 'Laici enim non sunt homines profani, sed membra Ecclesiae in mundo profano; unde characterizantur imprimis, non per opera saecularia, sed per operosam participationem in activitate Ecclesiae' (see second schema: *Schema constitutionis dogmaticae de ecclesia*, 1963, ii, p 15).

[35] 'Licet clerici et religiosi quamdam activatem "laicalem" aliquando exerceant, praesertim ad certas deficientias complendas, a v per modum suppletivum, universaliter tamen loquendo per huiusmodi activitate laicis substitui neqeunt' (*op cit*, *Relatio de* 36, p 133).

[36] This second theme was developed at a chronologically earlier date, especially as a result of the work of E. Niebecker, *Das allgemeine Priestertum der Gläubigen*, Paderborn 1936. For a bibliography relating to the 'priesthood of the faithful', see *Katholiek Archief* 11, 1956, pp 541–612.

[37] See, for example, *L'Apostolato dei laici. Bibliografia sistematica*, Milan 1957. See also R. Tucci, 'Recenti pubblicazioni sui laici nella Chiesa', *Civ Catt* 109, 1958, ii, pp 178–90; the bibliography compiled by B. Häring and V. Schurr in the German edition of G. Philips, *Der Laie in der Kirche*, Salzburg 1955. For the Dutch-speaking countries, these must be supplemented by the *Capita Selecta* published in *Katholiek Archief* 11, 1956, pp 541–612 and 1201–64; 12, 1957, pp 265–352 and 554–616; 13, 1958, pp 353–84; 14, 1959, pp 537–72. The most useful protestant publication is *Laici in Ecclesia. An Ecumenical Bibliography on the Role of the Laity in the Life and the Mission of the Church*, Geneva 1961.

[38] It is striking that, round about the year 1950, and usually independently of each other, catholic journals published articles on or even devoted special numbers to the 'theology of the laity'. Thus there were, for example, in France, in 1946, *La Vie Spirituelle and Masses Ouvrières*; in

1948, *Etudes*; in 1949, *Cahiers du Clergé Rural*; in 1950, *Supplément de la Vie Spirituelle*; in Germany, in 1950, *Geist und Leben*; in Switzerland, in 1948, *Orientierung*; in Belgium and the Netherlands, in 1948–49, *Nederlandse Katholieke Stemmen* and *Tijdschrift voor Geestelijk Leven*; in North America, in 1948, *Integrity*. It is therefore clear from this that this study of the christian laity happened at about the same time in the whole west European catholic church and as the result of the same contemporary christian situation (and, what is more, after a long pre-history) and that it cannot be called a 'French', 'German', 'Dutch' or 'Belgian' theology. In the chronological survey carried out in this section of my article, a selection has, of necessity, been made of the many contributions to this theme, in which I have concentrated exclusively on those by professional theologians. This does not mean, however, that I do not appreciate the value of the other articles. What is particularly striking in this context is that it was not in the purely theological journals that articles dealing with this question were first published, but in the journals of spirituality.

[39] The following studies of the christian laity according to canon law were published in 1950: H. Keller and V. von Nell-Breuning, *Das Recht der Laien in der Kirche*, Heidelberg 1950; O. Köhler, 'Der Laie im katholischen Kirchenrecht', *Stimmen der Zeit*, 146, 1950, pp 43–53.

[40] I. de la Potterie, 'L'origine et le sens primitif du mot "laïc" ', *Nouvelle Revue Théologique*, 80, 1958, pp 840–53; confirmatory material will also be found in J. B. Bauer, 'Die Wortgeschichte vom "laicus" ', *Zeitschrift für katholische Theologie*, 81, 1959, pp 224–8.

[41] In connection with this question, the following books and articles merit especial consideration: G. Philips, *Naar een volwassen christendom*, Louvain 1960; Y. Congar, in his articles or lectures in *Sacerdoce et laïcat*, Paris 1962; E. Schillebeeckx, in the three successive articles which draw attention to this christian aspect of the layman's relationship with the world: 'De leek in de kerk', TGL, 15, 1959, pp 669–94 (Engl tr 'The Layman in the Church', *Doctrine and life*, 11, 1961, pp 369–75; 397–408); 'Dogmatiek van ambt en lekestaat', TT, 2, 1962, pp 258–92; 'Een uniforme terminologie van het theologische begrip "leek" ', *Te Elfder Ure*, 10, 1963, pp 173–6.

[42] First published as 'Un nouveau type de laïc' in the collection entitled *La nouvelle image de l'Eglise*, edited by Prof Bernard Lambert, OP, Tours 1967.

[43] First published in the *Tijdschrift voor Theologie*, 1967, 7, pp 1–27, when it was entitled 'Het nieuwe mens- en Godsbeeld in conflict met het religieuze leven'.

[44] See, for example, P. Ricoeur, 'Prévision économique et choix éthique', *Esprit*, 34, 1966, pp 178–93, especially pp 188–89.

[45] A genetical and semantic analysis of the concept of 'secularisation' since the enlightenment and its relationship with the expropriation of the church's property by the state is provided by L. Lübke in *Säkularisierung, Geschichte eines ideenpolitischen Begriffs*, Munich 1965. See also M. Stallmann, *Was ist Säkularisierung?*, Tübingen 1960.

[46] Non-believers always have difficulty in accepting the matter of factness of the secularity of the world and feel constrained to give the secularised world an ideological substructure (nihilism, scepticism, a naive faith in a future paradise, to name a few examples). See Ottoheinz von der Gablentz, 'Die Krisis der säkularen Religionen', *Kosmos und Ekklesia* (Festschrift für W. Stählin), Kassel 1953, pp 243–61, especially pp 258–9.

[47] F. Gogarten was one of the first to work out this idea in powerful terms in his book, *Verhängnis und Hoffnung der Neuzeit. Die Säkularisierung als theologisches Problem*, Stuttgart 1953. He was later followed by J. B. Metz, 'Versuch einer positiven Deutung der bleibenden Weltlichkeit der Welt', *Handbuch der Pastoraltheologie*, II–2, Freiburg 1966, pp 239–67.

[48] We often unconsciously make religious statements when we should in fact be making statements about human society. Many events in the past which gave rise to an immediate appeal to God to intervene would appear now to be based, according to our present-day knowledge, on a lack of human technology, for example, or on scientific ignorance. But was the faith of christians then, in view of their circumstances, less authentic? Religious experience is, after all, always partly determined by existing social and historical conditions—it was in the past and is now. Surely man does not have to wait for authentic faith until correct scientific conclusions have been reached? In the modern world, which is so conditioned by science and technology, we simply have different occasions and incentives for religious experience. Our faith is not necessarily more authentic than that of christians in the past.

[49] I am, of course, not speaking about priests in general here, but of religious as such. I am not considering the priesthood with its own, special mission and tasks. Another question also lies outside the scope of this article —the repercussions of the priesthood on activities in a religious institution which was in the first place founded as a religious community of priests. (This is, of course, quite different from a religious institution in which the members are, as a result of historical circumstances, ordained priests.)

[50] The acceptance of these vows therefore also includes the approval of the community. The community cannot, on the one hand, be made subject to any one-sided bond, nor can it, on the other hand, accept the duty of recognising every arbitrary or even frivolous agreement. This has probably been all too frequently overlooked.

[51] This talk was given originally during the conference organised in 1962 by the 'Institution for Pastoral Training in the Archdiocese of Utrecht and the Diocese of Groningen'. It was later published as an article in *Nederlandse Katholieke Stemmen*, 59, 1963, pp 210–22.

[52] This term 'implicit christianity' has, of course, to be carefully handled. There is no intention, when it is used, of claiming non-christians as christians. It is simply a way of interpreting the authenticity of the lives of non-christians in a christian sense, that is, in the light of faith.

[53] Even Karl Rahner, who certainly cannot be accused of 'essentialism' and 'conceptualism', has felt constrained to point this out. See his *Gefahren im heutigen Katholizismus*, Einsiedeln 1953³.

[54] A paper read on 21 April 1964 to the General Conference of Religious Superiors in Belgium. I have omitted the introduction in this published version.

[55] There are also, of course, episcopal congregations. The bishop will not approve even an episcopal congregation unless he is satisfied that it contains an authentic charisma and then he will, in the light of this understanding, exercise authority over it.

[56] It should, of course, not be forgotten in this context that the church's office as such also has a special charisma. I have, furthermore, not provided any analysis of the apostolic function of the religious life as such, that is, apart from the priesthood. The apostolic value of the strictly con-

templative way of life would, for example, clearly be of fundamental importance in any study of this. It can even be regarded as the distinctively apostolic charisma of the religious life as such.

[57] I am using the word *paroikia*, 'parish', here in the theological sense, as the community of faith in the concrete, and not in the sociological sense in which we usually understand 'parish' and which also evokes all kinds of problems.

[58] First published, with a longer introduction, as 'Theologische kanttekeningen bij de huidige priester-crisis', *Tijdschrift voor Theologie*, 4, 1968, pp 402–34. ET published in *Theological Studies*, 30, 1969, pp 567–87.

[59] See especially, Neumann, 'Erwägungen zur Revision des kirchlichen Gesetzbuches', *Theologische Quartalschrift*, 146, 1966, pp 285–304, in which the author correctly reacts against the idea of 'irreversibility' defended by Rahner; see K. Rahner, 'Über den Begriff des *ius divinum* im katholischen Verständnis', *Schriften zur Theologie*, 5, Einsiedeln 1962, pp 249–77.

[60] A good historical and theological argument in favour of this has been provided by P. A. van Leeuwen in his article 'Grenzen van Kerk en Doop' in the *Jaarboek 1965–66 Werkgenootschap van Katholieke Theologen in Nederland*, Hilversum 1966, pp 71–102. Although van Leeuwen was discussing the question of the validity of baptism, his principles apply equally to the validity of the office.

[61] This idea, which has its basis in the early church but was later forgotten, is being reconsidered at the moment and is beginning to find unanimous recognition among theologians. See, among other works: M. Villain, 'Can there be Apostolic Succession outside the Continuity of the Laying-on of Hands?' in *Concilium*, 4, 1968, 4, pp 45–53 (Engl ed). The whole number contains articles on the apostolic succession. See also F. van Beeck, 'Towards an Ecumenical Understanding of the Sacraments', *Journ Ecum Studies*, 3 (1966), pp 57–112.

[62] The fact that younger candidates are no longer able to experience their reception into the office of the church as a 'reception into a college' because they feel strange in this, is, in my opinion, proof of an existing objective situation of conflict.

[63] With the passage of time, protestant exegetes and historians have also come to re-emphasise more and more clearly this aspect of being 'over and against the community' (in reaction against untheological misunderstandings and uncritically accepted secularising tendencies). The special operation of grace which accompanies reception into the office of the church has in this way been stressed once again in protestant circles. This was, also, the original inspiration of the reformers, but it was diluted in later controversies.

[64] The ancient church, from the time of Ignatius of Antioch onwards (*Ad Eph* 5. 1 ff), had clearly set the example for medieval theology in this.

[65] This is especially clear from Thomas' reflections that Christ, the high priest, did not himself need any 'character' (*Summa Theol*, III, 63, 6). The primary aim of his teaching about the character was to show that ministry in the church was simply a being taken into service by the one priesthood of Christ for the benefit of the community. This was unmistakably the reason for all his ontological constructions. This *'in the name of* Christ *over and against* the community' was therefore, in the case of Thomas, the only reason why he called the office of the church a special participation in Christ's priesthood.

[66] A similar problem faced the Greek fathers in connection with the term *sphragis* (seal), but this cannot be considered here.

[67] There was a long debate about the *cuius ratione* (the reason for the unrepeatable nature of the sacrament) and the term was ultimately weakened to *unde*. From the purely grammatical point of view, there was not much change in meaning here, but it is clear from the discussions that the aim was only to establish a factual bond between the character and its 'unrepeatable' nature, not a *de iure* connection. In other words, this was not a conclusion from the doctrine of the character.

[68] The character is given 'in ordine ad cultum *praesentis* Ecclesiae' (*Summa Theol*, III, 63, 2 ad 3). This was also the teaching of the second Vatican Council (*Lumen Gentium*, 48).

[69] For the present situation of this problem, see J. Peters, 'Is there a Place for Woman in the Functions of the Church?', *Concilium*, 4, 1968, 4, pp 65–71 (Engl ed).

INDEX

MAN, 78–81
image of God, 56, 58
Married life, 26, 40
Marxism, 72, 80, 81
Mass, the, 22, 183
Mass media, 30, 146
Vatican II on, 127
Matthew, St, 146, 155
Merleau-Ponty, 85
Message, evangelical, christian,
26, 35, 37, 38, 41, 61, 186
Metanoia, 12, 13, 45
Metz, J. B., 234
Middle Ages, the, 27–28, 44, 52,
120, 169, 223
view of marriage, 26
Mission, 44, 55, 68, 93, 96, 100, 105,
128, 198, 210
layman's share in, 94, 95, 96,
100, 103–106, 108, 109, 110,
114ff, 123–124
religious, not political, 68
Missions, the, 214, 215
Modernism, 27
Monastic life, 118, 119, 166, 169
Moulin, Leon, 193
Music, 31
Mystery, 32, 33, 38, 43–45, 75, 76,
79, 82, 86–87, 89

NAZI RÉGIME, THE, 158
'Negative theology', 41
Netherlands, the, 194, 202
Neumann, 235
New Delhi, 3
New testament, the, 218
Niebecker, E., 232
Nineteenth century, the, 27
Non-catholic churches, 68, 74, 228
ecclesial reality of, 5, 7, 8–9, 18,
22, 213

OBEDIENCE, 32, 34, 39, 130
religious, 154ff

Office, 175, 179ff, 189, 207, 209, 214,
217
charisma of, 171, 213, 214, 217,
228
of church, inseparable from
community, 189, 206
catholic understanding of, 205
in apostolic church, 206
validity of, 210, 212ff
twofold dimension of, 211
reception into, 216ff, 235
'character' and, 226
Old testament, the, 72, 83, 87, 111
Order, established, 85, 192
Orders, religious, 163ff, 168, 169,
170, 191, 193, 195, 201
and renewal, 164

PAGANISM, 139, 140, 145
Palestine, 214
Papal encyclicals, 31
Mystici Corporis Christi, 3, 4, 9
Parish, 178
Paroikia, 200
Parousia, 14, 66
Paul, St, 3, 16, 36, 65, 77, 82, 89,
146, 186, 189, 214, 215, 217,
219, 227
Pentecost, 15, 16
Peter, St, 1, 6, 11
Peters, J., 236
Petrine succession, 6, 11
Philips, G., 109, 232
Philosophy, 75
Pope, the, 4, 10, 31, 34, 36, 197, 229
Potterie, I. de, 111, 233
Poverty, 153
Presbyterate, 196
'derived priesthood', 197ff
Priest, Priests, 23, 69, 77, 101, 104,
106, 118, 119, 120, 122, 126,
127
and laity, 171ff
as 'organs of contact', 172ff

Schillebeeckx, Edward Cornelis Florentius Alfons, 1914–
 The mission of the church ₍by₎ Edward Schillebeeckx.
Translated by N. D. Smith. New York, Seabury Press
₍1973₎

 ix, 244 p. 22 cm. $9.75

 Translation of De zending van de kerk.
 "A Crossroad book."
 Includes bibliographical references.

 1. Catholic Church—Addresses, essays, lectures.   I. Title.